AF292054

Box of Lions

Box of Lions

First-hand Accounts of Stopping the Japanese at Imphal

Christopher Johnson

Pen & Sword
MILITARY

First published in Great Britain in 2026 by
Pen & Sword Military
An imprint of Pen & Sword Books Limited
Yorkshire – Philadelphia

ISBN 978 1 03619 468 0

Typeset by Mac Style
Printed in the UK by CPI Group (UK) Ltd, Croydon, CR0 4YY.

The Publisher's authorised representative in the EU for product
safety is Authorised Rep Compliance Ltd., Ground Floor,
71 Lower Baggot Street, Dublin D02 P593, Ireland.
www.arccompliance.com

For a complete list of Pen & Sword titles please contact:

PEN & SWORD BOOKS LIMITED
47 Church Street, Barnsley, South Yorkshire, S70 2AS, England
E-mail: enquiries@pen-and-sword.co.uk
Website: www.pen-and-sword.co.uk
or
PEN AND SWORD BOOKS
1950 Lawrence Road, Havertown, PA 19083, USA
E-mail: uspen-and-sword@casematepublishers.com
Website: www.penandswordbooks.com

Cast bronze plaque belonging to the author. A copy was presented to AOC officers' mess Delhi from the Lion Cubs of Kanglatongbi.

Contents

Foreword

by
Lieutenant General Gautam Moorthy, PVSM, AVSM, VSM (Retd),
former Director General Ordnance Services &
Senior Colonel Commandant Indian Army

This is a story of what was clearly a forgotten battle of a forgotten army of the Allies in the Burma Campaign during WWII remembered in the UK only by one intrepid, passionate and obstinate soul – Christopher Johnson from Norfolk, whose father had fought there in the spring of 1944.

It would not be an exaggeration to say that Christopher has devoted a better part of his life to unearthing unheard-of details of this exceptional battle. With the assistance of Yumnam Rajeshwor Singh and Arambam Angamba Singh of Manipur, and the Manipur Government, he has also helped in establishing a War Museum in Imphal, the capital of the Manipur state.

The battle which was fought mainly by the logistics elements of the IV Corps of Slim's 14th Army, with the IAOC in the main (the precursor of today's Army Ordnance Corps of India) and elements of the British Army, is however remembered by the Corps in India every year, along with the anniversary of its founding in the then Bengal Presidency during the English East India Company era that was on 8 April 1775.

The first time that the Battle of Kangla Tongbi, also called the Battle of the Lion Box, was commemorated jointly by both the Army Ordnance Corps and the children of the British personnel who fought there, who call themselves Lion Cubs, took place on the seventieth anniversary of the battle on 7 April 2014. That Christopher organised the participation of a delegation from the distant shores of the UK is a testimony to his involvement and determination in ensuring that this battle gets its due as a defining moment of WWII in the South East Asian theatre. He was present on that red-letter day along with eighteen others from the UK. He was present again with a delegation from the UK on the seventy-fifth commemoration of the battle in 2019.

Pieced together painstakingly from hard to locate British, Indian and Japanese sources, unearthing every little detail of the encounters, Christopher has vividly captured every twist and turn of this bitterly fought battle in which no quarter was asked for nor given. Indian and British soldiers, mostly logisticians, carried out one of the most difficult operations of war – a planned withdrawal, taking back with them to Imphal the stores and munitions of war entrusted to their responsibility. From 31 March to 7 April, Slim's brave men came under intense and persistent firing from the Japanese who had occupied the hills overlooking the Lion Box. Despite the enemy's repeated attempts at overrunning the Advanced Ordnance Depot, the men fighting against such impossible odds managed to evacuate about 5,000 tonnes of arms, ammunition, other warlike stores, general stores, clothing and vehicles.

The book per se is a formidable work of scholarship and research, and compiled with an eye for detail. Christopher has written not just a historical account of that battle but has injected into it the human element, painting a very vivid picture of what took place under such extraordinary circumstances. *Box of Lions* is the most authoritative account of what transpired in that one week of hell on earth in that forgotten corner of the world. But for Christopher's labour of love, this comprehensive yet meticulous account of that historic battle and the men who fought it would have faded away into the mists of time.

Postscript

A newsletter from 221 AOD, (the first from the unit) was published in the *IAOC Gazette,* September 1944. The letter commences with the words, *"This may be the first time a lot of you 'lucky people' have heard of us; to others (including those who redirect our private mail) it will serve as a reminder of our existence."*
Little did they know then that one Christopher Johnson, eight decades later, would ensure that their existence would never be forgotten.

Acknowledgements

It would be far too numerous to mention all who have helped individually, there are so many who have assisted me in one way or another over the years, and to them I give my wholehearted thanks. However, there is one person who stands out, so much so that I have invited him to write about his work and that of the Second World War Imphal Campaign Foundation in this book. Rajeshwor Yumnam, who lives in Imphal, has been outstanding in his commitment to keeping the memory alive of those who fought around the Imphal Plain, and together with the members of the WW2 ICF, of which he is co-founder member, will ensure the 'Forgotten XIV Army' is remembered, in Manipur at least.

Another person who has also made a major contribution to this book with her research in these latter years is Joan Baron. She was the niece of one of the Lions who fought at Kanglatongbi and has helped me contact many other families of the Lions, to share information and obtain the photos of those men I have written about. The digital recording by Joan of a myriad of official unit war diaries held in The National Archives has enabled me to pore over these records in the comfort of my own home, to glean even the merest morsel of information to add to details from private papers and letters sourced over many years.

The Reverend Doctor Andrew Sangster, a prolific and recognised published historian, has unselfishly volunteered to edit my work. My schoolboy English, poor punctuation and grammatical errors alone must have severely taxed him, to say nothing of the complicated nature of the narrative necessary at times to record the events accurately. I am pleased to say that not every page has had the editor's dreaded red pen treatment (actually, it was blue ink). I'm greatly indebted to him and his patience with my hobbyist attitude to writing.

Those keen-eyed readers who were lucky enough to read my original publication (only 250 printed) may have found several 'honest' mistakes or inaccuracies when compared to this revised copy. New information gleaned since then has helped rectify this; but no doubt, there will be others in this publication, for which I bear full responsibility.

Chris Johnson
Bergh Apton, Norfolk. 2026

Author's Notes

Just when *is* the right time to stop researching and commit to paper the hard-earned fruits of one's labour? This is the question I have been asking myself almost since the ink dried on my first book about the battle at Lion Box Kanglatongbi. With so much further information having been gleaned since then, my answer must be, what better time to revisit and rewrite this story than in the eightieth anniversary year of this little-known and overlooked action.

Since my initial six years of research and the subsequent publishing of my book in 2001, the Internet has become the wondrous and widely used tool of the researcher. Long gone are the days of my laboriously handwritten enquiring letters and the excruciating waiting for replies and answers to my questions. The advance in cyber communication has allowed a flow of information that with a mere touch of a button is almost instantaneous, and with the availability online of previously unreleased records, has added greatly to the story of Lion Box. All this, together with further veteran eyewitness accounts and photos sent to me by their family members and others, has prompted me to rewrite the story in far more detail than the original, when the objective was just to record the basic details before they were lost. I have no doubt that there is yet more information that will surface in the future, but that will be for others to record.

This story of Lion Box is not one of grand strategies by the General Staff, nor one of the 'ifs and buts' or the various theories of the revisionist military historians, but rather of the soldiers who were actually there, in some cases written in their own words. These were just ordinary men conscripted into wartime service or, as in the case of the Indian troops, as part of the largest completely volunteer army in the Second World War, who became embroiled in the harsh brutalities of war. Others were seasoned professional soldiers who had seen active service in the First World War or in other campaigns since then, whose experience was invaluable with the steadying or rallying of men when under stress. The vast majority of the garrison at Lion Box were men from the support arms and logistics, given the cruel nicknames of 'blanket-stackers, throttle-jockeys, pen-pushers and navvies'. They were normally non-combatant troops, and there to do the specific job for which they were trained, but when their time came, they rose to the call and fought hard to repel a ruthless, determined enemy. It is to these men that this book is dedicated.

In the course of this work, I have tried to state only the facts as I compiled them into a readable but complex account, and not to digress too far with my own comments or observations, apart from in some minor incidences when sets of evidence seemed to conflict or were unclear, needing further input. In such cases, I have used my instinct and knowledge in the narrative.

To say that Lion Box has been a large part of my life is an understatement, for it has changed my life and that of my family, too. I have been to Kanglatongbi three times (sixtieth, seventieth and seventy-fifth anniversaries of the battle) and my children and nephews have also followed their grandfather's footsteps across India and onto the battlefield at Kanglatongbi. I have had the great honour of laying wreaths at the Indian National War Memorial in Delhi, at the Kanglatongbi War Memorial and at the Imphal War Cemetery, where I visited the graves of those men I have written about. I have also had the honour to officially open the Imphal War Museum. But my greatest honour and joy are the many friendships I made with the veterans I interviewed during this time, sadly all deceased now. Lots of these friendships still continue through their families and with other families of those who fought at Lion Box and who are now collectively known as the Lion Cubs of Kanglatongbi.

Additional Note

For the interest of those who may have not seen the original publication of my book in 2001, set out here is the foreword from it, as it remains important:

> What started as the recording of my late father's twenty-one-years' service
> with the Royal Norfolk Regiment for our family records has now expanded

to this detailed account of an action fought fifty-seven years ago in the jungles of Assam.

As a family we knew very little of our father's war other than a few odd stories of when he was at the Siege of Imphal. The first breakthrough was the confirmation that he was at Kanglatongbi when he had written on the page in a book of war stories. At the bottom of a page mentioning Kanglatongbi he had written 'I was there for good shooting', his euphemism for a battle of some sort, and from there the trail grew, as did my curiosity and determination to glean the facts from whatever source I could.

Six years ago, I would never have thought that my quest would have led me to write countless letters all over the United Kingdom, India, Australia and even Japan. During this time, I have made real friends with some of the old soldiers who were there and have spoken with many veterans of the Burma Campaign who, in the main, were only too pleased to help with information and who seemed pleased to think that the younger generation were interested in the Forgotten Army.

Obviously, official war diaries were my main source of information as well as the many books written about the Burma Campaign, though none gave the real details of the action that I needed, adding to my determination to put the events on record. Gradually, several unpublished papers and accounts built up my file, as did the eyewitness accounts of the survivors of the action. I must mention here that the veterans I spoke to were very modest about their participation in the fighting (much to my frustration), saying that it was a job that had to be done. Now, after finally putting together their true story of the battle at Kanglatongbi, I hope I have done justice to the memory of those who fought there.

CSM George Johnson, Royal Norfolk Regiment, attached 20 Rft Camp.

Preface

History books are written in various styles, ranging from a broad sweep of the brush giving an overall picture of a selected area of study, to closing in and providing a more detailed account of an event. This book has used a 'history microscope' by pinpointing one battle in the Far Eastern War called the 'Box of Lions', when a mixture of non-combatant trained soldiers courageously fought back against a formidable thrust of the Japanese Army in the Imphal Campaign. The author of this book, Christopher Johnson, has studied this battle over many decades, travelled many times to the scene of the battle, met and talked with many of the veterans and accumulated a wealth of evidence from their reports, letters and many personal conversations with those who fought in this bitter hand-to-hand fighting. He has through his efforts made personal contact with many of the combatants, not just from the British and Indian side but also men from the Japanese side of this conflict, often quoting their conversations and correspondence. Very few histories manage to have contacts from both sides of the conflict, and this microscopic study therefore provides an unusually detailed day-by-day account of the conflict and its ramifications, but the emotions and events of the day are recorded in unbelievable detail.

As such, this book offers a detailed study of this battle based on the evidence left by those who fought, basing its findings on the value of the best oral traditions left by the men of that time. In terms of being an unusual historical approach, the author has used a major reliance on oral tradition, so critical in historical work. Oral tradition in history is important not just because it provides the personal views of those who fought, but also their hopes, fears, the sense of panic and distress, and by so doing opens the reader's mind to the reality of conflict – in this case, a jungle-type warfare. The author met many of the survivors and the families of those who survived and those who were killed. This enabled him to read their correspondence home, their daily notes on events, providing detailed accounts of particular skirmishes, and the nature of jungle fighting. This intense study therefore offers insights not only into the battle but also into the minds and feelings of those involved.

This book thereby explores not just the daily unfolding of events but involves the human element of combat. Various characters emerge, those who were incredibly brave, but also the reality for the deep human instinct of those who wanted to survive. It demonstrates those who followed the rules and regulations, those who kept their heads down, and some characters who stand out for a variety of reasons – one being Padre Brock, whose obstinate character and courage caught the attention of many on the battlefield. The nature of the personal insights almost helps the reader have the feeling that they knew these men. Above all, as mentioned above, these men caught up in the defence against the Japanese thrust were not trained frontline soldiers, but belonged more to what we call today the logistics corps, providing drivers, communications, signals and so forth, yet they fought tenaciously, as the Japanese discovered. This book captures the scene of everyday people, the John Does and Smiths of all nationalities caught up in one of the war's bitterest battles, mentioning by name many of them, from drivers to leading officers, from both sides of the divide.

The Reverend Dr Andrew Sangster

Introduction

After their defeat at Singapore in 1942, the remnants of the Burma Corps fought a valiant rearguard action over four months, through the jungles of Burma, crossing the Chindwin River and finally onto the Plain of Imphal in the princely state of Manipur in Assam.

For nearly 1,000 miles, this battered corps, consisting of British, Indian, Gurkha and Burmese troops, bravely and stoutly resisted the Japanese Imperial Army. With their 'tails up' after their victories in Malaya and elsewhere, the Japanese relentlessly pursued them until the monsoon, and having extended their supply lines, called a halt, and both sides then retired to regroup and re-equip. The cost of this retreat was around 1,500 killed in action with a further 12,000 wounded, missing or taken prisoner, but they had fought and held the Japanese longer than any other land-force formation at this time.

Back in India, General William Slim then set about the task of retraining the XIV Army ready to take the fight to the Japanese and retake Burma. This would all take time and entail the learning of new tactics, including that of even the normally non-combatant administrative troops being expected to fight. Air transport would in future play an important role in the supplying of the fighting men with all their needs, but the airfields would first have to be built. The roads, little more than jungle tracks in places, would also need building or improving, so that vehicles of the transport companies, now being formed, could deliver the supplies to the large stores facilities (also being built at the same time) at Kanglatongbi, Imphal and Palel.

By early 1944, the Allied victories against the Japanese in the Arakan area finally brought much-needed confidence as the plans for the retaking of Burma were nearing completion, but the Japanese were first off the mark with their plans for the 'March on Delhi'. Crossing the Chindwin River on 15 March, the Japanese 15th Army began Operation U-Go, causing a rethink of General Slim's strategy. Knowing how inefficient the Japanese lines of communication (L of C) were (depending on captured military supplies and the looting of civilian food stores), Bill Slim decided to pull back all his fighting divisions to the Imphal Plain, where on the ground of his choosing, and knowing he had air supply for his garrison, he would further extend the Japanese lines of communication before bringing them to battle.

The Battle of Imphal was not a single set-piece battle, but one of many smaller actions around an ever-shrinking perimeter, as the whole of IV Corps were besieged for three months. Although not always large in scale, they were some of the most ferocious and doggedly fought anywhere during the Second World War. One of these smaller and lesser-known actions was fought at Lion Box Kanglatongbi, 14 miles north of Imphal, where an Advanced Ordnance Depot (AOD) was situated and contained the supplies that the Japanese Army were now in need of.

Prologue

As we descended the steep slope towards the eastern side of Keithelmanbi, we hit dense jungle. Thick grass grew as high as my waist. The wide road became slightly more elevated, and a landmark stood at the side of the road showing the number of miles to Imphal. The road surface was a good hard paving, and I thought that of all the roads I had seen thus far, this was the best. We had crossed numerous mountains, and we had come through dense jungle so perhaps that is why this road seemed so grand. I was certainly surprised at the level of engineering of the enemy, which had enabled them to build this kind of road in such a remote region of India. As there was no one to speak of living in this isolated area, it had been built purely for military use. It was impressive, even in comparison with the road, which had been built under our command in Thailand during an earlier offensive. It stretched 15 metres across.

On the far side of the road, there was a great expanse of virgin jungle, with a background of mountain upon mountain interspersed with valleys of all shapes and sizes. It was an ideal landscape in which to conceal the movements of a military unit, and on the eastern side high mountains towered into the sky. Towards the south in the direction of Safarmaina stood four of the enemy's depot buildings on the western side of the road, where enemy trucks came in and out intermittently.

Just before dusk on 3 April 1944, the Fukushima Battalion [3rd Battalion, 60th Regiment] finally set foot on the Imphal–Kohima road. We branched out onto both sides of the road and launched a surprise attack on Safarmaina, but not noticing any obvious signs of the enemy. We continued southwards using the ravine on the western side of the road, assigned some of the mortars and machine guns to the 12th Company. Thus, equipped against any enemy attack from above the main road, the main body of the battalion continued to investigate the lie of the land and enemy movements further ahead and prepared our attack. Enemy planes incessantly flew scouting missions at a low altitude in the vicinity of the main road. All our movements so far had taken place in the knowledge that the enemy had complete mastery of the air, to which our troops were now accustomed. We could not escape from the roar of the planes. This ravine must have been a river in the rainy season, and great stones and rocks were still strewn about. Now, however, it was the dry season and, in order to get water for cooking, it was still necessary to go into the heart of the dense jungle. This made it unlikely that we would be spotted by enemy planes.

The Uchibori Battalion [2nd Battalion, 60th Regiment] continued their scouting operations on the eastern side of the road, and liaising with us, pushed southwards. Where this mountain ridge came to an end, the whole valley of Imphal stretched out, and Imphal itself could be seen lying in the centre of the valley. The rear supply route for the enemy was blocked off, and the battalion headed in a southerly direction in readiness for launching the attack. The western side of the road, which lay in our battalion's route, gradually turned into open land where there appeared to be an enemy base. Heavy vehicles were coming and going, and we could even make out enemy soldiers. We were nearing Kanglatongbi…

These pages were written by Lieutenant Chojiro Takahata, Adjutant, Fukushima Battalion (3rd Battalion, 60th Regiment), of the Japanese Imperial Army, April 1944.

Chapter One

The Build-Up

The main supply route for the forces building up at Imphal and further south into Burma was the Dimapur–Imphal road, which ran south from the railhead and huge stores facilities at Dimapur for 132 miles to Imphal. It was under the command of 202 Lines of Communication Area, which controlled the movement of supplies and the building of all the infrastructure required to keep IV Corps on a war footing. The work of the Royal Indian Army Service Corps (RIASC) to deliver all these supplies was truly an outstanding feat of logistics, unsurpassed anywhere at this time. The records of movements and statistics speak for themselves. When, for example, during the month of December 1943 alone, at a particularly busy time, the drivers of the RIASC drove a staggering 4,174,498 miles and delivered 46,101 tons of supplies and equipment. Colonel Robert John Holmes, the commander of Lines of Communication Transport, wrote:

> Speaking of the Indian Other Ranks generally, I have approximately 9,000 RIASC personnel under command, and I say unhesitatingly they are the finest lot of men I have ever worked with. Twenty-four hours a day, 365 days per year, they have given of their best that is in them, worked extremely hard and never complained. I would not hesitate to operate MT [Mechanical Transport] with these men in competition with the best in the Allied armies. Having much experience in the economic use of MT, I trust that my appreciation of the RIASC Driver will be duly recorded. I have often wondered when writing these progress reports if Officers reading them observing we have operated four and a half million miles in a month, or moved say approximately 2,000 tons per day, ever pause to think of the organisation and management required to achieve these results. Try it sometime. I'm still learning after twenty-odd years' intensive study of MT and problems relative thereto.

Colonel Holmes was known for his ruffling of the feathers of his superiors at times, as he sought to get the transport system up and running smoothly, with all the necessary vehicles and properly equipped workshops with which to maintain them. Not one to mince his words, he was greatly respected and well placed to comment on the efficiency of his men, having been a businessman involved with transport in Burma for many years before the war. His obsession with statistics greatly impressed his superiors, and during a visit by some American counterparts, they commented that 'it seems the only thing you don't know is what your drivers are thinking'. He probably knew that too.[1]

At a maximum height of 3,700 feet above sea level, the section of the road

Colonel Robert John Holmes, RIASC HQ Road Transport.

from milestone 19 through Kohima and onwards to milestone 92 just north of Kangpokpi was a designated hill sector and was, and still is, a tortuous and dangerous mountain road, twisting and winding through high peaks and deep gorges. Sadly, many drivers and their passengers and loads would end up at the bottom of these gorges because these treacherous passes took a heavy toll on experienced and inexperienced drivers alike, but the supplies still arrived. Kanglatongbi, milestone 118, at the northern end of the Imphal Plain, was where at last the road opened out from the jungle-clad hills either side and onto a level running all the way into Imphal. Though motorable for two-way traffic throughout its entire length, there were, except for designated areas along the roadside, few places to halt for the large numbers of trucks that ran night and day under a system called 'round-the-clock free running'. This system allowed for the free running of individual trucks back and forth, so that their various destinations would not be overwhelmed by

---

1. Joining the army at 16, Colonel Holmes served on the North-West Frontier of India in Waziristan before a spell in Shanghai, where he met and married his wife when he was a sergeant in the Royal Artillery. Upon leaving the army, he spent some time working in China and Burma and was on the list of the Burma Army Reserve of Officers when he was commissioned into the RIASC. He was awarded an OBE in 1945 for his valued services.

large convoy numbers arriving all at once for loading and unloading. Other specialist convoys, such as a complete unit being moved, would also be using the road at the same time. A service area called the Naga Service Station was set up at milestone 58; it was named after the 300 local tribesmen who did the work under the guidance of British officers, giving invaluable help in checking tyre pressures, water, oil levels and general maintenance for the trucks that plied this route. Located at various areas along the road were traffic control points manned by the Military Police, where convoy transport movements and discipline were controlled and logged with the use of a telephone line to positions in both directions. This greatly helped with the smooth running of operations, which would see many hundreds of vehicles on the move at any one time, with all the inevitable breakdowns, accidents and delays that inevitably occurred. Most delays were caused by the ever-present threat of landslides, especially during the wet season as the rain-soaked hillsides slumped onto the roads below or washed them away completely. A traffic census, conducted by the Lines of Communication Provost at Kanglatongbi for the month of March 1944, showed that the daily average density of traffic moving southbound on the main road was 663 vehicles, and northbound, 626 vehicles. Accidents reported for that same month were 157, of which, 5 were fatal, but this was an improvement on previous months when the drivers became more familiar with the road. It was noted, however, that almost as many accidents occurred on the flat straight runs as on the dangerous hill sector. This was attributed to the drivers speeding, and steps were taken to curb their zeal by Military Police checkpoints near to known accident black spots.

All along this route to Imphal were dotted the camps and installations of the various lines of communication administrative units; they ranged from small workshop recovery units through to large depots and hospitals, and even a pig farm. Mainly non-combatant, some of these units were moved time and time again, as the situation demanded them to carry out their vital work around the Imphal Plain and further afield into Burma.

Perched on a hillside overlooking the Imphal River and the small settlement of Kangpokpi was an American Baptist Mission compound and leper colony under the administration of The Reverend Earl Ernest Brock. He had been a missionary and teacher in Assam since 1927, and

Padre Brock's chapel at Kangpokpi.

continued with his work in Manipur in 1941, following the tragic death of his predecessor, Doctor Ahlquist, in a motor accident on the road to Kohima. The Reverend Brock also administered to the many Baptist churches in the district as he went about his missionary and teaching work, walking for days at a time over rough mountain paths and through thick jungle to visit his widespread flock. After the Japanese air raids on Imphal in 1942, a wave of fear seemed to have swept across the state, with the people fleeing back to their communities. At the Mission station, the hospital opened in 1920 by Dr Crozier was sadly closed and the work of the medical dispensary was withdrawn because those lepers who were able left for the safety of their villages. Overall, nearly 400 Naga and Kuki tribespeople moved away, though The Reverend Brock himself would stay in case they thought he had deserted them and would lose heart, writing, 'To leave people with a feeling that they have been more or less deserted would cause too many to lose confidence and hope. To fail them would be unfair to them, unfair to the people at home who are supporting the work, and unfair to the cause of Christ.'

The Mission compound covered a considerable area and contained several buildings, some large and well built with corrugated tin roofs, and

The American Baptist Mission compound at Kangpokpi, looking east towards the main Dimapur–Imphal Road.

others of the traditionally built basha type (bamboo and straw hut). Into this now largely vacant area with many buildings moved the headquarters of the General Reserve Engineer Force (GREF) at the end of October 1943. Previously they had been at Shillong, but as their operations moved ever southwards, it was decided that they needed to be nearer the units doing the work. Under the direct command of General Headquarters India, this formation had been charged in 1942 with the construction of the major engineering works in Assam and Burma, which included roads, airfields and pipelines. Unique in its make-up and achievements, GREF consisted of a variety of heavy engineering units, with their equipment and plant supported by large numbers of associated specialists, road transport companies, and pioneers totalling 26,000 men, and they were spread throughout the Imphal Plain and as far south as Tamu and beyond.

In command of this HQ at Kangpokpi was Brigadier S.A. Westrop, DSO, MC & Bar, with Lieutenant Colonel Agnew as Adjutant Quartermaster GREF. A small staff of 20 officers and 150 British and Indian other ranks and camp followers were also billeted within the compound. Captain Benjamin William Beasley of the Royal Indian Army Service Corps was a member of this HQ staff, and he came to know The Reverend Brock quite well during this period as he stayed with him in his bungalow; he remembered him as a determined yet very mild, unassuming man. By 1943, such was the good relationship the military had with The Reverend Brock that they actively encouraged and helped him to keep going what services he could for his flock, especially that of the school, which was

Sapper William Ernest 'Miff' Bowman, 864 ME Company Royal Engineers, driving a D8 bulldozer pulling an earth grader for road building.

kept partially open despite most of the pupils and teachers returning to their homes. The Reverend Brock, or Padre Brock, as he was addressed by the military, was invited to become an honorary member of the officers' mess, where he would often entertain them with his piano playing as they relaxed on the veranda after their day's work. As well as this, he also attended to the spiritual needs of those who assembled in his small, corrugated tin church overlooking the valley below.

Other units camped in the vicinity were also non-combatant, including Traffic Control Point 10, General Purpose Transport (GPT) companies, Headquarters No. 1 Mechanical Transport Regiment, 671 Indian Mechanical Excavation Company and 126 Heavy Wireless Transmitter Section of the Royal Signals. The latter unit was of particular importance to the HQ

Padre Brock and family in Assam, 1933.

GREF in keeping contact with all their units, which were widely spread over hundreds of miles, and for communications with GHQ back in India. Signalman Jack Ramsden was an operator wireless and line (OWL), and was part of this six-man unit, four of whom were also OWLs, the others being an instrument mechanic and a driver. Their equipment was a '33 set' transmitter with two receivers powered by a generator fitted in a 3-ton wireless truck. Another truck contained all their personal equipment, stores, spare parts and aerial masts when not in use. Brigadier Westrop was most impressed with the power output of this equipment, being able to transmit a couple of thousand miles, given the best conditions.

By early 1944, a settled routine was in place but by now, the rations were getting very monotonous. Captain Beasley took up the account:

> The Indian Other Ranks [meaning all ranks apart from officers] at the Mission, during their forays into the hills, found what they considered to be a useful variation to their khana [food] … in the cultivated garden of the leper colony on top of our hill. Their raids had to be stopped because not only did they frighten the lepers but also deprived them of their only food. I therefore decided to visit the colony at least once a week to see they were not molested. The top of the hill was a long steep climb through jungle with one or two small clearings on the way. After a few weeks I noticed that further clearing and building was in progress, which puzzled me because the Kukis on our side of the Imphal valley were head-hunters like the Nagas, and they only built on the top of hills as a precaution against surprise attacks by raiding parties. As the weeks went by the size of the long houses being built, and the unfriendly, villainous and surly looks of the builders made me suspicious too. So, I queried this building activity with Padre Brock, who was the contact between the villages and the Political Agent in Imphal who reported directly to the Maharajah of Manipur [His Excellency Bodhchandra Singh] for administrative and security purposes. In due course back came the answer yes, the villagers had been given permission to build a new village. I thought this very odd and checked again as the long houses grew in size and number. Still the same answer.

Captain Beasley's suspicions were not unfounded, and neither were Padre Brock's concerns for his flock, for indeed, the Japanese would later take over the Mission as their divisional headquarters of 15th Division and the newly constructed village was used for their No. 1 Field Hospital and depot.

Heading in a southerly direction just past Kangpokpi, the terrain opened slightly allowing for various installations to be erected on the relatively flat open areas between the road and the thick jungle-clad hills either side. At milestone 108, the Indian Army Medical Corps had set up 14 Light Field Ambulance next to where a large Base Ordnance Workshop area, complete with roadways and sheds, was being constructed by the steel riggers of 413

1. Milestone 108 unfinished BOD sheds; 2. abandoned grass airstrip; 3. milestone 109 meeting place of 2 Division and 5 Division, 22 June 1944.

Indian Steelwork Erection Section Indian Engineers. This unit, commanded by Lieutenant Shanley, was tasked with building twenty-four large steel-framed and clad sheds, some complete with overhead gantries for the heavy lifting of engines and machinery under repair. Other sheds being built were to be used for storage of Vote 9 stores. A small advance party from the Ordnance Corps commanded by Major L. Woodcock was on hand to liaise and advise with the construction, but with only a few weeks being allowed to complete this project, Lieutenant Shanley and his second in command, Lieutenant Rogers, were constantly under pressure; this was not helped by the shortage of labour and materials, and by amendments to the plans. Other delays were caused by the artillery units nearby as they practised their firing drills, and by the shipments of steel being delivered in the wrong order. They were supported by the pioneers of 1341 Indian Pioneer Company and the African Sappers of 32 (West African) Artisan Works (AW) Company. Since the beginning of March 1944, this company had camped nearby at milestone 114 under the command of Captain William Edward Pryde Watson, and they had been busily employed in the construction of sites ready for 14 British General Hospital, with 79 and 87 Indian General Hospitals within the same locality. A great deal of time had been spent constructing dams and laying pipework for a clean water supply, as well as brick-built operating theatres. Nearby, a temporary pig farm was built, big enough to house 40 boars and 400 sows, with a 2,500-acre vegetable garden set out near to milestone 110. A D4 bulldozer with a 6-furrow plough with 2 engineers from 864 Mechanical Equipment Company Royal Engineers was used to plough this land, where it was hoped that the 800 gardeners from three Pioneer Corps companies earmarked for this project would provide

Captain Pryde Watson, OC 32 Artisan Works Company West African Engineers.

enough fresh vegetables that could be airlifted to forward units, as well as for those stationed nearer. An emergency landing ground had been set out near milestone 108. However, this grass strip was only used occasionally for light aircraft, and it was abandoned once the airstrip at Imphal became operational.[2]

One of the few fighting units to be located alongside the main road in this area was the 3rd Carabiniers (Prince of Wales Dragoon Guards) with its General Lee medium tanks, being part of 254 Indian Tank Brigade. By this stage of the war, the American-built Lee tank had become obsolete in the European and North African theatres, because it was totally outclassed in every respect when pitted against the powerful German Tiger and Panther tanks. However, the Lee proved more than a match against anything that the Japanese had in armour, and during the only tank versus tank battle during the campaign, the Japanese were completely routed. Upon moving to milestone 109, the Carbs, as they were known, were heavily engaged with the 1st Battalion Seaforth Highlanders, who were also camped in the immediate vicinity, for training in the tactics of infantry support in thick jungle. Now, they were involved with learning the art of 'bunker busting'. The Japanese Army were expert at building bunkers and their complexes, which were difficult to dislodge once established. The Lee tank proved highly effective against these bunkers with their 75mm gun firing at close range, using solid shot projectiles. A series of bunkers modelled on the known Japanese designs were built into the jungle-covered hillside by the engineers, where live firing tests were conducted and tactics worked out. In early February 1944, the Supreme Allied Commander, Admiral Lord Louis Mountbatten, made a surprise visit to the regiment as they continued with their training. Trooper Malcolm Connolly remembered how the 'Supremo' gathered all the troops around him, giving them a rousing speech telling them that there was to be no more running away from the Japanese, because they would in future be supplied by air. It was noted by Trooper Connolly that

> We were ordered to wait out of sight until his jeep could be seen coming along the track into camp. Then the Regimental Trumpeter would sound the call 'Barrack Field Alarm', and then we all had to come running showing all the

---

2. On 11 August 1942, an RAF Lysander became the first aircraft ever to land in Manipur when it successfully landed on this airstrip.

signs of enthusiasm for this great honour. As we had been paraded at 08.00 hours and eventually when he did arrive it was 12.00 hours, everyone was so completely browned off with sitting around that we couldn't have cared less.

To highlight the importance of the work of the Carbs, further individual visits during the month were made by General Sir George Giffard, the Army Group Commander, IV Corps Commander Lieutenant General Geoffrey Scoones, and 14th Army Commander General William Slim, better known as 'Uncle Bill' to all the ranks throughout the Army, such was his popularity.

Located at milestone 110, Keithelmanbi was the site of the divisional reinforcement camp of 20 Indian Infantry Division, the only formation in the 14th Army to have trained throughout its inception specifically for war in Burma. Another normally non-combatant administrative unit, 20 Reinforcement (Rft) Camp held, equipped, trained and dispatched all the reinforcements for the division, who were now in the Kabaw Valley area south-east of Imphal. There were also the Engineer reinforcements destined

Trooper Malcolm Connolly, 3rd Carabiniers.

A 20 Indian Division sign.

for the Indian Engineer units of IV Corps. The unit had been formed in 1943 in Gaya, Bihar State, and sadly, in common with the reinforcement operations in general at this time, had been allowed to become a place where the men were neglected, and discipline had failed as despair set in. The accommodation, in most instances, was in dilapidated bashas with earthen floors, or in decaying tents with a lack of any amenities. The training and recreation were disorganised, and the troops crowded together from all different units with the esprit de corps suffering badly as a result. The permanent staff, with a few exceptions, were officers and non-commissioned officers (NCOs) who had no interest in their work, and who had been posted away as unwanted by their units. To combat this parlous situation, a cavalry veteran of the First World War, Lieutenant Colonel John Gradidge, OBE, formerly of the 10th Queen Victoria's Own Corps of Cavalry Guides Frontier Force, was appointed by General Slim as the Commandant Reinforcement Group. He was to completely overhaul the whole reinforcement operation. Immediately he set about this task by the staffing of the camps with good men and officers, namely those who had the necessary skills and experience to motivate and properly train the reinforcements to the standards required for fighting the Japanese. Most of these permanent staff came from fighting units, having had some pressure applied to their commanding officers to release them. Not wishing to lose valuable fighting men and officers from the front line, it was agreed that their posting would only be for a few months' duration in most cases. Gradually, the accommodation in the camps was improved, discipline was regained, and proper regimes of instruction and realistic jungle warfare training took place, where the former passive and defensive attitude was replaced by a more aggressive one. The men responded well to these improvements and the camps became places where their pride was restored and their fighting abilities honed.[3] For his valued work with this, Lieutenant Colonel Gradidge was awarded a Mention in Despatches in 1945, eventually retiring as a brigadier.

On 18 October 1943, after a term of eight months as President Courts Martial, Lieutenant Colonel Victor Henry Wells-Cole, MC, of the King's

---

3. It was noted in the war diary of the 2nd Border Regiment of 20th Indian Division how the condition and efficiency of the new reinforcements had improved considerably since the battalion's first arrival in theatre.

Own Yorkshire Light Infantry (formerly the OC of the KOYLI depot), took over command of 20 Rft Camp from Lieutenant Colonel Branscombe, Green Howards. Lieutenant Colonel Wells-Cole had previously been in command of 7th Battalion KOYLI for two years and oversaw their change of role to that of an armoured unit when it became 149 Regiment Royal Armoured Corps in December 1941. This unit went on to be heavily and successfully involved in the Battle of Kohima in 1944, supporting the British 2nd Division. The adjutant of 20 Rft Camp, Captain Thomas Andrew Sinclair

Lieutenant Colonel Victor Henry Wells-Cole, MC, KOYLI, CO 149 Regiment Royal Armoured Corps, CO 20 Rft Camp, Lion Box commander.

Lieutenant Colonel Wells-Cole, MC, KOYLI depot commandant, inspection on Minden Day, a regimental battle honour celebrated each year on the anniversary.

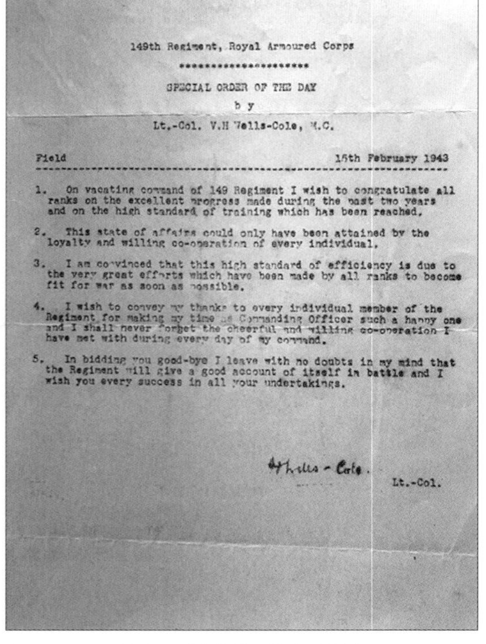

149th Regiment, Royal Armoured Corps

****

SPECIAL ORDER OF THE DAY

b y

Lt.-Col. V.H Wells-Cole, M.C.

Field   15th February 1943

1.   On vacating command of 149 Regiment I wish to congratulate all ranks on the excellent progress made during the past two years and on the high standard of training which has been reached.

2.   This state of affairs could only have been attained by the loyalty and willing co-operation of every individual.

3.   I am convinced that this high standard of efficiency is due to the very great efforts which have been made by all ranks to become fit for war as soon as possible.

4.   I wish to convey my thanks to every individual member of the Regiment for making my time as Commanding Officer such a happy one and I shall never forget the cheerful and willing co-operation I have met with during every day of my command.

5.   In bidding you good-bye I leave with no doubts in my mind that the Regiment will give a good account of itself in battle and I wish you every success in all your undertakings.

Lt.-Col.

Lieutenant Colonel Wells-Cole, MC, Special Order of the Day, 149 Regiment Royal Armoured Corps.

Captain Thomas Andrew Sinclair Charles, Worcestershire Regiment. Adjutant 20 Rft Camp.

Charles of the Worcestershire Regiment, remembered how, under the command of Lieutenant Colonel Wells-Cole, 'the unit was converted from a disintegrated, disorganised rabble into a smooth working unit of the Army which produced reinforcements to a standard that satisfied the division'.[4] Possibly to illustrate the efficiency of the camp, it was noted that unlike most of the other reinforcement camps, 20 Rft Camp received very few inspection visits from senior officers of the Reinforcement Group.

On 30 October 1943, 294 men from 20 Rft Camp left Gaya and arrived at Keithelmanbi on 7 November after a long journey, crossing the Brahmaputra and Ganges rivers on flat-bottomed ferryboats, with 160 tons of their baggage and equipment. Further personnel arrived in the following weeks and began settling into their routine. Completely unsuited for any real active defence, the site was chosen because of the training facilities nearby, as well as for ease of access, being located on the main supply route. In the shadow of Mount Koubru, to the west of the road, a tented camp was set out on an open plain bounded by nullahs (dried riverbeds), but a large landslide down the escarpment adjacent to the main road meant that the scheduled work on the site facilities was delayed, as the access to the camp was gained from a long slope leading up the escarpment from close to a bridge on the main road. This landslide had also caused delays to traffic as a one-way system was put in place lasting several weeks, while engineers and labourers cleared and stabilised the 300-yard-long slippage. At the top of this slope, in amongst a few trees, a small gate guard consisting of six Royal

---

4. Captain Charles's younger twin brothers, Arthur and Robin, both subalterns in the Royal Artillery, were at this time POWs of the Japanese, with one being held in Java and the other in Hiroshima, in Japan.

Former site of Lynx Box and 20 Rft Camp milestone 110, 20 April 1944.

Artillery gun fitters, awaiting posting to their unit, were located in tents. Gunner Bruce Betteridge remembered how the company sergeant major left them to their own devices so long as there was someone on duty at all times. There were no unnecessary parades, and to keep themselves occupied an old 25-pounder field gun and a Tata armoured car in the camp were overhauled and maintained in good running order. Gunner Betteridge also spent considerable time roaming the adjacent hills hunting to augment their

Gunner Bruce Betteridge, Royal Artillery, attached 20 Rft Camp.

rations, while Private Ray Dunn of the Devonshire Regiment remembered going out on patrol looking for signs of Japanese, but he 'bagged' a deer instead.

The 20 Rft Camp consisted of ten sections – two British and eight Indian – each commanded by the permanent staff of a captain, a company sergeant major and company quartermaster sergeant, or the Indian equivalent, and with help from a few reinforcement officers and NCOs, oversaw a varying amount of anything up to 300 men. The camp strength for the end of February 1944 was 227 British troops and 1,494 Indian troops. Of the eight Indian sections, six were of infantry and the other two were of support and administrative troops, namely engineers, drivers, pioneers and signallers, who were all commanded by the Indian Viceroy's commissioned officers (VCOs), with subedar majors (Indian rank equivalent to a warrant officer) as well. The two British Sections, No. 1 Section commanded by Captain Andrew Maurice Ewing of the Border Regiment and No. 2 Section, were

Captain Andrew Ewing, 2nd Border Regiment, attached 20 Rft Camp.

exclusively for British reinforcements destined for the front line with 20 Indian Division. The camp headquarters consisted of the colonel, the adjutant, the second in command, Major Norman Sinclair of the 7th/10th Baluch Regiment, Major Norman Algernon Chubb of the Duke of Cornwall's Light Infantry attached to the 19th Hyderabad Regiment, the chief training officer, Captain John (Jack) Alfred Archer Pannell of the 12th Frontier Force Regiment, the postings officer, Captain Thomas Penrice Kidman Royal Engineers, the assistant adjutant, and Captain Timothy Williams, the quartermaster. One of the Indian section commanders was Captain Rodney Walter Darragh Newton of the 14th Punjab Regiment. Known as Paddy because of his Irish birth, Captain Newton had been a tea planter with plantations in Ceylon. Sergeants Gleed and Eric Bailey of the Royal Artillery were the orderly room sergeants, and Cecil Garrod of the Royal Norfolk Regiment was a company quartermaster sergeant. The permanent staff formed a close bond with each other as the rest of the camp was in a constant state of flux, with large numbers of men being moved in and out continuously. As is usually the case in this type of situation, the men

Sergeant Eric Bailey, Royal Artillery attached 20 Rft Camp.

CQMS Cecil Garrod, Royal Norfolk Regiment, attached 20 Rft Camp.

and officers tended to mix more often, and the usual peacetime condition of the 'us and them' culture was not so strictly observed. The officers' and senior ranks' mess bars were run by a sergeant from the Royal Artillery and Gunner Betteridge, and his team of gun fitters were the beneficiaries of one or two half bottles of whisky 'donated' by him, in addition to their rum ration. The physical training officer was Captain Bernard Joseph Frances Goggin, a physical education teacher in a private school before being commissioned from the ranks into the Frontier Force Regiment. He would hold music evenings in his tent, playing a selection of his records on an ageing gramophone. He would also give a short talk about the music he was playing to those gathered, who would then sit in silence listening. It is not difficult to imagine the sounds of opera or Beethoven wafting over the jungle-clad hills in the stillness of the dark Manipuri night. While having a drink during one of these evenings, 2nd Lieutenant Jack Allen, another former tea planter of the 4th/3rd Madras Regiment, remembered how he, as a very young subaltern aged just 21, was told by Company Sergeant Major George (Johno) Johnson of No. 1 Section (the author's father) that he probably had more years' army service than his age. CSM Johnson was a pre-war veteran of the troublesome North-West Frontier Province of India, and he had already seen seventeen years of service with the Royal Norfolk Regiment by this time. Strangely, Lieutenant Allen and three other officers, Lieutenants Scott, Master and Halge, had been posted back to 20 Rft Camp in January from their unit, who were acting as divisional defence at their HQ at Shenam because the battalion was overstrength. Another Indian section commander was Captain Brian Hope Winstanley of the 9th/14th Punjab Regiment, who was posted to 20 Rft Camp on 17 March as a replacement

CSM George Johnson, Royal Norfolk Regiment, attached 20 Rft Camp.

for Captain J.C. Harrowing, also of the 9th/14th Punjabis, who had been there since the camp's arrival in November.

Despite this relaxed atmosphere, it was still expected that all ranks should follow discipline and that the CO's orders be carried out. Any transgressions were soon dealt with by the CO, and in some more serious instances, the offenders were put in detention within the camp. This was the case with two reinforcement riflemen of the 3rd/1st Gurkha Rifles, resulting in them not being posted to their unit until their sentences were served during February and March 1944. The adjutant, Captain Charles, remembered one incident when even an officer had to be disciplined:

A Major waiting for his posting to a unit was sitting having his food in the mess tent stripped to the waist, which was against standing orders. I approached him and told him to put his shirt on or he would be arrested. The Major protested and said he would report this to the CO, Lt Col Henry Wells-Cole, and I told him that that was fine. I then reported to the CO myself in his tent and told him what had happened, to which he replied, 'I think we had better have him in here to learn about discipline, don't you Andrew?' I stood behind the Colonel sitting in his chair as the Major marched in, properly clothed by this time. The Colonel gave him a dressing down and told him 'My Adjutant doesn't give the orders here, I do! … but what he does do is see that my orders are carried out.' When the Major was dismissed, the Colonel turned to me and said, 'I think we had better get him posted.' I replied, 'To the front or the rear Sir?' 'The Border Regiment will do,' replied the Colonel. He was in the jungle the next day!

Towards the end of February, 20 Rft Camp was informed that because of the need of further training of the Engineer reinforcements, an Engineer officer would be taken onto the camp's War Establishment for this purpose. Captain Eric Ivan Hamilton-Parks from the Madras Sappers and Miners, an architect in civilian life, took up his position and, aided by a training grant of 300 rupees for locally obtained materials such as bamboo poles, ropes and so forth, began his work with the reinforcements. Also, in a most fortuitous way, as will be seen later, Captain Hamilton-Parks was allowed to draw considerable amounts of explosives and detonators from the ammunition depot at 221 AOD Kanglatongbi, for the purposes of demonstrations of demolition and the making of booby traps. In addition to the training of the reinforcements within the camp, other units in the locality were also invited to send personnel for further weapons training and, on occasion, Lieutenant Colonel Wells-Cole gave permission for his instructors to visit nearby units for instructional purposes.

Another reinforcement camp was located near milestone 112, not far from Safarmaina. The 25 Rft Camp under the command of Lieutenant Colonel Brookman had arrived from Bangalore and was now the divisional camp of 23 Indian Division, taking over the role from 24 Rft Camp at Kohima, who were now to provide reinforcements for the 256 Sub Area. Also, near here, at milestone 114, was a vehicle park and dump for wrecked vehicles, where a detachment from 203 Base Ordnance Depot cannibalised and used them for spare parts whenever possible, because supplies were always short. The GPT units thereabouts were always stopping off at this vehicle graveyard to replace worn or broken parts. During the campaign, the Fourteenth Army became supreme masters of improvisation. There was no doubt it was the 'Cinderella Army' when it came to supplies and equipment, with priority being given to the European theatre of the war. Everything was used, reused, recycled and on tight rationing, especially later, as the Siege of Imphal began to bite.

Another armoured unit, the Indian 7th Light Cavalry, was based in the milestone 116–117 area for training with Indian infantry units, and with their Stuart tanks and armoured carriers regularly patrolled the main road almost into Kohima. A tank reserve harbour had been built along the western side of the road with associated sheds and facilities, but this was hardly used and was instead employed as a forward servicing station where, for a while, a three eight-hour shift system was used to ensure the road transport supply vehicles were maintained correctly. In the middle of February 1944, 43 GPT Company of the RIASC took over this position and found their new site very agreeable and well suited for their purposes. Commanded by Major Victor Clement de St Croix, a pre-war Territorial Army officer, formerly the battalion transport officer of the 4th Royal West Kent Regiment at Dunkirk in 1940, and his second in command Captain Cecil Miles Beddow, they began their work as a lines of communication transport company under the guidance of 242 GPT Company, who had already been performing these duties since 1943. Those men not required for immediate driving duties were

43 GPT Company OC Major de St Croix (right) and 2 i/c, Captain Beddow, next to him.

put to work by digging and constructing formidable defensive bunkers with interlocking trenches all along their roadside perimeter. In fact, the actual 117 milestone was in the middle of their location. However, these defences were never used by the company other than at the stand-to order because they were to be abandoned later, as were all the other defences north of Kanglatongbi as the Japanese advanced southwards. Possibly not up to the standard of their renowned bunkers and fortifications, the Japanese nevertheless made use of them. Other men of the company were used in the cutting of bamboo for the construction of bashas and charpoys (bamboo-framed beds) to make their accommodation comfortable, unaware that their stay would only be a short six weeks. A few days later, the company suffered their first serious road traffic accident, when one of their lorries

Captain Cecil Miles Beddow, 2 i/c 43 GPT Company RIASC.

Major Victor de St Croix and officers of 43 GPT Company RIASC.

43 GPT Company recovery vehicle and workshop personnel.

went over the khudside (side of a deep ravine) at milestone 89 and fell 400 feet. The driver and his passenger, though badly injured, had a lucky escape, and to emphasise the importance of road safety, Major de St Croix ordered that the now recovered wrecked vehicle should be placed beside the out gate of the camp, as a stark and timely reminder to others of the consequences of not driving carefully.[5]

A mile further south was the entrance to the largest Ordnance Depot on the Imphal Plain, located between milestones 117½ and 118½, west of the main road, covering an approximate area of over a square mile. It had been carved out of scrub jungle using bulldozers to make several thousand yards of connecting roadways and loading areas. An ammunition depot was at the northern end of the site, where thousands of tons of ammunition were stacked in separate bays as a fire precaution. The A and B Sub-Depots held all the other stores, which ranged from artillery pieces through to clothing.

---

5. Lieutenant Swailes of 137 GPT Company remembered how, when on road patrol duties checking on his drivers, he would sometimes come across a driver and his co-driver sitting on their haunches by the roadside. Having fortunately bailed out, the driver greeted Lieutenant Swailes with '*Gari niche Sahib*' (Vehicle is down there, Sir).

Lion Box and Ordnance Depot, 4 April 1944.

On the opposite side of the main road was 298 Field Supply Depot (FSD), where a detail issue store was established.

Various elements of the Indian Army Ordnance Corps (IAOC) were based here under the umbrella of 221 Advanced Ordnance Depot for the storage and distribution of these stores. Various technical, scientific and ammunition experts responsible for the safe storage and handling of important equipment and explosives were also on site, one of whom recalled:

> Then came my next assignment that took me to Kanglatongbi and the ammo dump. So off to Howrah Station where we boarded the train for the destination of the Dimapur railhead; here I found a conglomeration of all types of supplies heading for Kanglatongbi and Imphal. The Major I met at the Mess asked where I was heading for, and when I said Kanglatongbi

Lieutenant Shamsher Brar, Indian Army Ordnance Corps 221 AOD.

> he asked if I could ride a motorbike. Apparently, they had no room to take any more motorcycles so me and the Quarter Master Sergeant accompanying me set off for Imphal on two wheels. Our first stop was Nichugard where I had never seen so many Red Caps before. We were very tired and wet through when I finally found the Officers' Mess where I had a much needed and great night's rest. Next day I sent the QMS on ahead as I stayed behind to repair the generator for the station after someone had filled the fuel tank with petrol instead of diesel. This held me up for two days before setting off again when catastrophe struck as I rounded a bend. A landslide on the road caused me to brake hard and the bike skidded beneath me, and I ended up in the mud. Fortunately, a group of L of C wallahs who were nearby brewing char and bully beef and chapatis heard the crash and came to my rescue. It was a miracle I wasn't hurt, and the lads straightened the handlebars and the footrest. They gave me a feast and once again I was on my way. At long last I reached Kanglatongbi where I placed the bike at the Guardroom and informed the guard that someone would be coming to collect it. It did go in the end but who collected it I don't know. I felt sorry for the one who had to ride it!

The depot had originally been set up as an Ordnance dump in 1942 after the defeated Burma Army had retired from Burma. The men of 25 Indian AW Company Indian Engineers, under the command of Captain R.M. Bennett, had spent months constructing large basha-type buildings and infrastructure. Further work and improvements had been done by the pioneers of 22 Auxiliary Battalion Indian Pioneer Corps when more extensions and roads were made. This then became the site of the 56 Ordnance Depot in March 1943, but this changed again in October when it became an Advanced Ordnance Depot. 2nd Lieutenant Shamsha Brar was posted there at this time together with 2nd Lieutenant Nand Kishore and remembered how it was very basic, being built using local materials of bamboo and straw in what was an area prone to disease. Sergeant Bernard Hargreaves of the Royal Army Ordnance

Sergeant Bernard Hargreaves, 221 AOD.

Corps (RAOC) described the basha he lived in as a 'perfect little mansion'. He shared this accommodation with four others who were 'a grand crowd who pulled together which means more than creature comforts', though they had the luxury of a table and chair upon which they took turns in writing their ever-important letters home. Another luxury was an ancient radio, which provided them with news and sometimes music, despite the high hills that surrounded them interrupting the signal. Their water supply and that of other units at Kanglatongbi was drawn from a stream that ran down the hills near the Kangla Admin Commandant's office. Sergeant Hargreaves described its surroundings as:

> great jutting mountains, covered with huge jungle trees all knurled and twisted through years of torrential rain and terrible sunshine, and the creatures who inhabit these forests – squirrels, deer, jackals, wild pigs and birds, tigers, snakes, and panthers. We get a goodly assortment of nature here of which we never see any to speak of, which usually sheer off when humans occupy the place – wish the blinking Japs would do the same!

By early 1944, 221 AOD, numbering over 430 personnel, were now known to be a unit containing 'a very good assortment of fellows', had been specially trained for a mobile role during the Arakan campaign, and in January moved to Chittagong and left the depot under the control of a skeleton staff from 203 Base Ordnance Depot and 403 Base Ammunition Depot. They were augmented by personnel from other Ordnance units commanded by Captain Bristow. At about this time, Lieutenant Dennis Granville Buckingham was posted to 221 AOD after being attached to the IAOC from the Royal Norfolk

Lieutenant Dennis Buckingham, Royal Norfolk Regiment, attached 221 AOD.

Regiment. Also at this time, the General Staff deemed it was important for an intelligence officer to be attached to the depot, and Captain Gordon Frederick Duckworth took up his position there. Formerly of the Royal Artillery and now attached to the RIASC, Captain Duckworth set about his duties of passing information between the depot and his HQ. With the

Captain Gordon Duckworth, RIASC, attached 221 AOD.

Lieutenant Colonel Herbert Cunningham, CO 221 AOD.

launch of operation Ha-Go, the Japanese offensive in the Arakan meant that 221 AOD were now sent back again to their familiar site at Kanglatongbi. Under the command of Lieutenant Colonel Herbert Ian Cunningham (known as HIC), advanced elements of 221 AOD relieved 203 BOD and 403 BAD on 26 February, with the remainder of the unit returning by the 8 March to find that the stocks of the depot had been run down considerably. They then set about the task of restocking. At this time, the depot was an extremely busy place, with scores of lorries arriving with over 9,000 tons of all manner of supplies being offloaded and correctly stored by the labourers of the Pioneer Corps under the watchful eye of the Ordnance staff.

Major Herbert Scanes, 15th Punjab Regiment, Kanglatongbi Administration Commandant.

Organising the depot to be up and running again at full capacity was set back for a brief period by a series of widespread jungle wildfires that broke out, including at the FSD on the other side of the road, which destroyed some tentage and stores. These fires were taken under control by the staff, and other nearby units were drafted in to help, such as 15 AW Company West African Engineers (WAE). Because it was believed there were Japanese sympathisers in the area, it was decided that it would be prudent to keep a proper firefighting unit on hand within the depot. Sergeant William Sargeant was in charge of 508 Indian Fire Fighting Section, and with his small unit of firemen and their firefighting equipment patrolled the area checking vulnerable points, especially where the jungle had become tinder-dry. Three tall wooden fire-watch towers had been built by the engineers and erected around the perimeter, and they proved useful in the early detection of signs of fire by the picquets placed in that area. A forward marshalling yard was set out opposite the entrance to the depot, where the incoming supply trucks were held until called for to be unloaded. This allowed the roads within the depot to be kept clear from queuing vehicles, helping to minimise congestion and improving their turnaround times. All in all, this was a very busy and important place at a critical time.

Immediately adjacent to the southern boundary of the Ordnance Depot was the HQ of the Kanglatongbi Administration Commandant, Major Herbert James William Scanes, a veteran of the First World War. Formerly of the Pioneer Corps, he was now attached to the 15th Punjab Regiment. He and his staff of three British and four Indian clerks were better known as the 'Kangla Admin Commandant', and it was where many units of 256 Line of Communications Sub Area were based or controlled from. This had been an important staging post in 1942 as the civilian refugees from Burma struggled back to India, accompanied by the remnants of the defeated Burma Army, and sought refuge at 51 Rest Camp. It was also the site of a Public Works Department for the maintenance of roads and bridges in the area, which was administered from the Dak Bungalow close by. This was a pretty, colonial-era building, constructed by the British in 1898 as a transit point for government officials and postal couriers. However, the commandant's offices were further along a track in a group of basha huts beside a deep nullah at the base of a range of hills overlooking the valley from the west. This track came out onto the main road at milestone 118, with the Imphal Turel flowing north to south half a mile away. The western end of the Kanglatongbi Ridge ended here with the high mountains of the Molvom and Mapao Ridges towering beyond, overlooking Imphal.

During the month of March, there were just under fifty assorted units under this command who were camped between milestones 118 and 120. These were mostly support troops who ranged from field bakers, butchers, anti-malarial specialists, engineers, medics, drivers, labourers and postal workers. There was a canteen facility offering a twenty-four-hour service of hot meals and drinks for the drivers from the many GPT companies passing through Kanglatongbi, as well as a mobile tea van. This was most ably run by a detachment of the WASB (Women's Auxiliary Service (Burma)), which was also on hand. Though to some, the work done by these so-called 'soft' troops may have seemed mundane and inconsequential, it was nevertheless absolutely vital to the maintenance of operations in general, and for the morale of the fighting troops. The latter aspect should not be underestimated, and the effect of simply having a 'hot mug of char and a wad' while enjoying a smoke and reading the all-important mail from home was immeasurable to men who had been in the most difficult circumstances. Another morale booster was the playing of sport and the much-contested inter-unit football matches, with local units fielding teams of varying abilities, guaranteed to cause friendly rivalry. The 99 Mobile Workshop Company seemed to be the main host for these games, and one of the last of these matches played before security was tightened in early March was between 99 Mobile Workshop Company and 20 Reinforcement Camp, when 20 Rft Camp came out as clear winners in a 2–5 victory.[6]

Concert shows were provided by the Entertainments National Service Association (ENSA), and though it is unknown whether its most famous celebrity Vera Lynn ever performed at Kanglatongbi, she did elsewhere in Burma and was enthusiastically received by the troops. Noel Coward, however, did perform at Kanglatongbi with his own particular brand of humour and wit. A makeshift stage for him, complete with a piano, was erected on the back of a lorry. Another entertainer equally appreciated was 'Stainless' Stephen. Mobile cinema units proved very popular as well, especially with the Indian troops, and operated quite frequently at Kanglatongbi. With there being so many non-combatant and unarmed personnel in this area, the security for the Kangla Admin Commandant and the units thereabouts was provided by two platoons from C Company 27th/5th Mahratta Light Infantry, with the rest of their battalion spread out at various locations along the 202 Area L of C.

The last village of any appreciable size before reaching the outskirts of Imphal was Sengmai at milestone 121, where the HQ and Workshop Sections of 864 Mechanical Equipment Company Royal Engineers were based. This also was a GREF unit, commanded by Major Thomas Lindsay Gray, OBE. There, a large white-painted two-storey modern building was taken over by the HQ Section to administer the comings and goings of the four other sections of the company, who at times would have sappers with

---

6. Though not as well known as the famous Tennis Court at Kohima, the football pitch at Kanglatongbi was another sporting venue that later saw heavy fighting as it became the front line. To this day, the Kanglatongbi Football Ground is adjacent to where 99 Mobile Workshop Company's position used to be.

their heavy earth-moving equipment and plant detailed to work along the whole of length of 256 Sub Area L of C and beyond. Smaller details of sappers would be sent to wherever their expertise and machinery were needed, though their main work was mostly the construction of roads and airfields. To service and repair this machinery, basha-type workshops were erected in the area of the old Sengmai rice mill.

A little further along the road about a mile to the west of milestone 124, at the small settlement of Leimagong, the 41 Indian General Hospital complex

Major Thomas Lindsay Gray, OBE, 864 ME Company Royal Engineers.

Sapper Joe Ford standing in the middle with others from 864 ME Company Royal Engineers.

had been set out and built as a permanent site. The 17 Indian AW Company Indian Engineers had been tasked with its construction, taking many months to complete. Other medical units were based there as well, including an Indian field laboratory, an ear, nose and throat clinic, an X-ray unit, an anti-malarial unit, and transport companies.

As these support and administrative units and many others went about their daily tasks, the gradual build-up of the 14th Army continued in preparation for the campaign to retake Burma. The Japanese too had been busy preparing their campaign for the 'March on Delhi'. Their Operation Ha-Go was the attack on the Arakan in southern Burma and preceded by a month their main thrust of Operation U-Go, the capture of Imphal and Dimapur, which would leave wide open the door to India itself. On 15 March 1944, the Japanese 15th Army, consisting of three divisions, crossed the Chindwin River and advanced towards their objectives. The 31st Division were tasked with the capture of the all-important Dimapur railhead and stores facilities via Kohima, while the 33rd Division were to move to the south of the Imphal Plain. The 15th Division had the objective to cut the main Imphal–Dimapur road just to the north of Imphal, thereby completing the encirclement of the British IV Corps.

This move had been foreseen by General Slim, and plans had been put in place for the withdrawal of the divisions of IV Corps to the Imphal Plain, where it would extend the very doubtful lines of communication of the Japanese. It would be here on the ground of his choosing that Slim would stand and fight, knowing he had air superiority to enable the resupply of his huge garrison, while the besieging Japanese 33rd and 15th Divisions desperately sought supplies.

To counter the threat to Dimapur, General Slim ordered the British 2nd Division, now training in India, to move there while sending part of the 5th Indian Division to reinforce the small garrison at Kohima. This would all take time to put into place but as luck would have it, time was bought by the Indian 50th Parachute Brigade, who happened to be in the Sangshak area north-east of Imphal, and in the direct path of the advancing Japanese 31st and 15th Divisions. It was here that the time needed by Slim was paid for with the blood of this overwhelmingly outnumbered brigade, because the Japanese were delayed for three days and lost many men, which they could ill afford. This extra time also allowed the defences around the Imphal Plain to be altered and improved. As the few gallant stragglers of 50 Parachute Brigade made their way to Imphal through thick jungle to reform and fight again, the Japanese 31st Division moved on towards Kohima, while the 15th Division then split into three groups, each with their own objectives to the north of Imphal. The Right Assault Unit comprised the 2nd and 3rd Battalions of the 60th Infantry Regiment, 1st Battalion 21st Field Artillery, two Engineer platoons, and the 1st Field Hospital, which was under the command of Colonel Matsumura. Their objective was to advance to the north-west of Imphal and then, in conjunction with the other two assault units, move on Imphal. The Left Assault Unit under the command of Colonel Omoto comprised two battalions of the 51st Infantry Regiment, 3rd Battalion 21st Field Artillery Regiment, and one Engineer platoon, which were expected to capture Sengmai along with areas to the north-east of Imphal. The third assault unit was named after its commanding officer and was known as the Honda Raiding Unit. This was made up of elements of the 3rd Battalion 67th Infantry Regiment, 2nd Battalion 21st Field Artillery Regiment, and one Engineer platoon. Their objective was to advance quickly ahead of the other assault units and to capture Kangpokpi (always known as Mission to the Japanese) and to cut and hold the main Imphal–Dimapur road. The remaining units of 15th Division were held in reserve and were to reinforce where necessary.

Thus, the scene was set for two of the most critical and bitter British battles of the Second World War where, for a while, the entire fate of India was held in the hands of a few hundred desperate and brave men of the Kohima Garrison, and at Imphal, where the Imperial Japanese Army would finally suffer the worst defeat ever inflicted upon them.

Chapter Two

The Withdrawal

In anticipation of any Japanese advance along the Kabaw Valley or elsewhere to the south of Imphal, a plan of withdrawal of the GREF units working in these areas back to the Imphal Plain were put in place for safety reasons, in order that the fighting units of the divisions in place would not be impeded by the work or movements. Around the end of February 1944, the HQ staff of GREF at Kangpokpi began working on plans that superseded the previous one codenamed 'Bungy'. A false alarm and the sending of the coded message for withdrawal earlier had unquestionably revealed deficiencies in that particular plan. As such, Lieutenant Colonel Agnew and Captain Beasley, with their team, began working on a new and extremely complex three-phased operation, its implementation depending on the speed and level of the Japanese threat. This would ensure that each unit of GREF would know exactly where they should be at any given time, and what they should be doing. It also gave guidance as to what to do with their heavy equipment and machines used to make the roads and airfields.

At the beginning of March, IV Corps issued orders for the adoption of defensive areas or 'boxes' to all lines of communication units, to improve protecting themselves by concentrating in small areas around the Imphal Plain, centred on The Keep. The 256 Sub Area L of C were to adjust where units were placed to enable the best use of the fighting power available, and to ensure all units newly arriving in the area were allotted a box. Arrangements were to be made for the removal of all civilians from these areas, presumably for their own safety, but also because the defenders would not be impeded. Another reason for this was that it was known that there were Japanese sympathisers operating in Manipur who could prove a serious problem if they were within defended areas. Commanders for each box would be appointed who would then appoint their own staff officers from available units, and

Imphal Main runway and Keep area.

they would be responsible for their own defence. Communications would be by a No. 42 wireless transmitter or land line from each box to the HQ 256 Sub Area, who would in turn report to IV Corps. Each box was given its own codename and was expected to be self-sufficient with a Box Reserve of ammunition and supplies enough for fifteen days, though this was later reduced to eight. The 256 Sub Area had thirty-eight such boxes under their command at one time, but this was reduced, because the threat from small Japanese raiding parties was deemed greater than that of large-scale attacks or even air raids. Some boxes were then closed down or amalgamated with others and were moved closer to Imphal, where the Imphal Main airstrip could easily be used to resupply the garrison and evacuate the wounded, and any men or units surplus to requirements. The units within these boxes were expected to carry on with their normal duties during working hours, whilst leaving enough men to man the defences. Further work on improving defences would continue at other times when trenches were dug and strongpoints constructed. A system of patrol boundaries was set out around the perimeters, and the units were expected to know the lay of the land for which they were responsible. A minimum 25 per cent manning of defences during stand-to was put in place at first and last light, when an attack was most likely, with the men being stood down and sentries posted once the time of the threat had passed.[1]

It would be unfair to describe the situation around the Imphal Plain at this time as chaotic, but it was certainly confusing. Many units and large numbers of men found themselves moving to different areas and boxes, and sometimes returning to the same place, as IV Corps and the L of C Sub Areas juggled to get units into the correct position. Many were flown out of Imphal back to Chittagong and Comilla or elsewhere if their contribution to the build-up had been completed or was no longer viable. There was no point in maintaining high numbers of troops while literally eating into ever-decreasing levels of supply. All along the main roads into Imphal the traffic flowed heavily as General Slim's plan of withdrawal gathered pace. The 17th Indian Division to the south had to be reminded to 'keep your eye on the ball' and to disengage from fighting the Japanese, as there was a real danger that they would be leap-frogged and cut off further along the road. To the north, the 5th Indian Division were ordered to set up positions so that no enemy penetration was allowed south beyond Sengmai. On 15 March, the 7th Light Cavalry moved into the Oyster Box south of Sengmai at milestone 126, where they harboured and made their base, and on 18 March, the Carabiniers at milestone 109 loaded their Lee tanks onto transporters and

---

1. Not only was this a time of threat by the enemy but also by careless handling of weapons by inexperienced men, which caused several accidental casualties. The Sten gun in particular was known as an unreliable weapon. At stand-to on 31 March, Sepoy Shiv Raj of 43 GPT Company was accidentally killed by a negligent discharge of a weapon.

joined them. From there they would both patrol daily northwards on the main road to Kangpokpi and beyond.[2]

On 16 March, the order came through to HQ GREF to evacuate their units back to Imphal from their forward operating areas. The new codeword 'Smithfield' was sent out to all units, and within three hours thousands of men and vehicles and tons of equipment were on the move, back along the roads they had built just a few months previously. As this huge force swung into its well-planned schedule, Lance Corporal Arthur Coulson, the company surveyor of 58 Field Company Royal Engineers, remembered it well:

> The word came through during the day fortunately, but there was only time to destroy the road-making plant that had taken so long to set up, then cut the guy ropes of the few tents, snatch up as many stores as possible and depart to the other side of the river where we dug in and settled for the night. In fact, there wasn't much settling as the rattle of gunfire soon developed quite close at hand. The main crossing of the river was by the Bailey bridge high above the gorge a short distance upstream, and it appeared that some dispute was going on there for much of the night. In the meantime, we spent the time in our holes with rifles ready and bayonets fixed, and all scared out of our minds. After all, we were not overly used to this sort of thing in any big way and our chance as infantry had not yet arrived. Next morning when all was relatively quiet, an Indian unit replaced us, and we quickly loaded up and continued back along the road that we knew so well. Back up the escarpment staircase into the familiar hills we went, passing the milestone 62 quarry area, over the saddle at Khong Khang, around the steep pointed hill at Tengnoupal and finally at nightfall came to a halt at the Shenam Pass. This was supposed to be a position for a whole brigade, but our rather understrength company was given the task of occupying it for now. That first night we slept like logs in our blankets under the stars,

---

2. One such patrol of twelve men from the Carabiniers under the command of Lieutenant Burns in their wheeled infantry carriers left Oyster Box on 22 March and met up in Kohima with a platoon from the 2nd Battalion Suffolk Regiment (part of 5 Division flown in to protect Dimapur and Kohima) to patrol the road down to milestone 84 with the purpose of locating any enemy attempt to block the road. The Suffolks with the rest of the 5th Division, apart from the Royal West Kent Regiment, were eventually ordered into Imphal, but Lieutenant Burns continued with his patrols without any infantry support, and he became caught up in the defence of Kohima when he and his men found themselves on the wrong side of a Japanese roadblock. Here they were part of the scratch garrison that for two weeks held at bay the Japanese until relieved by the British 2nd Division.

not really being aware of the general situation but trusting that we were well ahead of the Japanese.

Back at the GREF HQ at Kangpokpi, matters were also moving up a gear as the IV Corps defensive scheme came into effect. With the same meticulous planning as went into the withdrawal, a box defence scheme was put into action. To be known as Loris Box, a series of trenches were dug, and strongpoints were established around the buildings of the Mission compound, with interlocking arcs of fire to cover any enemy approach. An inner keep was formed, for the HQ and a secure area, where reserves could be held ready to launch any counterattack. Into this well-set-out defensive area went the troops of GREF HQ, 126 Heavy Wireless Section and the HQ Commander Royal Engineers (CRE) 671 Mechanical Excavation Company Indian Engineers. A series of observation posts were set up to watch for any movement and patrols sent out in daylight hours, and more frequently during the hours of darkness. Provision was made for the HQ of 1 Mechanical Transport Regiment to join this box, but with the arrival in the area of the occupants of Monkey Box from milestone 99½ it was decided to open a new box, Lemur Box, and the HQ 1 MT Regiment went there instead. Monkey Box had been the most northerly on the main road, and being in an extremely isolated position was ordered to close down and move to Kangpokpi on 19 March. The position of Lemur Box was located further down the track from the Mission compound near to the Dak Bungalow, beside the main road, and into it went Traffic Control Point 10, a section of 327 Recovery Company, 325 Bulk Petrol Transport Company and 96 GPT Company.

Frustratingly for the men who did all this work, creating the defences at the Mission compound was to be in vain, because a few days later on 20 March, the HQ GREF received orders to move back to Shillong, where they would come under the command of 11 Army Group. On 23 March, Loris Box was closed down, and the HQ GREF began their move from Kangpokpi to Gauhati and on towards Shillong. The 126 Heavy Wireless Company was then moved into Lion Box, while HQ CRE 671 Mechanical Excavation (MEx) Company moved at the same time as 652 Indian MEx Company to Sengmai, in with 864 ME Company. By a cruel and ironic

Kangpokpi milestone 105, showing: 1. the American Baptist Mission and site of GREF HQ and Loris Box; 2. the site of Lemur Box; and 3. the downed bridge over the Imphal River.

twist of fate, the only ones to benefit from these defensive works were the Japanese, who took over the Mission compound a short time later.

With the removal of his fellow inhabitants and protectors of his Mission, Padre Brock was left in a quandary about what to do. He had been offered the opportunity to travel out with GREF by Brigadier Westrop, but he had declined in the hope that a place would be found in Imphal for him, rather than leave the area altogether. It was pointed out to Padre

Major Arthur Mackenzie, 1 MT Regiment RIASC.

Brock that because of the crowded situation in Imphal there would be no hope of accommodation there. The only option left for him was to approach Lieutenant Colonel Harry Stanley Kelly, the CO of 1 MT Regiment and commander of Lemur Box, and to ask if he could stay with them.[3]

Major Arthur Mackenzie, the second in command of 1 MT Regiment, described his first meeting with Padre Brock:

> It was six o'clock in the evening. We had had a hard day clearing the jungle around us to make an administrative box and defend ourselves against surprise attack. As I sat outside the HQ resting, I was brought to life by a strange apparition walking toward me up the drive between the trees. It was an elderly man in white cricket shirt and khaki shorts. Combined with this he wore brightly coloured ringed rugby-stockings and white rubber slippers. His face was very tanned, and his white hair was thinning, but the striking thing about him was the enormous calves of his legs.
>
> As he walked closer, I could see he wasn't an Oriental, but I was still uneasy and had my hand on my revolver. I got up to meet this stranger and

---

3. Lieutenant Colonel Kelly was born in Jubbulpore, India, and came from a military background on both sides of his family, with strong ties to India. His father was killed serving with the Punjabis in the First World War, and he enlisted into the Queen's Royal West Surrey Regiment in 1925 before being transferred to the Royal Indian Army Service Corps in 1934. His maternal uncle was General Lord Ismay of Wormington, Hastings Lionel (Pug) Ismay. Lord Ismay was Winston Churchill's chief military assistant throughout the Second World War and was the first Secretary General of NATO.

as I did so he called out 'Good evening' in a very American accent. I relaxed and joined up with him as he said, 'Ma name's Brock. I'm a Missionary in the hills and have just returned from a journey of five miles over the mountains. I found that the Japanese were in ma villages and so about-faced and came straight back.'

I noticed across his chest a strap slung over one shoulder and under the other. This I discovered later was a shoulder-holster containing a .45 automatic, slung American-gangster fashion. I took him to the Colonel and gave him some supper which we were about to have. His purpose in coming down was to ask if he could come into the protection of the camp as he was afraid the Japanese would soon overrun his hospital for lepers which he had built in the hills. The Colonel agreed but said as he was a civilian, he would have to go to Imphal and there be flown out of the area. This upset Mr Brock. 'Naw,' he said, and his accent fascinated us, 'I will not leave ma Flock. As long as they know I'm around they will keep heart. I want to see this out. I'm going up there to send all ma lepers to their villages and close everything up. Do you mind if I bring a few of ma belongings down here?' 'Of course,' said the Colonel. 'We will send a few men to help you clear your place up.' 'Do you mind if I bring ma wife's sewing machine?' asked Brock. 'I'm very worried about leaving that … and ma piano,' he added. Both the Colonel and I were dumbfounded. 'Do you mean to say you have a piano and a sewing machine up there?' enquired the Colonel, and looking at me he added, 'We could do with that down here, couldn't we Mac? But I'm afraid I can't accept the responsibility of either of them at the moment Mr Brock. Just collect what valuables you have and hope for the best.'

The next day we sent men in a 15-cwt truck with him up the mountain track and the stuff he brought back was no one's business, not forgetting a wardrobe, various sets of tools, a grindstone of some considerable size, and last but not least, an old, powerful, and very heavy Harley-Davidson motorcycle. We had overlooked his ideas on valuables!

Padre Brock moved in and spent the next few days being 'treated royally'.

The 20 Reinforcement Camp location at milestone 110 now became the site of Lynx Box on 16 March, where the men of the reinforcement sections began constructing strong defences. From the beginning of March, a defence scheme had been prepared and arrangements to patrol the main road and all areas thereabouts were put into effect. A mobile reserve of 400 men was placed on hand ready to move at a moment's notice to counter any threat, while trenches and weapons pits were dug along the escarpment overlooking the main road and along the nullahs to the south and north of the camp. A line of trenches and bunkers were built across the open space known as a maidan to the west, and the area within divided into three sectors. Into this box now moved large numbers of other non-combatant units as well, sometimes without warning, and at one time numbered 28 different units totalling roughly 10,000 men, mostly GREF troops freshly evacuated from south of Imphal. Two of these units were 414 Indian Light Field Park Company Indian Engineers commanded by Major R. Blagden, and the 8th Sikh Engineer Battalion Indian Engineers, less A Company, commanded by Lieutenant Colonel H.D.S. Page, both arriving on 20 March. The Japanese pressure on the 8th Sikh's defensive positions at milestone 109 on the Tiddim Road forced them to abandon their equipment and they began marching out, some acting as stretcher-bearers as they struggled along the road in the dark before being ferried out on trucks. Upon arrival at Keithelmanbi they immediately began digging in and manning the box defences. They stayed for just over a week, reorganising, and training, before being moved to Lion Box Kanglatongbi, where they took over part of the northern perimeter defences near to the field supply depot, manning the roadblock near milestone 118 on the main road. It was a similar story for the HQ 465 Army Troops Engineers, 442 Quarrying Company and 414 Light Field Park Company, and after ten days, with 20 Rft Camp at Lynx Box, where they had been part of the mobile reserve, they too moved into the Lion Box, on 30 March. Accommodating these large numbers of men and all their heavy equipment and vehicles was particularly difficult at this time, with relatively few fighting troops to man the long lines of the defences. It was therefore decided to link 20 Rft Camp defences with those of 25 Rft Camp in Leopard Box immediately to their south, who were also struggling to cope with these large numbers, and many of these units were placed in the vacant areas between them. The 1390 Company Indian Pioneer Corps had arrived at Leopard Box from Palel during the night of 25 March, and they were detailed to help at the site of 14 British General Hospital (BGH) milestone 113. However, with the hurried movement of the 79 Indian General Hospital (IGH) and 14 BGH with their personnel from the area on 29 March, it left a shrinking perimeter, leaving only the

1391 and 1407 Companies IPC and 25 Rft Camp in the box. It was decided that 1390 Company should move nearer 25 Rft Camp for their protection on the night of 1 April. Captain Maurice Browne, a former tea planter, moved his company a mile down the road, where the men slept in the jungle before moving back to their camp at daylight, packing up their equipment and burning the unit documents while they awaited further orders. These orders were not long in coming when Lieutenant Colonel John Fiddian Peart of the 2nd Punjab Regiment commanding 12 Group IPC arranged transport to move the company to Lion Box later in the day, while 25 Rft Camp closed down the Leopard Box and began their move to Prawn Box within the Keep area at Imphal.[4]

Another one of these 'floating' units, the 62 Indian Anti-Malarial Unit, had a very frustrating time while it was being decided exactly where they should go. It took them nine lifts in their sole 3-ton truck to move the unit and their equipment into this area, but they were unable to carry out any work on the anti-malarial drains, because certain areas had been put off-limits by the Box Commander, Lieutenant Colonel Wells-Cole. The unit was then ordered to move in with No. 3 Section of 20 Rft Camp, but three days later were told to move again, though no one seemed to know where, but they had to move. The Officer Commanding 62 AMU, Captain Ruzbeh Aderji Mehta of the Indian Army Medical Corps, by then a frustrated and desperate man, contacted the Kangla Admin Commandant for guidance, and he was told to report to the newly formed Lion Box, 8 miles away, though no extra transport would be provided. It was a thoroughly disgruntled group of men who finally settled in at Kanglatongbi.

As well as the anti-malarial units, there were field hygiene sections whose job it was to ensure the health of the troops was maintained to the highest level as possible in jungle conditions. With large numbers of congregated men, the possibility of disease breaking out was a constant threat, especially with the poor sanitation and untreated drinking water supplies. Great

---

4. Captain Browne led his unit out of Imphal along with thousands of other pioneers when it was decided that their presence in Imphal was no longer required, and were a liability given that supplies were running short. Because of the large numbers of men involved, flying them out would be time-consuming and would also tie up valuable aircraft usage, so a route was planned to march them out along the Silchar Track. This turned out to be an epic trek for the men of the Indian Pioneer Corps.

efforts were made in making sure that the men understood the importance of personal hygiene, and that just wandering off into the jungle to do what comes naturally was unacceptable. Proper 'long-drop' latrines were built and maintained by the unit's sweepers. The work of these lowly caste men cannot be overstated as they undoubtedly saved untold numbers of hospitalisations and deaths.[5] Despite the gallant efforts of these units, a breakout of cholera occurred amongst the No. 4 Khasi Porter Group while they were camped in Lynx Box. The whole unit was placed in isolation and were not able to carry out their duties until they were reported clear of infection by the Medical Corps.

As the numbers of units frequently changed up and down, this meant the defences of the two boxes had to respond likewise, being elastic enough to expand or contract to suit the situation. Thankfully for those involved, this state of affairs lasted a short time. By the end of the third week of March, most of these units had departed, enabling the long perimeter between the boxes to be abandoned and moved, reducing further the area they covered. This freed up troops to strengthen the open spaces of the western perimeter and elsewhere of the Lynx Box, which at this time was quite compact and of considerable strength with an outer defence line, and an inner keep consisting of a battle HQ, a regimental aid post with quartermaster's stores. Heavily fortified bunkers were constructed and sited for further protection.

Gunner Betteridge remembered this as a time of great activity with those reinforcements from the camp who had units to go to being posted away, leaving behind mainly newcomers. No one had mentioned to him the possibility of the enemy arriving and so he continued with his hunting forays into the hills. One evening, as it was getting dusk, he was making his way back to camp across the valley, and while crossing the river he thought he saw a movement by the bridge just outside the camp entrance. He stopped for a moment and watched but saw nothing more, putting it down to a figment of his imagination, and continued his way back to

---

5. In recognition of his bravery and commitment to his duty, Sweeper Kantu, attached to the 7th/10th Baluch Regiment during a particularly bad time in action on the front line, was awarded a Mention in Despatches authorised by the 14th Army Commander Bill Slim himself. John Randle in his book *Battle Tales from Burma* wrote, 'It was without parallel that anyone should get a "Mention" for shovelling sh*t.'

camp. Later that night a loud explosion followed by others was heard in the distance, and the whole of Lynx Box was stood-to. Gunner Betteridge knew then that he had indeed seen something earlier. The bridge on the main road, only a few yards from his tent, had been attacked. The company sergeant major arrived a few moments later from the main camp to assess the situation, but as there was no sign of anyone or any follow-up attack, it was thought that local Japanese sympathisers were responsible and had melted away into the jungle. At dawn, the bridge, codenamed 'Keith Bridge', was inspected, and was found to be intact with hardly any damage having been caused, certainly not enough to halt the movement of traffic on the main road. The camp's Tata armoured car was sent out along the main road to investigate other explosions that had been heard in the distance at the same time during the night, but nothing was found. Early that same morning, 24 March, Lieutenant Colonel Wells-Cole ordered that a roadblock be constructed near to the camp entrance on the main road. A standing picquet of twenty-four Indian other ranks under the command of a British officer was despatched to the hill codenamed 'Pork Pie', where they were to secure the high ground on the other side of the road to the camp, from where the whole 'box' was overlooked. From this vantage point, they would also be able to see the main road in both directions and the surrounding area, thereby being able to give advance warning to the box of any approaching enemy. This ridge was also patrolled as far north as milestone 108. The 256 L of C Sub Area then issued orders that patrols were to be intensified and sent out night and day up to a mile distant from the box. The patrols near the nullah along the north of the box were sniped at on several occasions on 26–27 March, but despite intensive searches of the area with a larger force, no one or anything was found. One of the patrols sent out further afield reported seeing a large formation of 400 Japanese troops and 100 mules moving along a track between Makeng and Molkon, 5 miles to the east of the box. This was later confirmed by another patrol, which had a brief engagement with the enemy in Makeng before withdrawing. On the evening of 29 March, the patrols reported hearing rifle and machine-gun fire further to the north, and the box was again stood-to.

*   *   *

Orders were received during the day at Lemur Box, milestone 105, to close down the box and retire to Lion Box. The main party of TCP 10 were soon packed up and moved away, with the bulk of 96 GPT Company not far behind. This happened as Warrant Officer Tom Ansell and his Madrassi mechanics of the Workshop Section finished working on the vehicles needing attention, while gathering their equipment and moving off as well. The headquarters of No. 1 MT Regiment packed their stores and equipment onto

Warrant Officer Thomas Ansell, IEME attached 96 GPT Company RIASC.

their seven vehicles, helped by Padre Brock, who by this time had acquired a rifle and ammunition as well as his automatic pistol, because he recalled feeling somewhat more vulnerable with this reduction in numbers of troops thereabouts. After a bit of customising of his rifle to fit him properly and some target practice, Padre Brock was satisfied that should the need arise, he was equipped to face the situation, recalling:

> We did have a number of trucks which made it look a larger unit. There were also some thirty-five Indian drivers and clerks, but they were distinctly second-line troops who like other non-combatant units such as engineers and construction workers had been trained for their special task but not for combat. If trouble had developed the brunt of the fighting would have fallen on four men … three British officers and myself. Because the order had not seemed urgent, men and vital supplies had been left in the old camp. As soon as a few trucks could be unloaded the Lieutenant rushed back to pick them up. When more trucks were available, I went back with the last two [having already ridden to Kanglatongbi on his Harley-Davidson motorcycle]. The

driver of the last one in which I was riding was a man from another part of India whose language I did not speak. However, I did know two words, 'jaldi, jao!' [go fast]. We did. In rounding a corner, we came very near taking the wheel off the Colonel's car. Then the air became livid. I was busy strapping a gun in place and only had a faint understanding of what was happening as we straightened out onto the main road and went faster. Later when we learned what it was all about the Colonel came with an explanation and an expression of regret for the force of the words I had failed to hear. At sunset we got out of the old camp with our seven truckloads of men and supplies. Shortly after dusk the Japanese began turning the British trucks into the road leading to the Mission Compound, bayonetting the drivers and leaving them there.

Travelling fast and light, and well in advance of the main force, the leading elements of Captain Honda's Raiding Unit of the 9th and 12th Companies from the 3rd /67th Regiment reached the main Imphal–Dimapur road on 28 March, where they began reconnoitring areas as to where best to disrupt this main line of communications route. On the evening of 29 March at about 21.00 hours, Japanese troops began harassing the GPT supply drivers still running with their vital loads, setting fire to a small blockage at milestone 107.

At milestone 105, two drivers, Sepoy Phul Khan and Sepoy Viran, were pulled from their trucks by a party of twenty-five to thirty Japanese. They had been forced off the main road and up the track leading to the Kangpokpi Mission compound, where they were bayoneted and shot. A third driver was left wounded. The bridge over the Imphal Turel a few hundred yards north was then blown up by Sergeant Toidoi with a squad from the Japanese Engineers, thus closing the only road supply route to Imphal. Fortunately, thanks to reports from other drivers who had managed to escape the trap, the TCPs and Provost along the road soon managed to halt all traffic movements before the telephone lines were also cut, unquestionably saving further casualties. One of the Military Policemen from TCP 10 set off for TCP 11 at Kanglatongbi on a motorcycle to warn them of the block, but he never made the destination. His motorcycle was found with the fuel pipe cut, but he was nowhere to be seen. Next day, while on their regular patrol the Carabiniers picked up the policeman when he stepped out of the jungle and flagged down their tank. Obviously still in a state of shock, he was dropped off at the Military Police post at Kanglatongbi when the tanks returned to their base at Oyster Box. Lance Naik Nur Mohammad of 137 GPT Company was one of those lucky drivers who escaped after being shot at, and abandoning his vehicle, marched through the jungle and returned to his unit the next day. Altogether, 137 GPT Company had twenty-eight vehicles unable to return to their base at Kanglatongbi, being the wrong side of the blockade, and together with other vehicles being stranded, turned around and headed back to Dimapur. In all, just two lorries were lost, one from 242 GPT Coy being burnt out, and one from 167 GPT Coy; the remaining abandoned vehicles caught up to the south of the blockade were retrieved the next day by patrols sent out to investigate.

The last complete unit to travel north to Dimapur was 413 Indian Steelworks Erection Section, who had been warned earlier of their pending move from Lynx Box into Lion Box with the GE 921 Works Section. This order was changed during the day on 29 March, and they were instructed to move at once to Dimapur, leaving their work at milestone 108 unfinished. Their move was going well and without incident until the lorry in which Masalchi Phatta was travelling broke down near milestone 105. Fortunately for him, this was north of the bridge at Kangpokpi, where repairs were made to the lorry, allowing him to reach Dimapur, where he rejoined his unit the next day. The unarmed Masalchi Phatta was another of those who had a providential escape when the Japanese cut the road, spending a very anxious time as he hid under the tents and equipment on his lorry, while the Japanese searched it before he made his escape. With the cessation of work on the Base Ordnance Workshop at milestone 108, Major L. Woodcock and his small party also made their way to Dimapur, after leaving important equipment with 221 AOD. Elements of 14 BGH, commanded by Colonel Humphreys, were also among those making a desperate dash northwards to Dimapur and eventually on to Comilla. Even at that late stage, they had still been preparing to receive large numbers of patients. The last unit to travel south down the road from Kohima to Imphal was the 2nd Battalion West Yorkshire Regiment, who would soon play a key role in the northern sector of the Imphal Plain, and they would come to know this road very well indeed, sadly much to their expense.

Imphal was now cut off; the only way in or out for the next three months was by air as IV Corps was besieged.[6]

*   *   *

The Advanced Ordnance Depot at Kanglatongbi now became part of Lion Box, and the work began on making strong defences around their extensive long perimeter at the northern end of the box. Significant efforts were made to secure the area with well-sited bunkers and trenches, but the lack of barbed wire supplies meant that very few places could be wired in properly, and at best, only a few strands of cattle fencing were erected. Work continued in the depot issuing and receiving stores despite the continuing withdrawal of the divisions and units back to the Imphal Plain. The large Ordnance Depot at Moreh milestone 109 on the Tiddim Road was abandoned under enemy pressure and 52 Ordnance Field Depot moved from there into the IV Corps Keep area in Lobster Box, to where 221 AOD were now sending all their monsoon stocking stores. At about this time it was decided by IV Corps that all unit anti-gas equipment and clothing should be put into storage at 221 AOD. The small party of five privates from the 1st Battalion Seaforth Highlanders were detailed to return their battalion's equipment to the depot and now found themselves temporarily taken on the strength of 221 AOD. Sergeant David Campbell was commanding this detail and shared the quarters of Sergeant Sargent of the Fire Fighting Section. Unknown to them at this time was how important their presence at the depot would be.

---

6. One of the more unusual groups, whose route back to safety in India from the advancing Japanese Army that was now closed, was that of the Elephant companies. Commanded by Lieutenant Colonel J.H. Williams, or 'Elephant Bill' as he was known throughout the XIVth Army, these units with their powerful and intelligent beasts were vital with their ability in moving large timbers for bridge building, and in the construction of boats for the numerous river crossings during the campaign. It was decided by Elephant Bill after a reconnaissance that there would be enough forage and water for his herd of forty-five elephants along the Barak River valley for them to withdraw through, but that evening the very bridge at milestone 105 which he had sat upon making his decision was blown up by the Japanese. He was therefore compelled to change plans and an alternative route and epic and legendary journey via Haochin climbing over 5,000-foot-high peaks to Silchar was taken. Part of this tortuous route was also taken by the Pioneer groups who marched out of Imphal as the siege began to bite. Among these Pioneer units were those who had recently been evacuated from Lion Box.

The large hospital site at Leimagong, just west of Sengmai, had by now become Kinkaju Box under the command of Major G.S. Bal from 20 Rft Camp, with his detachment of one of the Madrassi sections from 20 Rft Camp providing the bulk of the defenders. Because of the vulnerability and isolation of its location, and with such a small force of fighting men available to protect the large numbers of non-combatants, along with the patients in 41 Indian General Hospital with several other medical facilities and the Powerhouse, it was decided that this box would close, and its occupants were moved on 30 March into Mussel Box in the Keep area at Imphal. The contingent from 20 Rft Camp then returned to Lion Box, though a small picquet was left to guard the Powerhouse.

Llama Box, at Kanglatongbi, was now closed and also incorporated into Lion Box at the same time. Under the command of Major David Mudie Dewar of 99 Mobile Workshop Company, this box had been in the area just to the south of the Kanglatongbi Dak Bungalow, where, on either side of the main road, three transport companies and the Garrison Engineers 921 Indian Works Section were placed. Because of the more static nature of the Mobile Workshop companies than the GPT companies they served, it had been arranged in advance that in case of any enemy threat that some boxes would be formed around the location of a workshop, but this policy was changed after an update from IV Corps orders. This now meant that these mobile workshops would, like all other units, move to larger and more defendable boxes. When the main road was cut, those GPT companies to the south of the roadblock, Nos 43, 96, 167, moved to Lion Box with their Workshop Sections moving in with 99 Mobile Workshop Company to become a temporary Mobile Workshop Company Group. The 137 GPT Company, already in Lion Box, moved their Workshop Section there, where they worked together until their eventual evacuation to Imphal. Several other GPT companies who had sections or small contingents who had been isolated found themselves part of this mixed garrison. Major Scanes, the Kangla Admin Commandant, and Captain J.G. Nicholson, OC of 15 WA Artisan Works Company, now jointly commanded this very large and busy box where, despite the continuing defensive work, it soon became apparent that its size meant it would be very difficult to defend, mainly because large parts of the perimeter were open to infiltration. At about this time, Japanese sympathisers had somehow managed to erect loudspeakers in the hills, from where they tried to exhort the Indian sepoys to rise up against the British to liberate India. No doubt there were some who were influenced by this, but overall, the Indian troops remained loyal and referred to the Indian National Army (INA) as the Traitor Army or Japanese Indian Forces (JIFs) and if encountered were given a particularly tough time.

The 221 AOD still continued with their work until, on the evening of 29 March, the whole depot was stood-to and manned the defences

Major John Boyd, 221 AOD.

after a telephone message was received at 22.30 hours telling them the road had been cut. Major John Peter MacBryde Boyd of the Royal Army Ordnance Corps, the Deputy Chief Ordnance Officer, was then detailed to take a mobile patrol of seven British other ranks and an Indian havildar from 221 AOD to investigate the report. Major Boyd had been commissioned from the ranks of The Queen's Regiment into the Ordnance Corps in May 1941, so he was well placed for this role having been trained originally as an infantry soldier. At around 23.30 hours, Major Boyd telephoned the depot from 20 Rft Camp at milestone 110, explaining that he had just returned from near milestone 108, where his patrol came across twelve abandoned lorries, in one of which was a wounded sepoy. The driver was able to tell them of the blown bridge at milestone 105, how his convoy had been attacked by a party of Japanese, and how some of the other drivers had escaped. Major Boyd then went on to explain to Lieutenant Colonel Cunningham that he and his patrol were going to investigate further along the road with support from a strong patrol of Gurkhas from 20 Rft Camp, where Lieutenant Colonel Wells-Cole had already ordered Captain Winstanley to investigate reports of Japanese harassing trucks at milestone 106. Major Boyd also asked for more ammunition and an armoured car to be sent up from the depot to meet him. Two volunteer BORs were dispatched but nothing further was heard from Major Boyd or his patrol until at 04.00 hours on 30 March, when three members of the patrol returned to the depot. They confirmed the reports of the downed bridge at milestone 105, and that Major Boyd was holding this with Captain Winstanley. It was understood that his patrol had seen no signs of the enemy, though it was believed there were about twenty-five involved. Therefore, IV Corps were informed of this, and at once orders were issued that the evacuation of all ammunition and demolition explosives to the Keep at Imphal would begin at 07.30 hours.

When word of the attacks and cutting of the road came through, Lieutenant Colonel Kelly of No. 1 MT Regiment together with an Indian officer and his Indian driver made themselves ready to leave the box at first light in search of a few missing men, who were feared to have been caught up in this action. This was done, even though it was known the enemy were present. They were at once joined by Padre Brock jumping into the vehicle with them, and despite the protestations of Lieutenant Colonel Kelly, made off up the road to Kangpokpi. Upon arriving near to their old site, the driver was told to turn the car around and wait for their return, as this small band set off on foot in their search. Padre Brock wrote in his account:

> This was not the place for a before breakfast stroll. I have heard of men sweating under such conditions … I didn't. I was distinctly cool, uncomfortably so, in fact almost chilly. We pressed on with our search through the abandoned camp and Mission Compound. Feet moved forward in an almost unconscious tiptoe and shoulders dropped to a semi-crouch while the finger rested inside the trigger guard and the thumb pressed lightly on the safety catch of the cocked gun … ready for instant action yet knowing that if trouble came it was almost inevitable the other man would get the first shot. The only hope was that he would miss, and the range was exceedingly close.

The search for the missing men was in vain, though the wounded sepoy was collected and taken to 20 Rft Camp for medical attention. The search party had been lucky to come away unscathed, but Padre Brock almost seemed disappointed, noting, 'Devastating as it may be to personal ego, there are advantages in being considered relatively unimportant, or at least not worth shooting.'

It was not bravado that drove Padre Brock, but the cold fact that he was very experienced in the handling of weapons and had been a proven marksman for over forty years. The other overriding factor in him joining such a risky venture was his sense of responsibility, not only to those missing and wounded men, but also to Lieutenant Colonel Kelly and his officers, who had taken him under their wing during his time of need. As Padre Brock wrote:

> This was not the ideal place for a missionary who is supposed to be a man of peace. Yet, what else was there to do? I had asked protection from a group that was not a fighting unit. It would hardly have been playing the game to have expected freedom of responsibility while men less trained than I bore the brunt of defence.

*   *   *

The Kangla Admin Commandant was informed of the damaged 70-foot-long Hamilton bridge at Kangpokpi, and they contacted Major Walter John Madden, the Garrison Engineer of 921 Indian Works Section, to dispatch a party to begin emergency repairs. The original and much smaller stone-built bridge over the river there had been replaced by the adjacent Hamilton bridge and though now in disrepair, it remained as such. At about 07.15, Lieutenant Corden arrived at 32 AW Company lines at Leopard Box milestone 114, with orders that a party of sixty African other ranks (AORs) under the command of a British officer and British NCOs, should proceed to the bridge at milestone 105 to ascertain the situation and carry out repairs necessary to open the road. This party, consisting of

Lieutenant George Stout, 32 AW Company West African Engineers.

Lieutenant George Russell Stout with Sergeants French and Layland and fifty AORs, loaded onto two lorries, set off, with Sergeant Harry Thorpe and nine other AORs with all their tools and equipment following in their unit lorry. Presumably because of their road-building experience, some sappers from 864 ME Company, including Sapper Walter Wolsey Elvin, were also detailed to go with the West Africans and arrived with them at the bridge site at about 08.30, where they quickly debussed and met Major Madden, just at the same time as Major Boyd and his party left. With the African sappers sitting by the roadside under cover, Lieutenant Stout and Major Madden examined the damage and worked out how best it was to go about their task. It was decided that one half of the force should commence work on the north side of the breach, while the other half started from the south. Just before 09.00, as the party made their way down the sides of the deep nullah to the northern side, they came under heavy mortar fire from the hills about 800 yards to the east. The mortar rounds fell about 40 yards to the west of the bridge, scattering the sappers, with Lieutenant Stout calling for them to cross the road and find cover on the hillside to the east for better protection. After urgent consultation, it was decided that it was too dangerous to possibly carry out any repair work without a large covering party being present for their protection. Consequently, plans for their evacuation were set in place as the sappers were recalled to their transport. Sergeant Layland and about ten AORs of his party, still hiding in the jungle on the northern side of the breach, failed to hear the orders being shouted by Lieutenant Stout and remained in their positions. As the drivers then went to fetch their lorries, the enemy mortar barrage opened up again, with one bomb exploding next to Driver Obiernu's lorry, causing it to overturn. Because there was no way of contacting those who had not heard the shouted orders to

Lieutenant Jack Swailes, 137 GPT Company RIASC.

withdraw, the remainder of the party quickly loaded up on the remaining two lorries and moved off to safety.

Others caught up in this bombardment were three road transport officers, Lieutenant Colonel Bristow, Major Taylor and Major Dewar, who had come to survey the situation. Lieutenant John (Jack) Gilbert Swailes of 137 GPT Company remembered how this news was rather light-heartedly reported in their officers' mess that evening:

> Bristow, Dewar, and Taylor went down there this morning to inspect the damage. Dewar was then turning the car around when 'crump!', a mortar bomb exploded twenty feet from the road on the hillside. Bristow fell flat on his face (howls of laughter in the Mess on hearing this!) and Dewar is alleged to have said, 'Come on, I think we'd better get help,' with which he trod on the gas and three thoroughly shaken officers tore back to Kanglatongbi and phoned to Corps!

The bridge repair party of West African Sappers made their way back to their camp, calling in at 20 Rft Camp on their way, where Lieutenant Colonel Wells-Cole was then informed of what had happened, and asked if he could provide help in locating and escorting those sappers who had been separated at the bridge. Upon the return of the three transport officers to Kanglatongbi, a request was sent for airstrikes on the Japanese positions, while a company patrol under the command of Major Chubb from 20 Rft Camp was made ready and dispatched. At 10.25, a flight of two Hurricanes from No. 1 Squadron Royal Indian Air Force (RIAF) took off on an offensive recce from Imphal Main airfield, piloted by Flying Officers Abdul Hafeez and Anand Pandit. Arriving at Kangpokpi, they quickly located the position on the hills where the Japanese mortar was most probably thought to be situated, and they began their strafing runs. In all, they made 5 runs and expended nearly 800 rounds of ammunition before returning to Imphal, unsure of how many casualties they had caused.[7]

The standing mobile patrol of the 7th Light Cavalry and their platoon from the 15th/11th Sikh Regiment arrived at the scene of the destroyed

---

7. Flying Officer Hafeez was killed when his plane crashed in thick cloud near Palel on 29 July 1944. Flying Officer Pandit was awarded the Distinguished Flying Cross in 1945, his citation stating: 'his outstanding courage and determination have enabled him to secure valuable information and photographs.'

bridge from their new base in Lion Box at about 10.30, although they were not called into action, and when Major Chubb and his patrol arrived at the bridge, they spent an anxious time going all the way through Kangpokpi village and the Mission grounds unmolested. No doubt, the RIAF Hurricanes machine-gunning the area to the east of the road had kept the Japanese heads down. This allowed Major Chubb's patrol to contact Sergeant Layland and round up what African sappers they could, before collecting all their tools and equipment and loading up on the lorry provided by the patrol. A recovery vehicle from 326 L of C Recovery Company arrived at 13.00 to collect the overturned lorry, and by 14.00, the sappers were back in their camp, with the rest of the few stragglers eventually returning to camp early the next day. A further patrol from 20 Rft Camp was sent out the following day, commanded by Captain Norman William Hocken of the 8th Gurkha Rifles, who again went all through Kangpokpi and as far north as milestone 103, and they were not engaged by the enemy. The standing mobile patrol also returned to the location, spotting a patrol of ten Japanese with a mortar moving in the distance, but they were not fired on. This lack of any serious engagement seemed to suit both the British and Japanese. The Japanese did not at this time have sufficient forces present in the area to repel a serious effort to break the blockade, and moreover, the plans made by General Slim were not to become involved, to allow the Japanese to continue their advance, because it would further stretch their supply routes.

Despite the strong defences now in place and being on a high state of alert, Lieutenant Colonel Wells-Cole at Lynx Box had grave doubts about the situation as it began to unfold with the road cut just 5 miles to his north, and patrol reports were coming in of large numbers of Japanese troops on the move, some just 4 miles to his east. They and the Leopard Box, who were in the same predicament, were the most isolated and northerly outposts between Imphal and Kohima, and they were 8 miles from the nearest defended area at Kanglatongbi. Lieutenant Colonel Wells-Cole informed IV Corps of the situation, suggesting the withdrawal of the whole of Lynx Box at Keithelmanbi as soon as possible. The IV Corps then gave orders that those reinforcements of the British infantry battalions who were ready were to be sent to their respective units in 20 Indian Division, and on 31 March began moving out. The 1st Northamptons at Palel were busy refitting and reorganising before their move to Bishenpur received a large draft of 119 men, while the 2nd Borders and 1st Devons in the Shenam area received their reinforcements as they began preparing their defences. At 21.00 hours on Friday, 31 March, the order was given for Lynx Box to close, and the occupants were to retire to Lion Box at Kanglatongbi. Most of the units in Leopard Box had also by this time already made their move to the Keep at Imphal, just leaving 25 Rft Camp, 15 AW Company WAE and two Pioneer companies packing their equipment ready to move. Earlier in the month, IV Corps had issued an instruction that all reinforcement camps were to move into the Keep area at some time in the future, as and when the situation permitted. The 20 Rft Camp were to go to Maiba Khul at the northern end of the Imphal Main runway. The speed of the Japanese advance now meant this movement was cancelled, and 20 Rft Camp would instead be used to bolster the defences of Lion Box at Kanglatongbi.

A conference was called at the CO's HQ tent, where the officers were informed of the order and plans that would normally take days to organise and complete were put in place for the evacuation. Lieutenant Colonel Wells-Cole later confided with his adjutant, Captain Charles, saying that he hoped they were quick enough before the Japanese surrounded them or cut the road between them and Imphal. The evacuation began almost immediately without waiting for assistance with transport from IV Corps, and the darkness making things immensely difficult. The first lorry load moved away before midnight using the unit transport of seven 3-tonners. Because of the large numbers of men involved, around 2,300, and the static nature of its duties, 20 Rft Camp's War Establishment lists included the holding of large quantities of food, ammunition, stores and tentage. This would take quite a while to be cleared, so the priority was given for the removal of all of the fourteen days' ration of food and ammunition in case the road was cut between milestones 110 and 118, or the box attacked, as these supplies would have been of enormous assistance to the Japanese. Anything remaining would be cleared afterwards. The arrival of 20 3-ton lorries, urgently dispatched from Imphal, helped speed up the slow work of moving 3,000 3-inch mortar bombs, as well as 250,000 rounds of ammunition throughout the night by the troops under cover of darkness, while others kept a wary guard for any Japanese movements. Foot patrols were also sent out as a screen to give advance warning of any approach by the enemy. The Kangla Admin Commandant, Major Scanes, was informed of the 20 Rft Camp's impending move into the box, and in the early hours of Saturday, 1 April, it was decided that because the ammunition depot was now in the process of being emptied, 20 Rft Camp should move there and take over the box defences on the north-western perimeter from 221 AOD.

At 11.00 hours, officers from 20 Rft Camp arrived at the Ordnance Depot and informed Lieutenant Colonel Cunningham that they were now ready to start moving into the ammunition depot, and they would be taking over the area for its defence. Back at Keithelmanbi, the loading of the various units' transport continued, and the move to Kanglatongbi was going well, until the lorries arriving at the ammunition depot at around 13.00 hours became mixed up with the lorries clearing the last of the ammunition from the depot to Imphal. Until it was finally rectified, this caused considerable confusion and delay. It had been hoped that all the food and ammunition would be cleared from Lynx Box during the day, and the personnel, still now manning the defences, would march out with the loading parties by 15.00 hours at the latest. This timetable was now seriously delayed, and the personnel finally moved off after 16.00 hours, regardless of the amount of equipment left behind at milestone 110, including all personal kit bags, tents and stores. A small force of about sixty men with a radio set were left guarding the site overnight. The evacuees began arriving at Lion Box at 18.00 hours and started organising their defences before it became dark, but because there were no tents, would spend an uncomfortable night in the open. The mobile patrol from the 7th Light Cavalry on its way back to base in Lion Box reported that they had encountered large numbers of transport and marching men on the main road all the way from 20 Rft Camp's position. Some of the Indian troops and camp followers seemed to be in a state of confusion, possibly because of the urgency and speed of the evacuation, and were reluctant to leave the safety of the box as darkness now began to fall. Some had to be urged onwards by the use of sticks even though they knew the enemy was not too far behind them.

It was arranged that evening that a covering force would be supplied early next day to return to milestone 110 to collect all the remaining kit and stores. At about 07.00 hours on 2 April, the standing mobile patrol of two infantry carriers of the 7th Light Cavalry commanded by Jemedar Jagmel Singh, together with their platoon of Sikhs, set off with Lieutenant Colonel Wells-Cole and Major Sinclair. This force, with a platoon of British other ranks (BORs) from 20 Rft Camp and the loading party, reached the camp at milestone 110 without incident or sight of any Japanese and commenced clearing the site, ensuring that nothing of use to the enemy was left behind and that all their defensive emplacements were destroyed or rendered ineffectual. When the loading was completed and the men and escorts were safely on their way back to Kanglatongbi, the 7th Light Cavalry proceeded further north along the road to milestone 108, where the Sikh platoon moved off into the hills on an overnight reconnaissance patrol.

Upon his return to Lion Box, Lieutenant Colonel Wells-Cole found the defences of 20 Rft Camp in the now nearly empty ammunition depot to

Kanglatongbi and Lion Box looking south-west from old Japanese positions on Isaac, 1944.

Kanglatongbi and Piquet Hill, 2019.

the north and north-west of the box were completed and fully manned, but during the day news came of the decision to abandon this northern part of the box, moving the Ordnance Depot a mile to the south, situating it in the area of the Dak Bungalow for better protection.

The GOC of the 5th Indian Division, Major General Briggs DSO, arrived from Imphal and chaired a conference of senior officers held in the Kangla Admin Commandant's office, where Lieutenant Colonel Wells-Cole was appointed as the Box Commander. Lieutenant Colonel Wells-Cole decided that his Box HQ would be set up in the Dak Bungalow, where a wholesale reconfiguration of the box layout was planned by him and his staff, because the box in its present form was too big to man and defend properly.[8] The

8. Lieutenantt Ralph Bird of 137 GPT Company remembered that at this time he was making a 'mobile generating lighting plant' for use by his unit, made from spare parts scavenged from the vehicle dump at Safarmaina. Somehow, Lieutenant Colonel Wells-Cole heard of this and put in a request for a similar plant to be installed in the Dak Bungalow, but with the rapid change of the circumstances, this was never done.

The Kanglatongbi Dak Bungalow, battle HQ 1–6 April 1944.

Ordnance Depot was ordered to complete its move within forty-eight hours if possible, and they were also put on standby for a complete withdrawal from the area within four or five days, or earlier, depending on any Japanese advance. The possibility of abandoning any stores and just evacuating personnel only was also mooted, although the decision for the demolition of any stores had yet to be made.

With their escort from the 7th Light Cavalry and the Sikhs, the depot's move had gone well, with only one or two problems for the Ordnance personnel and pioneers as their huge task progressed. Major Edward Cornelius Hubbard, the Deputy Assistant Director of Ordnance Services, had arrived at the depot from Imphal on the morning of 30 March with the details of how the ammunition and stores would be removed. He met and liaised with Lieutenant Colonel Cunningham and Captain Andrew Boyd Spence, a staff captain (labour) from 256 Sub Area L of C. Captain Spence, who was a former tea planter, had recently been appointed to organise the labour requirements with the Pioneer groups, as well as those units requiring their services along the L of C, especially with 221 AOD and their huge workload. Adding to the difficulties of his job was the ever-present possibility that his workforce could be taken away or reduced at any time for other duties by higher authorities. The work of the pioneers was in great demand during this period.

Warrant Officer Dennis Malton, the Chief Clerk of IV Corps Supplies and Transport Branch (S&T), had also travelled to Kanglatongbi with

Major Hubbard to collect Sten guns and ammunition for himself and the officers at S&T, in addition to their revolvers, as the threat of a Japanese attack loomed closer. He later wrote:

> Having collected the Sten guns I found that Major Hubbard was staying on for a time, and as the OC of our Field Security Section was also there, I asked him if he could take me back. He said he could take me but as two of his men were somewhere along the road to Kohima where the Japs had cut the road, he wanted to go along and see if they were alright first, but if I didn't mind, I could go with him. I agreed to go, and it was an uncanny experience. Whereas the road was normally busy with trucks bringing supplies, it was very quiet apart from a few birds singing and a distant crackle of small arms fire. We proceeded along the road until we came to an armoured car and were not allowed to go any further.

Despite the loss of the Cochin State Labour Company attached to the Ordnance Depot, the pioneers of 1351 Pioneer Company Indian Pioneer Corps and the drivers of 43 GPT Company worked exceedingly hard with little or no rest, and they moved 600 tons of ammunition. Other stores were sent to 52 Ordnance Field Depot, and by the end of the day sixteen 3.7 howitzers, twenty-five 2-pounders, fifteen 40mm Bofors guns and five 25-pounder artillery pieces from the Artillery Group had also been moved. Vehicles from the Vehicle Reserve Group (VRG) were sent to the Transport Park. One serious incident occurred when a lorry carrying phosphorus shells ran off the road while going over a bridge and exploded. This caused quite a stir around the Imphal Plain because it lit up the sky for miles around and throughout the night. Sergeant Les Smith of 189 Heavy Anti-Aircraft Battery, stationed at the end of the Imphal Airfield, watched. Along with some other units, they were at stand-to, thinking they were under attack. Several 'pungent' remarks were made in heated phone calls between IV Corps HQ and the Ordnance Depot at this time. It was probably because of the possibility of an incident of this kind happening that the Director of Supplies and Transport had earlier ordered that there were to be no night movements of transport, with loading duly halted at dusk. This admonishment from IV Corps caused no loss of sleep to the men of the Ordnance Depot, who had already lost what little sleep they could manage.

For a time, confusion reigned, when at 19.15 hours there was a telephone call from the Deputy Director Ordnance Services (DDOS) IV Corps to the depot, ordering the immediate evacuation of all gun equipment with transport and escorts provided. At 21.30 hours, another phone call from IV Corps cancelled these arrangements, but at 22.30 hours, the Assistant Director of Ordnance Services (ADOS) of 5 Indian Division and Deputy Assistant Director of Ordnance Services (DADOS) IV Corps arrived at the depot to collect this gun equipment and transported them away. Next day, the scene was again a hectic one at the ammunition depot, as the lorries continuously shuttled back and forth to the Keep until at last, all the 2,000 tons of ammunition had been moved and it was safely under the command of Captain Gill at Imphal. This work was done while still issuing the ammunition demanded by the various units on the front line. It was agreed that this was an excellent achievement by the ammunition personnel of the depot and the pioneers and drivers who had worked so hard during those two days.

Even though the ammunition depot was now cleared, there would still be no rest for the 221 AOD personnel, because the plans for the removal of the whole depot were now set in motion on 3 April. The area that was to be the new location of the depot was in scrub jungle just to the west of the Dak Bungalow, where bulldozers had cleared large areas and carved roadways for access to a dozen bashas, which had earlier been used by the staging sections of the Medical Corps.

Lieutenant Colonel Cunningham, Chief Ordnance Officer 221 AOD, wrote:

> At 6 am everyone was keyed up for the great move. Only a hundred lorries and 700 Pioneers arrived. This was a nasty set-back. Because of operational reasons further lorries were not forthcoming, but the best had to be made with what we got. There was nothing for it, and by 6.30 pm that night when all movement had to stop, we had moved about 750 lorry loads of stores to the new site and about a hundred loads of vote 9 and special stores to the Keep.

At the conference the previous day, it had been agreed that Lieutenant Colonel Cunningham's request for 1,000 labourers and 300 lorries for each day of the movement would be ordered. However, IV Corps had overruled

5 Indian Division's instructions, using these vehicles and labour for other purposes. In a signal to IV Corps, Lieutenant Colonel Cunningham pointed out that at this rate, it would take five days to move the stores instead of the two days as ordered by them. The reply came that the order would stand, and no extra transport and labour would be forthcoming and that, until the depot was cleared, nighttime picquets were to be posted to the outlying stores. Not to be beaten by this, what lorries from the VRG that could be started were pressed into service and driven by those officers and BORs who were able to drive. This amounted to another thirty lorries being used. Nevertheless, time was short. In order to gain what precious hours they could before movements were stopped at dusk, it was decided to turn the vehicles around more quickly by offloading the stores without stacking or properly recording the amount moved; this could be done later. However, no help with this sorting and stacking after dark was forthcoming, despite requests to the Kangla Admin Commandant and the OC of the pioneers, who were no doubt just as tired as the Ordnance personnel. Besides this, they all had their own responsibilities of manning defences to contend with. It was another long night for 221 AOD as they adjusted and accounted for their precious stores.

*　*　*

During the end of March and beginning of April, several Engineer units of the GREF began arriving at Lion Box, and they were placed to man the perimeter defences in Sectors 1 and 2 at the northern end of Lion Box, under the command of Lieutenant Colonel Frederick Donald Peacock, Commander Royal Engineers 671 Indian Mechanical Excavation Company IE. On 28 March, the HQ and Workshop Sections of 864 ME Company RE, together with HQ CRE 671 MEx Company from Koala Box at Sengmai, began arriving at Lion Box. Leaving their heavy spare parts and stores behind as well as the plant being repaired in the workshops, the personnel of 864 ME Company took their positions on the corner of the box perimeter, 50 yards opposite the now vacated offices of the Kangla Admin Commandant. There, above the deep nullah that ran along the north-west part of the box, they dug weapons pits and constructed sandbag pillboxes. The

864 ME Company Royal Engineers HQ and Workshop sections.

remaining sections and detachments of 864 ME Company had by now made their way back from beyond Tiddim and from other places, and they were concentrated at milestone 4, on the Tiddim Road near the Tulihal airfield and close by to the Imphal Main runway. Lance Corporal John (Jack) Welsh, a diesel plant fitter of 36 Section, remembered how their machinery, when loaded on transporters, reminded him of a circus on the move with all their paraphernalia and caravans. On their way back to Imphal, his job entailed riding a motorcycle in advance of the convoy, and he was greatly pleased to reach Bishenpur, 16 miles south of Imphal. This was the first village of any appreciable size they had been to for nearly nine months of living in the jungle while continuing their

Lance Corporal Frederick Martin, Army Catering Corps attached 864 ME Company Royal Engineers as a cook.

Sapper Tom Paston (wounded 7 April 1944) and Driver Bert Kadwill, 864 ME Company Royal Engineers.

road building. After stocking up with fresh fruit, vegetables and eggs, 36 Section moved off the next day to their new site at Trout Box to make a new dry-weather fighter airstrip at right angles to the end of the Imphal Main airstrip.

Along the top of the same nullah, on the left flank of 864 ME Company, were 705 Section and the Workshop and HQ sections of 652 Indian Mechanical Excavation Company IE, who had moved from Sengmai at the same time. The OC of this unit, Captain Stanley Frederick Knight, found himself short of manpower, because 706 Section had been sent back to Palel to help with the evacuation of equipment and stores. The few men of C Section of 70 Mobile Workshop Company moved from Lynx Box and became part of the Sector Reserve, located next to the HQ CRE 671 MEx Company, near to the new site of the Ordnance Depot. On 1 April, two sections of 58 Field Company RE arrived from Shenam and became the mobile reserve for the box with their two remaining armoured scout cars. They were also located close

Lance Corporal Jack Welsh (left), 864 ME Company Royal Engineers.

to the HQ CRE 671 MEx Company with No. 2 Section, commanded by Lieutenant Ernest Walter Collier, later being detailed to take over from 8 Sikh Engineering Battalion at the box roadblock on the main road, when their remaining section arrived from Dampol on 5 April. Because the area they now found themselves in was dense scrub jungle and open country, they were able to make a reasonably comfortable encampment by clearing the jungle and drawing their vehicles into a laager, and by draping tarpaulins over the sides of the vehicles, made themselves adequate shelters. This unit had by now travelled from the most southerly line of defence of the Imphal battlefield to the most northerly. For another unit whose purpose was to build roads, this happened to be a case of jumping out of the frying pan and into the fire. Next to arrive at Lion Box were 517 AW Company Indian Engineers from Khong Khang near Palel, where the OC, Major Thomas

Henderson MBE, and his unit had a noisy and busy time clearing equipment as the Japanese pressure in their area grew.[9]

Upon their arrival they were placed on the western perimeter, where Major Henderson then sent out Captain William Thomas Charles Walker and Lieutenant Eric Oswald Purser to contact the adjacent units to ascertain their dispositions. On their right flank was 652 ME Company on the opposite bank of the deep nullah, which turned eastwards and bisected the box as it passed under the culvert on the

Major Thomas Henderson, MBE, 517 Artisan Works Company Indian Engineers.

9. Major Henderson's family came from a long line of British engineers who worked on the Indian railways. He was 3 years old when he arrived in India and by 1922 had passed his engineering apprenticeship. In the mid-1930s he served in the Auxiliary Forces and later joined the Calcutta Scottish Regiment. Although being 41 years of age, he was commissioned into the Indian Engineers in 1941 and in 1943, Major Henderson was awarded the MBE for his 'conscientious work and great energy' under bombardment and machine-gun fire while placing a boom over the river at Prome during the retreat from Burma in 1942. Two weeks after the action at Lion Box in April 1944, during which he and his unit were again under fire, playing a vital role in repelling the enemy, he was arrested by the Military Police at Imphal and marched away under escort and his personal belongings searched and seized along with his company's documents. Thus began a saga that would run for almost eight years as Major Henderson fought to clear his name in what became known as 'The Burma Fraud Case'.

An extraordinary set of circumstances throughout this time meant that the case against him and some Indian contractors of defrauding the Burmese Government by claiming for unused materials and signing off work that was never done could not be completed. With the end of the war and Independence and the religious violence during the partition of India and Pakistan, the tribunal set up to investigate the fraud ground to a halt, leaving Major Henderson, still a serving officer, on bail and in limbo. He was mistakenly repatriated to the UK by the Pakistani military in 1948 after receiving assurances from them that his case would be dismissed. He then became the subject of a lengthy extradition battle, with the Indian Government keen to flex their newly gained powers. With all his assets and those of his wife having been seized since 1944, and the surety of £4,000 given by his brothers also held, his intention was to return at some point to clear up the matter. His discharge from the Army by this time had left him with no income and no access to his assets to pay for the passage to India, and his defence costs meant he had to delay his return until he could fund both. In 1949 he was extradited to India for trial even though by this time many of Major Henderson's defence witnesses had died or moved on, making it impossible to call them for evidence, and in November 1951 was found guilty and sentenced to six months in prison and fined £750.

One of Major Henderson's older brothers, Major William Glidden Henderson, died while serving with the Defence of India Corps in July 1945.

main road, just to the south of the Dak Bungalow. Their left flank joined the right flank of 137 GPT Company Royal Indian Army Service Corps, at a track that led from the main road to the hills to the west. The 137 GPT Company continued to garrison the perimeter southwards along to another large nullah at the southernmost point of the box. The 528 AW Company IE, also from Palel, commanded by Major Robert Francis Douglas, arrived at this time, and they found themselves on the northern perimeter looking towards the area where the Ordnance Depot had been. Their positions were along the track that led to the Kangla Admin Commandant offices between the roadblock at the main road on their right, with the right flank of 864 ME Company. Other Engineer units arrived and left almost at once, such as 362 Field Company, who arrived from Khong Khang at 16.30 hours on 2 April, and they were gone again by 10.00 the next day, moving to Bishenpur just south of Imphal, leaving a small party behind looking after their stores. Another unit that had made its way through to Dimapur before the road was blocked was 655 Indian Mechanical Equipment Company. Under the command of Major Nightingale, they had previously moved into Lion Box, where they had been employed on defensive works, but they had moved out leaving loading parties behind at Kanglatongbi and Palel. Their detachment from Palel, loading heavy equipment onto transporters, later joined Lion Box, where Captain Richard Stewart Biddulph Madeley and Quartermaster Sergeant Owen and their sixteen Indian other ranks (IORs) were placed with the Box Reserve. The last Engineer unit to arrive was 440 Quarrying Company IE, who left Shenam early on 4 April, but because of their late arrival they were temporarily placed just in front of 58 Field Company for that night. Next day, the 8th Sikh Engineer Battalion, now commanded by Lieutenant Colonel Stevenson IE, moved out to the Silchar Track at Bishenpur, leaving one company behind, and 440 Quarrying Company took over these vacant positions on the north-east corner of the box to the east of the main road. No. 1 Section were placed at the north and No. 2 Section at the south of the perimeter, but because of the shortage of men within the company it was impossible to man all the trenches that had been dug, so only the alternate ones were occupied until when, it was hoped, a company of the 4th Assam Rifles from Imphal would arrive to bolster the defences in this part of the box.

Of all these GREF Engineer units, both Royal and Indian, only 58 Field Company had been in any actual fighting as designated infantrymen before. The remainder, especially 8th Sikh Engineers, had experienced themselves a certain amount of 'rough handling' under heavy fire during the defence of their respective boxes, and on their trek back to Imphal from down south. Upon their arrival at Shenam during these evacuations, 58 Field Company now found themselves being used as infantry to fill the gaps in the line as 20 Indian Division organised its withdrawal. This role would last for two weeks, and the company would sustain nine casualties during an engagement near Tengnoupal before they were relieved by the 2nd Battalion Border Regiment. It was here that Driver Illingworth of this company was awarded a Certificate of Gallantry. Lance Corporal Coulson recalled:

> Back at Tengnoupal No. 2 Section was left there as a temporary garrison, but the rest returned to Shenam, and once again to try and look like something resembling infantry. We spread ourselves to defend the whole area, quite a forlorn hope. This time our positions were dug with more deliberation but there did seem to be so few of us for such a big area, even less than last time we were here. We were encouraged to keep in pairs and Sapper Chunkie Johnson and I gravitated together. He was a good steady influence on me that I was pleased to have at this time. We found a nice pit already part dug with a steep cliff immediately below which made this spot not easily crept up on. Daily we made improvements to it with a cover of timber topped with earth. One of us remained in there at all times with our grenades and spare ammunition by our side while the other slept close at hand or got meals. So, the days went by, watching for the hordes of little yellow men expected daily. At about this time I was promoted to Lance Corporal and for my sins began to be sent out with three others on patrol in the local jungle to see what was about. It was assumed as Company Surveyor and possessor of a prismatic compass I could make sure that the group always found its way back. After spending a whole day wandering about the bush unable to see no more than a few yards ahead, or in any direction for that matter, it surprised me that somehow, we always did manage to get back before dark.

Now that this northern area of Lion Box was manned almost entirely by engineers with heavy earth-moving equipment, IV Corps at last gave permission to the Box Commander for 652 MEx Company and other

units' D8 bulldozers to be used to clear fields of fire for the defenders, instead of just being used to make roadways. Under cover from their infantry escort, three bulldozers were used, with Sappers Ernie (Miff) Bowman and Wally Elvin of 864 ME Company being some of those engineers detailed to do this work. The areas of scrub jungle outside the perimeter were cleared to a depth of 50 yards with even larger swathes being cut where necessary. This buffer zone would deny the Japanese any cover from which to launch surprise attacks, while further work around the whole perimeter of the box ensured the units within were as prepared as possible, given the lack of

Sapper Walter Elvin, 864 ME Company Royal Engineers.

time and limited supplies of barbed wire, despite IV Corps having released 10 tons of this material. To make up for this shortage of barbed wire, makeshift booby traps of tripwires and hand grenades were carefully hidden and strategically placed in areas where enemy infiltration or movements were thought likely.

Opposite: Enlarged aerial photo of Lion Box, taken 4 April 1944, showing tents and buildings, and areas cleared of jungle by bulldozers.

Chapter Three

The Defence of the Lion Box

The new defensive plans for Lion Box, which had been devised at the meeting with the General Officer Commanding (GOC) 5 Division and the Box Commander on Sunday, 2 April, were now put into effect while 221 Advanced Ordnance Depot continued ferrying their supplies to the new site. Lieutenant Colonel Wells-Cole decided that his Box HQ should be set up in the Dak Bungalow, from where he and his selected staff tackled the job of keeping the movement of units and supplies into and out of the box running smoothly, also ensuring that the defenders had all they needed to hold this vital location and protect the stores within. All units were relatively well armed and supplied with ammunition, though there was a great lack of hand grenades. This shortage was partially rectified by the enterprising and resourceful Captain Hamilton-Parks of 20 Reinforcement Camp, who now made use of his expertise and the stocks of explosives and detonators that he had accumulated while training his Engineer reinforcements. By scavenging empty tins of Player's cigarettes and packing them with explosives and broken glass he was able to make about fifty of these improvised grenades to augment their stocks. The locations of defences and strongpoints were established, and the personnel organised to offer maximum firepower. This was organised as Lieutenant Colonel Wells-Cole had planned his strategy to defend this large open area with daily inspections of the defences, to ensure his orders were carried out to his satisfaction. The box was now divided into four sectors, with boundaries mostly being defined by the lines of nullahs and roads or some other defensive feature, and because of this, they were of an unequal size. This was problematic when trying to cover such a large area with the troops available who were capable of fighting. Each sector, numbering one to four in a clockwise order, had its own commander who was responsible for their all-round defence, and they were expected to have a force held in reserve should those manning the perimeter need reinforcing at any time. The box's external perimeter was around 4 miles in length, while at its furthest point, north to south, it was 1 mile long as the main Imphal–Dimapur road bisected the entire box. High jungle-clad hills to the east and west towered over the flat area, which funnelled south and out into the Imphal Plain. The ground was covered with dense scrub interspersed by tall trees with barer broken ground in places, especially in Sectors 3 and 4. About 1,000 yards to the east of Sectors 2 and 3 and across the Imphal Turel was the Kanglatongbi Ridge leading away eastwards to the higher ridges beyond. At a height of about 400 feet, the hill feature at the nearest end of the ridge (Point 2720) overlooked the whole of Lion Box, providing an important vantage point overlooking the main road in both directions. Because of its strategic value, Lieutenant Colonel Wells-Cole ordered a force of twenty men of the 9th/12th Frontier Force Regiment from 20 Rft Camp, led by Lieutenant Lal Singh of the 14th Punjab Regiment, to establish a picquet at the top of this dominant observation position and to be prepared to defend it when and if necessary.

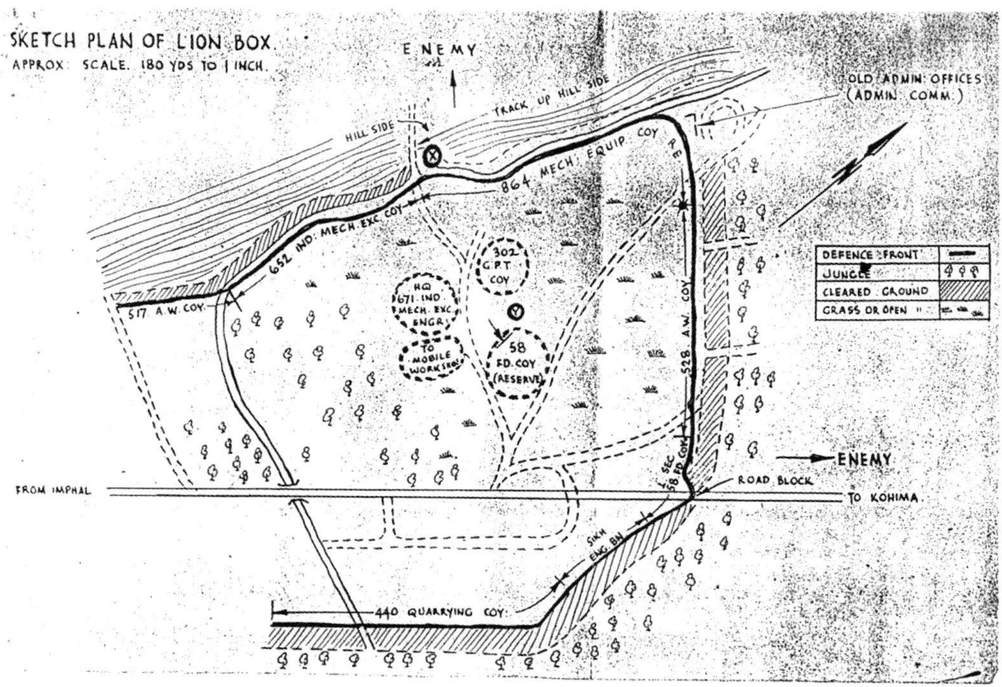

Sketch map of Engineers sectors of Lion Box.

Sectors 1 and 2 were at the northern end of the box, where the engineers were commanded respectively by Lieutenant Colonel Peacock (Commander Royal Engineers) and Lieutenant Colonel R.M. Stevenson of 8 Sikh Engineering Battalion, who had now taken over command from Lieutenant Colonel Page, but when the latter unit moved out, Lieutenant Colonel Peacock took command of both these sectors. In total, these two sectors had an approximate strength of 2,000 men; 1,500 were Indian and 500 British. When Lieutenant Colonel Wells-Cole was appointed Box Commander, his second in command of 20 Rft Camp, Major Sinclair, took over command of the unit, and when they moved to the south-eastern corner of the box, where 74 GPT Company had been, he also became the Sector 3 commander. The move from their previous position in the partially empty ammunition depot on Monday, 3 April was not

Major Norman Sinclair, 7th/10th Baluch Regiment, attached 2i/c 20 Rft Camp.

without mishap, for when at 21.00 hours, the duty officer from 221 AOD on making a tour of inspection discovered that one side of the perimeter was totally unmanned. The personnel from the depot were quickly ordered out to occupy the defences, while officers from 20 Rft Camp were informed because this had been their responsibility.

Quite how this oversight came about was not known but it is probable that during the confusion of all these movements and reorganisation of the defences, clear instructions had not been given to 20 Rft Camp on continuing a presence at the old ammunition depot perimeter, until they had been given orders to move once relieved. It was at about 01.00 when the Ordnance Depot personnel were finally relieved by a force from 20 Rft Camp and returned to their beds. As 20 Rft Camp settled into their new position, their third in three days, they began digging their trenches and bunker positions, but they found the local ground very hard and stony, making it difficult work, even to these men who by now were well-accustomed to digging, having

A recently uncovered trench dug by 20 Rft Camp above the escarpment in Sector 3, clearly showing how stoney the ground was.

been doing this since the beginning of March. The northern end of their sector was along the southern bank of the nullah that ran under the Dak Bungalow bridge on the main road, with the engineers of 440 Quarrying Company holding the perimeter on the opposite bank. The eastern side of the sector was along the top of a small escarpment of 25–30 feet in height, overlooking a wide area of paddy fields and scrub leading to the Imphal Turel. This area gave a good field of fire, but the large nullahs and smaller watercourses, now mostly dry, were ideal cover for any unseen approach by the enemy, and therefore a fire plan was co-ordinated to cover this whole area with light machine-gun (LMG) fire based on fixed lines. The entire No. 5 Section, about 150 men of the Gurkha Rifles, was now assigned as the Box Reserve, with a mobile reserve of 50 men from No. 3 Section, who were placed all along the road near the Dak Bungalow with their transport. Part of the area within the sector was the site of the driving school, where several bashas were commandeered and taken over as the sector HQ. This sector, manned entirely by 20 Rft Camp, had a strength of about 1,500 men, of which 400 were British, but they were very short of officers, there being about one British officer, one VCO and six NCOs to every 300 sepoys. An added difficulty was the fact that the officers did not know their men, and vice versa, as they would have done had they been an established unit. The two British sections, Nos. 1 and 2, who were by this time very depleted in their infantry reinforcements, found themselves thinly spread along part of the southern perimeter and most of the eastern perimeter as well. The south-eastern boundary was a small salient; it was about 200 yards south of a deep nullah, which cut across the main road where a roadblock was put in position to control traffic movement, thereby preventing enemy infiltration. In this salient by the roadblock, 921 Garrison Engineers, 1341 Pioneer Company and other auxiliary troops held the line. This, however, was evacuated on Wednesday, 5 April, and the occupants moved further back into the box, where 921 GE went into Sector 4 and 1341 Pioneer Company moved to the old position of HQ IV Corps in Sector 3 from when they were there in 1943. This move then enabled the sector perimeter to be straightened out and the roadblock pulled back to the bridge over the nullah and strengthened. A small diversionary track and bridge next to the main road bridge was then sealed off, and the northern bank of the nullah

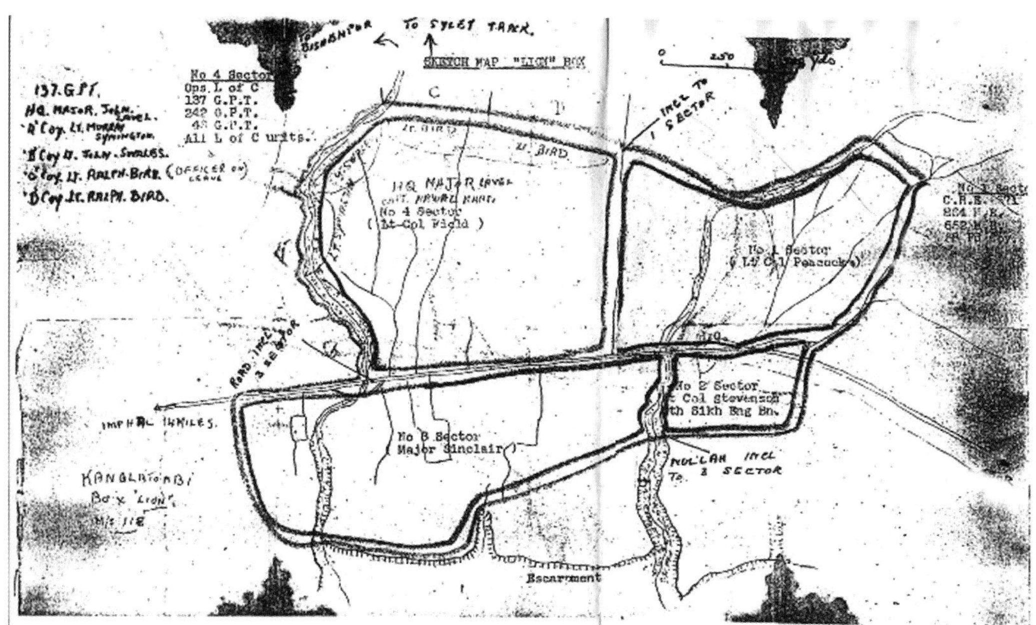

Sketch map of Lion Box issued to Lieutenant Bird, 137 GPT Company.

became the southern boundary of Sector 3. This area was then manned by about eighty sepoys of the 4th/3rd Madras Regiment from No. 6 Section of 20 Rft Camp, commanded by Captain Gnanadesikan Seturam, after being relieved of their duties at Kinkaju Box. No. 1 Section was also positioned in this vulnerable part of the sector. At the same time, it was decided that 517 AW Company in Sector 1 needed bolstering, and No. 4 Section of this company's position on the perimeter was taken over by a platoon of the 9th/12th Frontier Force Regiment from 20 Rft Camp as well.

Sector 4 was in the south-western corner of the box and was manned almost entirely by men of the lines of communication transport units commanded by Lieutenant Colonel Edward Styring Field, of the Operations L of C, with a strength of about 1,500 men. His offices had been evacuated from their long-established position on the west of the road by the bridge at the box southern roadblock, and they had been moved into a more northern part of the sector with other various L of C units. Faced with the situation of not being able to provide enough men for driving duties within the box and elsewhere, as well as for manning the long defensive perimeter,

Lieutenant Colonel Field ordered that 137 GPT Company should now become the Defence Company for this sector. This entailed that 137 should give up their vehicles to 43 and 242 GPT Companies, having their War Establishment strength made up from other Northern Indian class of L of C personnel stranded at Kanglatongbi. These two units and their trucks were placed within the sector along the main road, mainly for ease of access as they headed out to their allotted daily tasks for IV Corps. Further reserves for the Defence Company came from 96 GPT Company and 323 and 325 Bulk Petrol Transport Companies, with any other men or units not on the perimeter being placed near to the 99 Mobile Workshop Company Group at the northern end of the sector. At this time, 167 GPT Company became a reserve company upon which other companies and units could draw manpower to assist with their duties. Because 43 GPT Company had now taken over the vehicles from 137 GPT Company and were being brought up to strength, they drew heavily upon 167 GPT Company, and as such, Major J.D. Pearce, the commander, found himself and almost all of his men temporarily posted to 43 GPT Company.

A few others of the company were posted to 99 Workshop Company, 167 Workshop Section, and the 325 BPT Company. The boundaries of this sector ran northwards from the southern roadblock, along the main road to a track just south of the nullah near the Dak Bungalow, and then it followed this track westwards until it came to the left flank of 517 AW Company in Sector 1. There the line headed south to another large nullah and eastwards back to the southern roadblock. To further help this already stretched unit, 137 GPT Company, approximately 200 yards of their southern perimeter from the road westwards was placed under the command of Sector 3

Major John Levell, OC 137 GPT Company RIASC.

defences. This now enabled Major John Levell, the OC, and Captain Narwaz Khan, his second in command and a much respected regular soldier, to form a sector reserve using the HQ Section of 137 GPT Company, when they moved out of the line. The two Muslim sections, A and B, on the southern boundary, were commanded by Lieutenants James Murray Symington, formerly of the Cameronians, and Jack Swailes, respectively, with the two Hindu sections, C and D, on the western boundary, both commanded by Lieutenant Ralph Bird at this time.[1] Their front faced thick scrub jungle, and although the bulldozers had cleared large swathes, there were still

Lieutenant Ralph Bird, 137 GPT Company RIASC.

areas untouched, including the whole southern bank of the nullah along the southern perimeter. The 298 Field Supply Depot, commanded by Major Berry, was now placed in the B Park area of the sector, as this would enable easier access for units collecting supplies from their detail issue store, not hindering the work of moving the Ordnance Depot a few hundred yards further to the north. The 43 GPT Company had transported 298 FSD's stores from their previous site east of the road near to milestone 117, and now with their work completed sent their trucks to milestone 40 on the Tiddim Road to help 242 GPT Company move 23 and 17 Indian Divisions back to Imphal.

This was a very difficult time for all those in the Lion Box, because not only were the units expected to continue with their usual daily work, but they also had to man defences and provide men for patrol duties outside

---

1. Lieutenant Bird had been a motor mechanic by trade before his commission into the 1st West Yorkshire Regiment and upon his eventual transfer to the RIASC was the only officer in 137 GPT Company who had had any previous experience of vehicles and their maintenance and repair.

the box as well. Much of this work was hindered through no fault of their own, but by there being about 5,000 non-combatants, mostly pioneers from four companies, and camp followers dispersed within the box. They had been placed here for their own protection, though it had been feared that if there were to be a large-scale attack or bombardment, they would stampede, causing further problems for the defenders. With these large numbers of personnel within a defended area, the Military Police and Regimental Police had a difficult task of checking identities, as it was assumed that the Indian National Army would use this as cover to insert Fifth Columnists as spies and sabotage operations. Other disruptions were caused by numerous air-raid-red warnings at various times although the box itself was not targeted.

Communications from the units on the perimeter to the sector HQs at this time were mainly by runner, with only two units, 864 ME Company and 440 Quarrying Company, having direct telephone links with the Engineer HQ. The box signals officer, Lieutenant Edward Guy Fuller McCann, and some Indian Electrical and Mechanical Engineers, had a hectic time with his team laying cables to ensure that each sector HQ had a telephone connection with the Box HQ. Lieutenant McCann had been an obvious excellent choice as the box signals officer, having been a telephone engineer and the former manager of the Shanghai telephone exchange before the war. Contact with IV Corps at times was by telephone and by radio from the section of 126 Heavy Wireless Company, which was especially helpful when co-ordinating artillery ranging from C Troop 247 Battery 8th Medium Regiment Royal Artillery with their 5.5-inch guns in Sardine Box near Imphal. Further artillery support came from the 25-pounders of D Troop 522 Battery 4 Field Regiment RA 2 miles away at Sengmai. Their observation post spotters and signallers moved into the box at the same time as Captain Keith Thornton D'Aure Baker, with his two 3-inch mortar sections from C Troop 3 Battery 28 Jungle Field Regiment RA. These twenty artillerymen were

Lieutenant Edward McCann, IEME, Lion Box signals officer.

battle-seasoned troops having already experienced heavy action at Maungdaw in the Arakan region a few weeks previously. The section of two mortar teams commanded by Sergeant Wally Sheppard were placed where Captain Baker had made his command post near the Dak Bungalow. The ammunition quad driven by Gunner Stappleton was also placed here, where ammunition for the mortars was collected by jeep, while the other mortar section, commanded by Sergeant Lister, was placed in Sector 2 with 8th Sikh Engineer Battalion.

Captain Keith Baker, 28 Jungle Field Regiment Royal Artillery, commander box mortars.

Direct communications from Captain Baker's command post to the 8th Medium Regiment was established so that direct fire could be called upon at any time to assist the mortars should the need arise, with the guns of both batteries now being registered on pre-arranged positions around the box.

While the work continued in preparation for any threat to the box, IV Corps were in desperate need of positive intelligence to evaluate what they were up against and to confirm enemy strengths and compositions. The

A contemporary newspaper cutting showing Sergeant Wally Sheppard and a mortar team in action a few weeks before Lion Box.

mobile patrols of the 7th Light Cavalry continued from their base within the box, taking their Sikh platoons out to locations along the road where they would patrol the hills overnight before being collected the following morning. Japanese troops were spotted at various times and a roadblock made of large stones was found between milestones 114 and 115. Although there was not always any engagement during these patrols, a patrol to the downed bridge at milestone 105 on 2 April came under fire from four machine guns in positions to the east of the road. Their armoured carrier, which had stalled, could not be started again and during attempts to retrieve it caught fire and was burnt out. Four Japanese were thought to have been killed in this clash with possibly three others before the patrol withdrew. On 4 April, two British troops were met by one of these patrols who said they were heading for the old reinforcement camp position at milestone 110 to retrieve certain important items left behind during the evacuation, but the warnings not to go further went unheeded. Fifteen minutes later, the same two troops returned after seeing about thirty enemy troops in the vicinity, and during a brief skirmish claimed to have killed three.

Sergeant Walter Sheppard, 28 Jungle Field Regiment Royal Artillery, box mortar team.

A four-day-long deep penetration patrol to Kangpokpi was sent out on Sunday, 2 April, conducted by Major Graham Sell and his platoon from C Company 3rd/9th Jat Regiment to try to establish strengths and locations of the enemy in this area. This patrol finally returned on 7 April after extremely heavy going through dense jungle and steep high hills, but this brought back with them valuable information (although too late to be of use to the defenders of Lion Box). By observations and talking with local villagers, they established that around 3,000 Japanese troops were in the area of Thumion Khulen, just east of Kangpokpi, where they had extremely strong positions covering the three tracks that merged at this point, and where men from the Nepali lines near Kangpokpi had been forcibly taken to and were being used as coolies along the Japanese L of C route. A further 1,000 troops were in position on a spur east of milestone 104, just north of the Mission compound. Though the bridge at milestone 105 was blown and impassable, the Japanese were using a ford as a diversion for their transport. A large mule camp was found at Thumion Kongai and the nearby villages occupied by Japanese troops collecting food. Later, the patrol came across a soldier from the Assam Regiment hiding in the jungle with his wife and children. Subedar Lal Kholet had been part of the picquet guarding the bridge at milestone 105 when they had been attacked by the Japanese and had scattered into the jungle. He was able to confirm the enemy strengths and locations and stated that they were in occupation at Karong as well. Large numbers of motor transport and mule convoys were seen moving up and down the main road from a stone quarry opposite the Dak Bungalow at Kangpokpi to the area where 20 Rft Camp had been at Keithelmanbi, but it was also noted that some supplies were being hidden in culverts under the main road, presumably to avoid observation from the air. On the night of 3 April, two Japanese light aircraft were seen to have landed and later taken off from the road at milestone 109.

On their return route, the patrol had to pass through Nurathen, which was being used as a staging point on the Japanese supply line where another large mule camp was found. Two Japanese sentries were killed as the patrol charged through their positions on the track and headed for base. Six days later, Major Sell was killed in action at Nungshigum, north-east of Imphal. Other clandestine operations by 'V' Force operatives were carried out to the north of Imphal as far as Kangpokpi, at this time collecting further information. Daily stand-to orders were now issued for the 100 per cent manning of the defences from first light between 05.00 and 06.00 hours, and a 50 per cent manning at last light from 18.30 to 19.30 hours. Passwords were issued and stringent orders given regarding firing and movement after dark, with a curfew placed on all non-military personnel. Despite now being used to spending their nights manning slit trenches and pillbox defences, some of these untried troops were, understandably, in a state of nervousness as tales of Japanese ruthless brutality were well known. At around 02.00 hours on Tuesday, 4 April, something spooked a sentry, causing him to fire his weapon. Within minutes, the whole of Sector 3 began firing wildly into the jungle. This spread like wildfire throughout the whole box apart from Sector 1, and it seemed that every man who had a weapon was loosing it off blindly, with shots flying low and high and in all directions.[2]

Large numbers of red tracer rounds were seen going out from the box perimeter as well as into the box and up in the air. Captain Seturam and his Madrassi men remained in their positions on the southern perimeter as the tracers illuminated the sky, coming from about 300 yards to their north. Flares also appeared in every direction, with Seturam noting that 'this led me to believe that the enemy was all around us but since we had kept quiet, we had not been spotted. The patrols I sent out at dawn could not find the enemy and they must have disappeared into the jungle.' After a while it became apparent to the more experienced troops that there was no enemy incoming fire at all. The officers within their sectors struggled to get this indiscriminate fire under control, only to find it flaring up again and again somewhere else. Eventually, after twenty minutes Sector 3 became quiet and Sectors 2 and 4 sometime afterwards, with the whole box eventually settling down after an hour and a half. This lamentable display of fire discipline, although understandable considering the calibre of the troops involved, was totally unacceptable, because not only did it give positions away, but it also wasted thousands of rounds of ammunition that could be ill-afforded. The only possible redeeming factor was relieving the tension of constant strain with the troops, who had been under pressure for several weeks and, for some, it had given them the opportunity to fire their weapons for the first time other than on a range. It also gave the chance for the officers to re-instil the importance of correct fire discipline. The men, especially from 20 Rft Camp, had had very little sleep for the past ten days, and had been on jungle patrols for weeks. Japanese jitter parties were believed to have been responsible, or JIFs operating within the box, but it was known that Japanese reconnaissance

---

2. Possibly this was due to the fact that a lot of those engineers in this sector had recently been under fire, and they appreciated the necessity of not shooting unless a target was identified. 58 Field Company in particular had experienced this at Moreh, when thousands of rounds were expended needlessly.

patrols were also about, as the small piquet from 20 Rft Camp, guarding the power house to the south of the box, reported seeing a group proceeding north to south a few hundred yards from their position at this time.[3]

The entire box remained on full alert for the rest of the night, with only the occasional shot being fired. Just after dawn, the men were stood down to begin their usual daily tasks, though some would remain in their positions at vulnerable points. One of these men was Havildar Dulip Singh Rathore of 221 AOD who, for three days, manned a Bren

Havildar Dulip Singh Rathore, 221 AOD.

gun post on the bridge on the main road just to the south of the Dak Bungalow. The rest of 221 AOD personnel continued with their evacuations of the stores at 06.00 when 600 pioneers and a 110 lorries arrived to start moving the Armoured Divisional Troops (ADT) stores. The stocks of 17 Indian Division remained untouched as instructions were given that they were to be collected in due course by their own transport, but time was running short as the deadline for the removal approached and only half of the ADT stores had been moved. By the time of the closure of the depot at 18.00 hours, about 15 per cent of the clothing and barrack stores and the entire stores of 17 Indian Division were left behind. It was a disappointment

---

3. Another possibility was that a water buffalo wandering in the jungle had caused a sentry to shoot. Both Major Boyd and CSM Johnson separately recounted after the war the tale of a water buffalo being shot by mistake. CSM Johnson enlarged upon this, saying that the troops on the perimeter had heard noises in the jungle to their front one night and opened up with their machine gun in that direction. The noises continued and moved closer, causing the gunners to lose their nerve. Grabbing the machine gun from them, CSM Johnson continued firing until the noises stopped and at one point thought he had been shot himself when a hot empty cartridge case fell inside his shirt, burning his chest. At daylight, the area was searched, and a dead water buffalo was found riddled with bullets not far from where CSM Johnson had stood his ground.

to those men of the Pioneer and Ordnance Corps who had worked so hard to clear the depot to have to leave these stores. They had worked tirelessly with 43 GPT Company for two days, loading and then unloading around 800 lorry loads to move nearly 3,000 tons of stores as well as 6,450 gallons of fuel. The next day an enthusiastic staff captain from 17 Indian Division arrived with several trucks to collect their stores but was informed that if he wished to collect them, he may have some difficulty as they were still there on the loading ramps of the old depot, together with a Japanese machine-gun crew. The 17 Indian Division had missed the boat!

*   *   *

Late in the day of Monday, 3 April, the Japanese forces began arriving in strength to the area north of Kanglatongbi. The 60th Infantry Regiment, commanded by Colonel Matsumura, still recovering from their previous engagements, was already under-strength because their 1st Battalion had been ordered away to support operations in the Moreh area. In addition to this, the 2nd and 3rd Battalions were each deficient of a company who had been earmarked for operations to the west of Imphal. Nevertheless, the number from this regiment now ranged against the defences of Kanglatongbi and Sengmai totalled some 2,500 men. Support for these two battalions came from the HQ Battalion, which was comprised of companies or platoons of artillery, machine gun, mortar, engineer, signal, medical and mule transport. As well as this support, each battalion had their own embedded artillery, machine-gun, mortar and medical units.

The 3rd Battalion, commanded by Major Ginichi Fukushima, were to the west of the main road and now gathered information about the dispositions and defences of Lion Box in preparation for a night attack planned for Wednesday, 5 April. To the east of the road, the 2nd Battalion, commanded by Major Jiro Uchibori, were busy patrolling at Modbung with the view to capturing the Kanglatongbi Ridge and Point 3813. With their supply routes and dumps now in position to support their forward troops the Japanese began digging formidable bunker systems on key positions overlooking the main road all the way back to their HQ set up in Padre Brock's Mission at Kangpokpi. Booby-trapped roadblocks of trees and rocks were placed in strategic positions on bends and bridges, and they were well covered by machine guns and mortars to thwart any attempts at proceeding along the road. The patrol from the 7th Light Cavalry were sent out to investigate reports of one such roadblock between milestones 116 and 117 and came under fire before making a hasty retreat to the box.

After sunset on Tuesday, 4 April, further Japanese reconnaissance and jitter parties were sent out to probe the defences all around the box perimeter, but there was to be no repetition of the previous night's display, and fire discipline from the defenders was much improved, with only a few odd shots being fired wherever positive targets were observed. To the east of the box, up on Picquet Hill, the Japanese patrols from Major Ichihori's battalion were very active, trying to ascertain the strength of the British garrison. Several mortar bombs and grenades were fired at the picquet, who responded with rifle fire, and during the ensuing heavy firefight claimed at least four enemy wounded for the loss of one wounded of their own. A search of the area in daylight could find no bodies, though.

As daylight was breaking on Wednesday, 5 April, enemy movements were spotted in the old Ordnance Depot area, and some were seen moving towards the roadblock at the northern end of the perimeter being manned by 8th Sikh Engineer Battalion. This unit had received orders to move out at first light to Bishenpur, but this was now countermanded by the Box Commander because of the possibility of an impending attack. At about 04.30, B Company of this unit opened fire on a party of Japanese seen running eastwards across the road, but nothing further developed, and at 06.30, A Company were finally allowed to take over the positions as the remainder of the battalion made ready to move. A convoy of 3-ton trucks from Imphal arrived and were promptly engaged by the enemy, putting one vehicle out of action, while the men were being sniped at as they quickly loaded as

Driver Edwin (Ted) Tinnams, 58 Field Company Royal Engineers.

A Lynx armoured car similar to the one lost by 58 Field Company.

much equipment as they could onto the other trucks. Fortunately, there were no casualties as the convoy finally moved off at around 08.00 hours.

There was now a lull in reports of enemy movements from those units on the northern perimeter, so at 05.00, Lieutenant Colonel Wells-Cole sent orders for Major Leonard Arthur Pearce of 58 Field Company to send out their two Lynx armoured scout cars along the main road as far as milestone 116, to ascertain the enemy's whereabouts and strengths. Lance Corporal Edward (Taffy) Rowe, Driver Ronald Fessey, Driver Edwin George Tinnams and

Lance Corporal Edward 'Taffy' Rowe, 58 Field Company Royal Engineers, KIA 5th April 1944.

Sapper H. Lucas were detailed for this duty. On arriving at the vehicle park, they found that the scout car that was to be driven by Driver Fessey would not start because of a flat battery. This was soon rectified as the car driven by Driver Tinnams gave Driver Fessey's vehicle a tow, which soon started the engine. Both vehicles then set off along the track from their lines to the main road, with Driver Fessey leading and with Lance Corporal Rowe acting as the Bren gunner, and Driver Tinnams and Sapper Lucas the Bren gunner for that vehicle which followed. At the roadblock at the northern end of the box both vehicles had to wait several minutes while the Sikh Engineers manning the barricade cleared a path for them to pass through. Because of some oversight with the arrangements, the two scout cars left the box with no infantry support and set off along the road northwards with Driver Tinnams now leading the way. After travelling about 1½ miles, they came to a slight bend in the road where a blockade consisting of two bullock carts and a number of ration boxes and tins blocked the way. Strangely, a British steel helmet was hanging on a piece of wire on the barricade, and because of this, the patrol initially thought it was an old British roadblock. The two vehicles stopped and waited as they decided what to do next. Because they were still short of the location they had been ordered to patrol, and there seemed to be no enemy present and the blockade looking flimsy, Driver Fessey shouted to Driver Tinnams that he was going to attempt to push through it. Just then there was a shot, and a bullet smacked into the side of Driver Tinnams's car, causing both drivers to start up their engines ready to move off, but the battery of Driver Fessey's car had insufficient charge, and the car failed to start. Heavy machine-gun fire was now being directed at both vehicles from both sides of the road as the Japanese sprung their ambush. Driver Fessey shouted above the din of gunfire for Driver Tinnams to tow-start him again but, knowing it would be suicidal for either Sapper Lucas or himself to leave their vehicle to hitch a towrope, Driver Tinnams turned his car around in an attempt to push-start the other car with his. In doing so, he ran off the road and into a ditch, where the car stalled. After a few anxious moments for the occupants the car finally restarted, and after seeing how precarious the situation had developed into with both vehicles coming under heavy fire, Driver Tinnams and Sapper Lucas decided their best option was to return to the box for reinforcements. By then, Sapper Lucas had been badly wounded in the head, and blinded by his own blood, he was unable to return fire. The Japanese machine gunners seemed to be targeting the drivers' vision apertures and the Bren gun slits, and Driver Tinnams was also then wounded in the face by bullet 'splashes'. With his tyres now being shot to shreds and bullets peppering the vehicle, Driver Tinnams, also now loosing blood, managed to keep his vehicle on the road as he made the best possible speed back to the box, where the sounds of gunfire had alerted the defenders. Lance Sergeant Neil McMillan of 58 Field Company had heard the shooting, but now he could hear the sounds of a vehicle in difficulties approaching and suggested to Major Pearce that it must be the scout cars returning. Major Pearce sped off in a jeep to meet them at the roadblock to ascertain what had happened. Upon hearing their brief details and seeing the condition of the two bloodied and wounded men, Major Pearce ordered Driver Tinnams to report to the medical officer of 864 ME Company for immediate treatment, while he reported to the Box HQ with this information. A few moments later, the badly shot-up scout car rattled and bumped along the track past Lance Sergeant McMillan and 58 Field Company lines to the medical inspection (MI) room of 864 ME Company further along the line, where the occupants had their wounds tended by Captain Henry Adams Young of the RAMC and his assistant, Corporal D'Rosario. By this time, Sapper Lucas was in a bad way and had passed out through loss of blood and was later evacuated to hospital in Imphal. Driver Tinnams was more fortunate and once treated for his injuries, immediately reported back for duty. A further tragedy then occurred at 58 Field Company, when the acting Mechanical Transport sergeant wanted to go to the assistance of the missing men and recover the stalled armoured scout car. Major Pearce gave orders to Lance Sergeant Harvey Joseph

Captain Henry Adams Young, RAMC, and Corporal D'Rosario, IAMC 864 ME Company medical officer and orderly.

Lance Corporal Christopher Wright, 58 Field Company Royal Engineers, KIA 5 April 1944.

Maurice Adams not to do this, but instead to fetch the car driven by Driver Tinnams from 864 Company MI room and bring it back to the 58 Field Company lines for repairs. Unfortunately, for whatever reason, Lance Sergeant Adams either disobeyed his orders or mistook them, and together with Lance Corporal Christopher Wright took a Chevrolet 1,500-weight truck and proceeded through the roadblock and up the main road to the ambush site. Neither of these men were ever seen again, and it was presumed that they met the same fate as the crew of the scout car they went to retrieve, not least because more firing was heard from that direction. This tragic and needless incident was a blow for the men of No. 1 Section of 58 Field Company, who had been together since the unit was raised, but worse was to follow in the coming days.[4]

When news of this incident came through to the Box HQ, Lieutenant Colonel Wells-Cole sent out a search and rescue party for the missing men. Lieutenant Terence Frederick Bertram Helge of the 4th/3rd Madras Regiment led a patrol of 9th/12th Frontier Force Regiment from 20 Rft Camp, leaving the box at around 07.00 hours and heading up the main road. When the patrol arrived within 500 yards of the roadblock at milestone 116, they too were fired on by Japanese machine gunners, and during this brief engagement, Sepoy Mawaz Khan was killed and another wounded. They

---

4. The Chevrolet truck was later found burnt out on the side of the road and the Lynx armoured car was recovered three weeks later by the 3rd Carabiniers, but no signs of any bodies were seen.

then withdrew to the box having not been able to find the missing sappers from 58 Field Company. Further foot patrols were also sent out to locations all around the box perimeter at this time, even as far as Makan, 2 miles to the west, but there were no reports of any Japanese.

In view of the attack on Picquet Hill the previous night, it was obvious that the Japanese wanted to capture this high ground from which to direct their operations. Therefore, a further twenty-four men from 20 Rft Camp were sent out to strengthen the garrison. The picquet commander, Lieutenant Lal Singh, reported himself sick at this time. He was relieved by Lieutenant Dennis Reynolds of the East Yorkshire Regiment, attached to the Punjab Regiment, when he arrived with his reinforcements. A telephone line was run up the hill by Lieutenant McCann and his box signallers, and ammunition and more rations were sent at the same time as it was not known then how long the picquet position would last.

At Sector 4, it had been a quiet night until about dawn, when a movement was observed close by the Garrison Engineers' positions in their small salient,

Piquet Hill from Sector 3, clearly showing the two knolls that Lieutenant Reynolds and his men defended.

and a sentry fired a burst from his Bren gun on the figures crawling under the wire. These turned out to be some engineers going out on patrol, and some very irate sappers, including Garrison Engineer Major Madden, who had a lucky escape, but no blame could be laid at the sharp-eyed sentry as he had not been informed of the patrol. An unusual occurrence had happened at stand-to at about 05.30 when a Gurkha JIF was taken prisoner after he gave himself up. Lieutenant Bird of 137 GPT Company was alerted by one of his sentries who had noticed a movement to his front about 75 yards away from the western perimeter. Lieutenant Bird wrote:

> There was a tree stump where the movement occurred, and I waited a few minutes when I saw a figure step out from behind the tree stump and stand very still. I took a rifle from the Sepoy standing next to me and fired one round overhead in the direction of the form, a man promptly raised his hands in surrender. I called to him to approach me slowly keeping his hands raised above his head in the direction he was facing, and I would give him further instructions. He did this and I waited until he was about twenty paces from my slit trench. I told him I was an officer, and he was to approach me very cautiously as I had a rifle trained at his chest. He did as he was ordered, and I took him prisoner. After talking to him, I discovered he was Nepalese, and he had been taken prisoner by the Japanese in Singapore at the time when Subas Chandra Bose was offering all Indian Army personnel a chance to march on Delhi and free India from the British. He had taken the chance to join the Indian National Army with the sole purpose of giving himself up at the first opportunity having only been used as a coolie to carry mortar bombs on his back. Making sure he had no arms on him I sent him back to my HQ with instructions to be handed over to the Military Police.

Under interrogation, the Gurkha prisoner was able to give useful details to the intelligence staff at IV Corps of the Japanese unit he was with, including the fact they had fourteen days of food supply but were running low on ammunition. Strangely, he had in his possession several hundred rupees' worth of Japanese printed banknotes.

There were further comings and goings at the box during the day, and changes were made to the defences, as the defenders now settled into their routine of patrolling and manning their posts at stand-to or during an air-raid warning. The remaining subsection of 58 Field Company arrived from

Dampol, which enabled a working party of fifty-four sappers from No. 1 Section to be released from the box defences, to build a Hamilton bridge over the river near the Keep at Imphal. Lance Corporal Coulson belonged to Lieutenant Jones's party, and while surveying the area where the bridge was to be built, was oblivious of just how lucky he was to have left Lion Box.

The 5th Indian Division were now placed in operational control of the area north of Imphal, where real concerns were being raised about the numbers of Japanese present and the speed of their advance. It was decided that Lion Box needed extra support during daylight hours and 2nd Battalion West Yorkshire Regiment, the mobile reserve to the division, were put on standby to ensure the box was not overrun, and that no enemy came any further south than their positions at Sengmai. The West Yorks just a few weeks earlier had been involved with the Arakan operations, specifically for the defence of the Admin Box there. They would now find themselves at Kanglatongbi in a very similar position of protecting a large defensive area from Japanese attempts to capture much-needed supplies. The tanks of C Squadron, 3rd Carabiniers were called on to provide support but would also retire to their defensive areas and laagers overnight at Sengmai.

Enemy movements in the old depot were again reported during the morning of Wednesday, 5 April, and undoubtedly, because of the failure and loss of life of the earlier patrols, the Box Commander sent a request for assistance from the more experienced and better-equipped 5 Indian Division mobile reserve, who were then ordered to move into the area. At about 14.00 hours, 5 and 6 Troops and half of HQ Troop of the Carabiniers and two platoons of B Company West Yorks arrived at the Box HQ, where they were briefed of the situation. It was decided that 6 Troop, commanded by Lieutenant George Leslie Scott-

Lieutenant George Scott-Dickins, 3rd Carabiniers.

Dickins, formerly of the 14/20 Hussars, and one platoon should move up the road as far as the old depot area while the remainder wait on standby in the box. As the patrol made its way northwards through the box roadblock and along the main road, outlaying Japanese sentries alerted Lieutenant Yamaguchi, 12th Company Commander Fukushima Battalion, of the approach of the tanks with their infantry escort. He immediately ordered his men to conceal themselves on either side of the road and wait for their approach and his commands. A Japanese sniper was spotted hidden in a tree by the West Yorks platoon commander, who informed Lieutenant Scott-Dickins but had difficulty explaining the position using the tank's external telephone, so he then climbed up alongside Lieutenant Scott-Dickins on the turret to point out which tree. A round of canister shot was fired at the sniper just at the same time as movements were seen in some basha huts 50 yards to the west of the road, about 300 yards from the roadblock. The tanks opened fire with machine guns and 32mm high-explosive rounds. This brought a heavy response from the Japanese machine guns further along the road, firing from every direction at the tanks and infantry, who scattered into cover on both sides of the road. Bursts of fire whistled over Lieutenant Scott-Dickins's turret as he felt a heavy thump on his head, and upon inspection found a hole in his steel helmet and a 1-inch-long groove in his skull.[5] The platoon commander of the West Yorks now sent in a section of men to the basha area, who then moved forward to where Lieutenant Yamaguchi and his men had been preparing for their night attack. They were met with a hail of gunfire and grenades, which seriously wounded both Corporal Walter Pearson and Private John Lawson, causing the rest of the section to withdraw. The tanks had by now manoeuvred into position and began firing back. The leading tank was joined by another and began pounding enemy positions along the road and other bashas. This weight of fire was too much for the Japanese, who retired with around ten casualties, including Lieutenant Yamaguchi, who was hit by shrapnel from an exploding shell and died at dawn the next day. Several dead snipers were left dangling on ropes tied to the trees in which they had been hiding, and two machine-gun crews were

---

5. Two weeks later, Lieutenant Scott-Dickins was seriously wounded when, on 19 April as he and his tank crew were attempting to recue another tank, they were blown up by enemy shellfire. Three of his crew were killed and two others were wounded.

destroyed. The patrol carried on further along the road engaging various targets with 75mm high explosives including an abandoned truck, possibly the one lost earlier in the day from 58 Field Company, before returning to the box. On the way back the tanks manoeuvred themselves into a sheltered area where Private Lawson was picked up and loaded onto the engine deck of Lieutenant Scott-Dickins's tank for protection. Upon their arrival at the field dressing station, Private Lawson was found to be dead and Corporal Pearson was admitted, receiving medical attention before his evacuation.

These proceedings just to the north of the box were watched with a certain amount of glee by those working in the new depot area 200 yards south, because the Japanese could be seen scurrying about as the tanks continued with their bombardment. Unfortunately, an Indian other rank was wounded in the arm by a stray round from this action while unloading stores. At this time, the Box Commander instructed Lieutenant Colonel Cunningham that he should now make ready by providing seventy British other ranks to act as a mobile patrol reserve for the box, with the possibility of also being used as an attacking force outside the box. Major Boyd was detailed to lead this patrol and being prepared for considerable action, put in a requisition for 40,000 rounds of Thompson machine-gun ammunition and magazines, which were provided by 20 Rft Camp. Two platoons of about thirty men each, commanded by Captain Duckworth and Lieutenant Buckingham, were formed, with a headquarters platoon of ten men under Major Boyd making up this scratch unit. Though not experienced in this type of role, the men of the Ordnance Corps were keen to get cracking, and they were well supported by the infantrymen on attachment to the depot such as the six soldiers from the 1st Seaforth Highlanders and others. In addition, there were senior warrant officers and sergeants from the Royal Army Ordnance Corps to give guidance, among whom were Conductors Eugene French, Ronald Parker and Charles Slaney, and Sergeant Bernard Hargreaves. Conductor Slaney, formerly of the Sherwood Foresters Regiment, had already seen action at the Fall of Singapore in 1942. He was one of a lucky few who avoided capture when he escaped in one of the last boats as the Japanese closed in. After spending two weeks at sea in a small launch and a tramp steamer, he finally made it back to Colombo and was later posted to 221 AOD.

It was not long before Major Boyd's mobile patrol was called forward when, just before stand-to, enemy movements and digging were reported to the west of the perimeter in front of 652 MEx Company's defences in Sector 1. Shots were fired by this unit, which dispersed the enemy. A reconnaissance was then carried out by Major Boyd, but nothing was found, and the patrol returned to the box, just as further reports came in that about 100 Japanese troops supported by a further 700 had been sighted just 2 miles from the box.

At 19.30 hours, the Assam Rifles, who had earlier been promised to reinforce the box during the day, were finally ordered out from their positions at Imphal. Commanded by Lieutenant Colonel E.D. Murray and

Conductor Charles Slaney, 221 AOD.

accompanied by Captain Selwyn Fraser-Smith, 104 riflemen of 4th Assam Rifles reached as far as the Oyster Box at milestone 124, where they were halted and then recalled to Imphal as Lion Box was presently under attack, but no guides could be sent out to escort them to their positions. In preparation for dealing with any further casualties, the Box Commander asked that an advanced dressing station (ADS) be set up in the box, and at 19.00 hours, B Section 14 Light Field Ambulance were put on a two-hour standby to leave their position in Oyster Box. This was then put back to 06.00 hours the next day, but a telephone message was received at 21.00 hours for the immediate departure of a 3-ton lorry with a medical officer, one BOR and four ambulance sepoys to Lion Box. This group, under the command of Lieutenant Krishan Lal Chopra, set off with an escort of two armoured carriers at 21.50 hours, with the remainder of B Section to follow early on 6 April. Upon his arrival at the box, Lieutenant Chopra contacted the battle HQ, where he was directed to set up his ADS in the area nearby to the Dak Bungalow, and almost immediately began receiving casualties, eight of whom were evacuated to 89 IGH at first light.

*   *   *

By making good use of the intelligence gained by their reconnaissance patrols, the Fukushima Battalion now planned their night attack. It had been noted that because of the many secure and well-positioned lookouts on the eastern perimeter, it would be difficult to launch an attack across the open area of paddy fields. It was therefore decided that the best means of attack would be from the west where the thick jungle gave cover, and by approaching in a roundabout way the element of surprise would be maintained. Scouts would be sent out earlier under the command of Lieutenant Hayashi to set up markers in the jungle to guide the way, and once all the units were in position and the signal given, they would then break through the defences in one quick swoop right through to the main road. The 12th Company would be the advanced guard and once through the defences would secure the area from any attack from the direction of Imphal. The 10th Company were to follow closely behind 12th Company and would then hold positions to their right flank. Major Fukushima and his group would then attack the main camp behind 12th Company, while the Machine Gun Company and the Artillery Platoon followed and held the main road. The 11th Company and all the other units were to stand by in their present positions and await further instructions.

*   *   *

At around 19.20 hours, the Japanese began a mortar barrage on the northern defences and on the No. 1 Sector HQ, fired from positions in the old Ordnance Depot. Captain Baker with the box mortars responded and also called in a direct-fire barrage from the 25-pounders at Sengmai. This caused the enemy to cease fire, but almost immediately heavy firing began at the nullah between Sectors 2 and 3, where it was thought that the enemy were trying to infiltrate into the Box HQ as a diversion from their main attack. It was just then that the ordnance officers, including Lieutenant Colonel Cunningham, were having themselves a well-earned 'peg' in their mess tent in the officers' compound after their hard day's work. As the bullets cracked and whizzed about, the officers dived for cover, leaving their drinks, though one officer's hand was seen to be groping for his glass on the table under which he was sheltering.

Concerns were again raised about Japanese Indian Forces being within the box, as fire was also noted to be coming from the Workshop Group area of Sector 4 at this time, when bullets also whistled through the office of Lieutenant Colonel Field while he was making a tour of the area. He was convinced that JIFs were responsible and ordered a check of the weapons of the Workshop personnel. This was held later but none were found to have been fired, though a pioneer havildar from one of the Pioneer units nearby was placed under arrest for firing without orders. The 20 Rft Camp defenders in their positions along the top of the nullah between Sectors 2 and 3 had spotted the enemy movements, and they bore the brunt of the action as they beat off the Japanese attack. However, they were unable to confirm having caused any casualties despite laying down heavy fire.

A quiet period followed as the Japanese regrouped, but after a while the sentries all around the Engineers' perimeter reported hearing the rustling of bushes and clicking of rifle bolts. Others reported shouting and the throwing of thunderflashes, all typical jittering tactics to draw fire, though no shots were fired by the defenders. Just before midnight, the section from 58 Field Company under command of Lieutenant Collier, who were manning the northern roadblock, had seen a patrol of ten Japanese troops approaching along the road in the light of the full moon. At about 200 yards away, eight of the men moved westwards into the jungle and disappeared while the other two continued along in the middle of the road towards the block. At 20 yards, one man stopped while the other moved forward cautiously, until he was shot dead as he attempted to climb through the roadblock. The roadblock was then raked by machine-gun and rifle fire from the jungle, but this was soon silenced by bursts of Bren gun fire from the defenders. With reports now coming into the Box HQ from the Engineers sectors of increased enemy activity all along their front, it was thought that the enemy were massing for an attack. Lieutenant Colonel Wells-Cole then ordered Captain Baker to place an immediate direct-fire barrage from the three artillery units on standby, and the areas concerned were pinpointed and heavily bombarded by 3-inch mortars, 25-pounders and 5.5-inch shells.

This was a busy period for Gunner Stappleton with the ammunition quad, because Sergeants Sheppard and Lister and their mortar teams used up huge amounts of mortar bombs during this time. This barrage was noted to be the most accurate and effective, and even some bodies were observed thrown by the blasts out of the jungle and onto the road. The Japanese mortar teams responded with their 3-inch mortars, which mainly fell along the perimeter being held by 528 AW Company opposite the old depot. Several casualties were taken during this time: Sappers Battan Saha and Bengali Mistri were killed, and Sapper Keshwar Bhagat and Havildar Jamil Husain, who later died from their wounds. Another seriously wounded sapper of this company remained at his post in a forward position on the perimeter all night, despite having had part of his hand blown off. Sapper James Sidney Winestein of 58 Field Company was also wounded. The attack gradually fizzled out and broke off for a while, allowing both sides to regroup and take stock of the situation.

At about 01.00 hours on Thursday, 6 April, the Japanese resumed their attacks and attempts at infiltration. On the northern perimeter, heavy machine-gun fire was directed at the roadblock while 528 AW Company's positions were also raked by machine-gun fire from the old admin commandant's offices. The work of the bulldozers in clearing the scrub jungle in front of 528 AW Company's perimeter allowed them to bag several Japanese foolish enough to cross this open ground, and it was noted how the steady and controlled fire by this company held the Japanese from making any headway. At 04.00, a further direct-fire barrage was called down on the Japanese positions to disperse any build-up of troops, but unfortunately during this bombardment the second in command of 864 ME Company was seriously wounded. Captain Norman (Pat) Pritchard had been touring the company defences checking on his men when it was believed he was struck by shrapnel from a mortar bomb that had dropped short. He was evacuated to 89

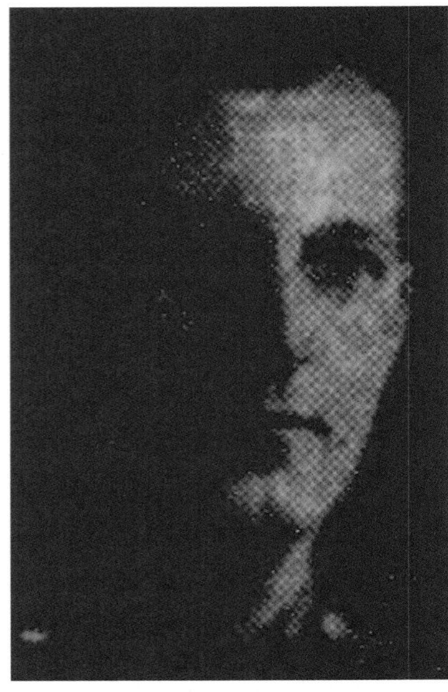

Captain Norman Pritchard, DOW 8 April 1944.

IGH but died of his wounds two days later. Major Boyd's mobile patrol were placed on standby near to the Box HQ, but they were not required other than when a mortar bomb had cut the telephone wire to the Engineers' sector HQ. Once the break was located, Lieutenant Buckingham, Sergeant Boyle and three other BORs spent an anxious and risky time as they relaid and reconnected this vital communication cable under the supervision of Lieutenant McCann. Further breakages in the line to Box HQ during the action were found and repaired in the darkness by Lance Naik V. Anthony and his three signallers. Under bombardment, Signalmen Faquir Mohd, Sanwar Shah and Shah Hussain crept out from their positions in the Dak Bungalow to join the broken cables, thereby restoring communications. Returning to their positions, they remained on standby throughout the night in case of more breakages.

Areas to the west and south of the box were relatively quiet and free from enemy infiltration at this time, but a careful watch was kept throughout the hours of darkness as it was known that the Japanese were very close to the perimeter. Bearing in mind Major Sinclair's strict orders regarding correct fire discipline, Captain Seturam and his men on the southern perimeter beside the large nullah there remained silent. At about 02.00 hours, a group of Japanese estimated to be of platoon strength made their way along the nullah shooting and firing mortars as well as shouting to draw fire from the defenders. Captain Seturam wrote, 'We did not open fire as we could not see them. Since we were in bunkers and trenches their fire did not cause us any harm and as we kept silent, the Japs who came within a hundred yards of us moved off to attack another position.'

The box was then subjected to a heavy and sustained artillery and mortar barrage with Sectors 2 and 3 bearing the brunt, which continued until daybreak. Very little sleep, if any, was possible as the defenders hunkered down in their trenches and pits for protection. So intense was this at one time that the Sector 3 commander, Major Sinclair, who had been sharing a trench with Captain Charles and Lieutenant Colonel Wells-Cole, commented to the Box Commander, 'I wonder how long we can stand this?' Lieutenant Colonel Wells-Cole rather pithily replied, 'This is nothing … you should have been at Passchendaele in 1917.' Lieutenant

Colonel Wells-Cole was a decorated veteran of the First World War and no stranger to heavy shelling.[6]

Padre Brock was also caught up in this barrage after moving with HQ 1 MT Regiment near to the operations L of C office just inside the northern perimeter of Sector 4. When they withdrew from Kangpokpi on 29 March, they were first placed in Sector 1 in the area just behind 652 MEx Company, where they spent several anxious days and nights, so much so that Padre Brock slept with both his rifle and pistol fully cocked in case of emergency, writing:

> The cocked gun seemed almost an exaggerated precaution but if trouble had developed the difference between the time needed to cock the gun and to release the safety might have meant the vital fraction of a second necessary in an emergency. The camp was guarded by a thin line of inexperienced troops and at no time were we very far inside that line. The fact that caution was necessary, and that possibly the precaution of the cocked gun was not exaggerated, was indicated by the capture of this part of the camp in which we were first located.

At their new location Padre Brock shared a slit trench with Major Mackenzie at stand-to or times of attack. Sleeping in these conditions at this time posed a problem, as usually when they had gone to sleep in their tents the enemy would open up with mortars or artillery, needing a rapid dash for cover in slit trenches. Upon thinking a barrage had finished, they emerged only to find another salvo coming in. This situation became so tiresome that Major Mackenzie suggested they should remain in the trench and sleep there. Padre Brock recalled:

> With backs braced against the ends of our little one and a half by four-foot foxhole, legs wrapped around each other, and guns placed carefully by our side we made the attempt. I did get my forty winks, but the Major was not

---

6. Lieutenant Colonel Wells-Cole's Military Cross citation: 'For conspicuous gallantry and devotion to duty. When the situation was very obscure during an action he went forward and ascertained the dispositions of the leading battalions and brought back most valuable information. The whole operation was carried out under continuous heavy shellfire.' On 4 October 1917, Lieutenant Victor Henry Wells-Cole, while on a reconnaissance, he twice had to pass through the worst barrage put down by the Germans. His two orderlies were killed, and he was present at battalion headquarters when a shell killed almost everyone. Upon his return to his headquarters, he was slightly wounded by a shell and had most of his coat destroyed and puttees torn off by another.

so comfortable. 'You seemed to sleep alright,' he reported, 'but I didn't get a wink.' Either my toes wriggled too energetically against his ribs or the feeling of responsibility for a non-combatant unit only seventy-five yards inside a doubtfully defended line made it impossible for him to get his rest.

The bombardment in the early hours of 6 April was exceptionally bad. 'The last experience was the worst. The enemy seemed to have picked our own particular corner for special attention,' with many 75mm shells landing in the vicinity of where Padre Brock was sheltering. Lieutenant Colonel Kelly's car, parked close by, received a peppering of shrapnel, and Padre Brock's trusty Harley-Davidson motorcycle 'qualified for the Purple Heart' with a hole clean through its fender. Another shell hit a tree between two trenches and showered the occupants with shrapnel, wounding one man. Had this shell not hit a branch and exploded in mid-air it may well have scored a direct hit on the trench where Padre Brock and Major Mackenzie were crouching. The unit's civilian cook and dishwasher also had a narrow escape when a piece of shrapnel landed in their charcoal fire as they cooked breakfast, scattering hot embers in their tent. During a short lull in the bombardment, there was a brief moment of light entertainment as the unit's Indian sweeper was observed crawling from one foxhole to another with an empty 5-gallon fuel can on his head for protection. He was eventually found at the far side of the camp by the morning, still clutching his improvised steel helmet and remaining within range of the Japanese guns. One person not perturbed by all this din and commotion and who was determined to have his night's sleep was Sepoy James Elliah Boddy, an officer's 'bearer' (servant) from 20 Rft Camp. A cheerful and smiling young Madrassi lad, he tied a length of cloth around his head and over his ears, and stretching out he slept throughout the bombardment, oblivious to the shells bursting around his trench.

Despite the best efforts of the defenders, some Japanese had eluded them, and limited incursions took place, some along the main road from the southern perimeter held by No. 1 Section of the 20 Rft Camp. A Japanese sniper was shot out of a tree in this area, and Gunner Betteridge of 20 Rft Camp remembered that by some means a few Japanese had still worked their way into the cookhouse area, and they took what little food was available. The next day, the Indian civilian followers and cooks packed up their pots and pans and headed off to safety. The 1341 Pioneer Company were also subjected to infiltration when three or four figures were spotted slowly proceeding along in the gloom of their company lines. The OC, Captain Hem Bhattacharyya, fired five rounds at the figures before they disappeared. He reported this to Lieutenant David Sparkes-Calcutt of the 14th/13th Frontier Force Rifles from the 20 Rft Camp commanding the Mahrattas, who were guarding the perimeter in their part of Sector 3.[7] The pioneers were mostly unarmed, with less than twenty rifles being issued to the whole company. The

Lieutenant David Sparkes Calcutt, 14th/13th Frontier Force Rifles, attached 20 Rft Camp.

previous evening, while making a tour of his company lines ensuring his men were all safely in their trenches, Captain Bhattacharyya had two rounds fired at him and his orderly, narrowly missing them both. Another officer, Captain Arthur Ernest Upfold, the OC of 440 Quarrying Company, also had a narrow escape when he too was shot at by his own men.[8] He and his second in command, Lieutenant W.S. Evans, with their ten-man patrol, were just returning to their lines in Sector 2 from going out on patrol after

---

7. Before his commission into the Frontier Force Rifles of the Indian Army in 1942, Lieutenant David Sparkes-Calcutt had been a territorial soldier of the Oxfordshire and Buckinghamshire Light Infantry, and an original volunteer member of 12 Commando, and was involved in the highly successful raids on the German-held Norwegian islands of Lofoten in 1941. He was an unarmed combat expert and demolition and sabotage instructor as well, until injury ended his commando career, though he was still fit enough to command a mule and camel transport section on the North-West Frontier Province of India before being sent to Imphal.

8. Captain Arthur Ernest Upfold had been a mining engineer in Africa before the war and was given a governor's commission into the African Colonial Forces in 1939 before joining the Royal Engineers. His experience in mining in the Gold Coast colony made him well suited to command a Quarrying Company, one of only three of these units within the 14th Army.

the evening stand-to, when a number of shots were fired. One of the Indian sappers sustained a fractured leg when he was shot, but there were no other casualties. It was believed at this time that this incident too was due to the heightened tension of the sentries, but the next day a more sinister possibility became apparent. During that evening, the company head clerk and another reported to Captain Upfold that they had overheard about a plot to have him killed. The company subedar together with a havildar major and the company armourer had hatched a plan to kill the OC in the hope that the unit would then be moved to a place of safety, on the grounds that there would be no one to command them. Captain Upfold immediately had these three men placed under close arrest and sent them into detention at the HQ of IV Corps Provost in Imphal, where they would await trial. Officers from 20 Rft Camp also reported being persistently fired at from their west when leaving Sector 3 HQ, and yet again, no one could be found responsible.

As dawn broke, the Japanese artillery and mortar attacks ceased, their patrols broke off and returned to their stronghold and laying-up positions to regroup and reorganise. After the morning stand-to, the defenders took stock of the situation and they began their usual daily tasks while foot patrols were sent out around the perimeter. Many heavy bloodstains were found all around the wire where the wounded and dead had been dragged away, but no bodies were recovered other than that of the Japanese soldier who had been shot dead while trying to break through the northern roadblock. He was identified as a superior private of 10th Company of the 3rd Battalion of the 60th Regiment, confirming that this unit was indeed in the area. His body, his rifle and equipment were sent back to the Box HQ for further intelligence purposes. The patrols also found many empty Japanese small arms cases in positions not cleared earlier by the bulldozers, especially around the old Kangla Admin Commandant's offices on 864 ME Company's front. It seemed that the enemy were concentrating in that place, so the bulldozers were put to work again opening up better fields of fire.

Half a mile east of the box, up on Picquet Hill the night had proved to be a difficult one for the defenders, because the Japanese again assaulted their positions on this important vantage point. The picquet had been holding their positions on the highest knoll of two on the extreme western ends of the Kanglatongbi Ridge, but they had to fall back to the lower knoll under increased pressure from mortar bombardment and infantry incursion. During these clashes a sepoy was wounded and had to be carried, as Lieutenant Reynolds and his small garrison carefully extricated themselves down the jungle-clad hill, up the next knoll, and organised themselves there. Having lost communications with the box and unable to call for assistance or guidance, they found that this position was also gradually being overwhelmed, and fearing they would be overrun, Lieutenant Reynolds gave the order for his men to disengage and make their way as best they could down the hill and across the Imphal Turel, back to the safety of the box.

Lieutenant Dennis Reynolds, 9th/14th Punjab Regiment, attached 20 Rft Camp.

Avoiding Japanese patrols along the way was a risky moment for the men of the picquet, because as they approached the perimeter the keen-eyed and trigger-happy sentries were on full alert, but after the correct passwords were exchanged, Lieutenant Reynolds and his men passed and reported to the Box Commander. The whole of the Kanglatongbi Ridge and Point 3813 were now in the hands of Major Uchibori and his 2nd Battalion of the Japanese 60th Regiment, where they now dug formidable bunker positions to observe and control all movements along the main road and along the Iril Valley, and more importantly, over the entire Lion Box. For the loss of this important outpost Lieutenant Reynolds was charged with the serious offence of 'Shamefully abandoning a post' and faced a court martial at a later date.[9]

Though the Japanese now held the Kanglatongbi Ridge, their main objective of taking the box and Ordnance Depot had been thwarted by the good security of those on the perimeter, who were supported by the accurate

---

9. Lieutenant Reynolds was acquitted of all charges by the court on 30 April 1944, when the eminent barrister, William Arthur Fearnley-Whittingstall, now serving as an artillery officer at Imphal, successfully defended him and proved his innocence. Lieutenant Reynolds later joined his unit, 9th/14th Punjab Regiment, and was heavily engaged in the fighting to retake Burma until he was wounded in action in 1945 and sent home. At his wedding, a Japanese officer's sword that he had bagged was used to cut the wedding cake. Lieutenant Reynolds finally retired from the Army in 1972 as a colonel in the Royal Army Ordnance Corps.

and effective fire from the artillery and the two mortar teams in the box under the command of Captain Baker. Major Fukushima and his 3rd Battalion had seriously underestimated the difficulty of a co-ordinated night attack in the thick jungle to the north and west of the box, and for a second night in a row the Japanese had been beaten back. Not only had their attempts been frustrated but they had also taken many casualties.

If there had been any doubts amongst the General Staff at IV Corps of the Japanese intention to capture the Ordnance Depot, they had evaporated, and orders were received first thing in the morning for its immediate evacuation. At 08.00, Major Hubbard and the Assistant Director Pioneers and Labour arrived at the depot, with instructions from IV Corps to organise the removal of all stores to the Keep at Imphal. They brought with them 200 pioneers and 200 lorries from 43 GPT Company to help the depot staff move all the stocks, with priority being given to the clothing, transport and camp groups, and by the end of the day around a further 1,000 tons of stores had safely been moved. Again, the men of the Ordnance, Labour, Transport and Pioneer groups all worked exceedingly hard throughout the day. They lived with the ever-present anxiety of knowing the Japanese were observing their every move from their new vantage point high up on Picquet Hill, from which to direct their intermittent shellfire.

Royal Air Force tactical reconnaissance patrols from 28 Squadron RAF, on their way to Kangpokpi (where they shot up some enemy MT), reported seeing fires burning to the west of the road at Kanglatongbi, which were presumably from the overnight bombardment. Another patrol of Hurricanes reported seeing two tanks just to the north of the box as they returned to base from Kohima. In both cases, there were no reports of any enemy movements. When the West Yorks and the Carabiniers arrived at the box from Sengmai for their daily tasks, it was decided by Lieutenant Colonel Wells-Cole that they should be split into two patrol

Major Alec Charles Dunlop, Commander B Company 2nd West Yorkshire Regiment.

groups, one taking the south and west perimeters of the box, and the other the north and east perimeters. Major Alec Charles Dunlop, the B Company commander, sent one of his platoons to escort the tanks of Lieutenant Christopher Leonard Rowe-Wilson's 7 Troop as they patrolled the southern and western perimeters, looking for any Japanese stragglers who might still be hiding close by following their failed night attack. In light of the Japanese presence on Picquet Hill and the threat it posed, a

Lieutenant Christopher Rowe-Wilson, 3rd Carabiniers.

reconnaissance patrol was organised, hoping to dislodge the enemy or at least keep their heads down while all the movements in and out of the box continued. The 5 Troop tanks commanded by Lieutenant John Allan Cole and their infantry support tasked with patrolling the eastern and northern perimeters manoeuvred themselves into position, and an artillery and tank barrage commenced as movements had been seen on the hill. Lieutenant McDonald led the patrol from the 20 Rft Camp and was joined by Lieutenant Reynolds to act as guide as he knew the ground, and together they made their way across the Imphal Turel and up the steep slopes after the barrage was halted. This barrage had proved successful, and bodies were seen to fly in the air. A trophy of a heavily bloodstained Japanese officer's sword was found and bagged by Lieutenant McDonald just before enemy pressure forced their withdrawal at about 15.30 hours. The tanks resumed spraying the hill with machine-gun fire and high explosive at intervals, but as there were insufficient troops capable of taking and holding the entire Kanglatongbi Ridge, the attack was called off having not sustained any casualties.

The patrols at the northern perimeter and in the old depot area were less fortunate and took two casualties, both fatal. Corporal Thomas Henry Clarke's section under the command of Lieutenant Alfred Meredith (Billy) Pocock of the Lincolnshire Regiment attached to the West Yorks had been patrolling through the basha areas in the old depot, throwing grenades into likely Japanese hiding places to flush them out.[10] As they were then coming to the end of their patrol and were making their way in single file back to the box along a track that led to the main road, there was a burst of machine-gun fire, and Private Joseph Walker, who was the leading scout, fell to the ground screaming and clutching his throat with both hands. Lieutenant Pocock, 5 yards behind Private Walker, ran to him and, as he bent to tend to him, there was another burst of fire and Lieutenant Pocock shouted and fell beside Private Walker, rolling around on the ground. The rest of the section

Lieutenant Alfred Pocock, Lincolnshire Regiment, attached 2nd West Yorkshire Regiment, KIA 6 April 1944.

dived into cover, though Corporal Clarke had to grab hold of Private Swift and restrain him from going to the aid of his friend Private Walker. Corporal Clarke then ordered the rest of his section, Privates Gill, Naylor, Stephenson and Porter, to retire while he made his way back under machine-gun fire towards Lieutenant Pocock and Private Walker to work out how to rescue them both. After a pause of a few minutes, Private Porter was able to rejoin the rest of the section as he had been in an exposed position and could not move for fear of being shot as well. Just then, there was an explosion of a hand grenade, and when the dust had cleared, Corporal Clarke could see that Lieutenant Pocock now lay motionless. This was the last grenade that the patrol had left, and Lieutenant Pocock had been holding it in his hand with the pin out in readiness for any action as they moved along the track. Realising that their situation was now impossible, Corporal Clarke, with his section, made their way back through the cover of the jungle and came

10. Corporal Clarke was killed in action in Burma on 15 May 1945. Lieutenant Pocock was part of the prestigious racing boat building family who had left England and set up their company in Seattle, America, in 1911. Their rowing boats are still sought after to this day.

out just in front of the roadblock and reported the events to Major Dunlop. Lieutenant Pocock, a former private in the Royal West Kent Regiment and survivor of the Dunkirk evacuation, had only been with the battalion a matter of a few weeks. He had had little time to know his men, but this was a blow to B Company to have lost an officer and two men in two days in almost the same spot.

While all the action was going on outside the box, there was also a great deal of activity going on inside. Not only was the heavy and steady flow of traffic moving the depot stocks causing disruption around the Box HQ, but there were also more movements of units in and out. Therefore, it was decided that Lieutenant Colonel Wells-Cole would move his HQ from the Dak Bungalow about 1,000 yards south into a more central position in the now vacant basha of 99 Workshop Company office by the main road in Sector 4. This unit had ceased their usual work a few days earlier because Lieutenant Colonel Field had given orders for them to pack all their equipment in readiness to move at short notice, while still manning their defences. Once again, Lieutenant McCann had a very busy time as all the telephone lines from the sector HQs had to be relaid and connected to the new site of the Box HQ. By 18.00 hours, Lieutenant McCann and his team had completed their task, and the HQ became fully operational after Lieutenant Colonel Wells-Cole and his staff had spent the day moving in, and they began preparing for what the night would bring. A field dressing station was also opened during the day nearby in the old bashas of the Provost Company, ready to receive any future casualties.

The first unit to move out during the day was the small rear party of 362 Company Indian Engineers under the command of Sergeant Longyear, who loaded all their unit stores, and they were on their way to Bishenpur by midday. Next to leave were 1351 and 1475 Pioneer Companies. With their invaluable and much-appreciated work constructing defences and moving the ammunition and Ordnance stores completed, they moved out to Imphal. Not only were these men much relieved to be moving out of danger, but so were those whose job it was to protect such a large number of non-combatants.

At around 06.30 hours, the advance party of the 302 GPT Company under the command of Lieutenant Morphy left their positions at Palel and arrived at the box during the morning. They began settling into their

Lieutenant John Cooper Somerville, 864 ME Company Royal Engineers.

Captain Matthew Cork Revell, OC 36 Section 864 ME Company Royal Engineers.

position as part of the reserves in Sector 1 behind 864 ME Company, and next to 58 Field Company lines. Major Leslie William Greenberry, the OC of 302 GPT Company, now joined the advance party in the box because his planned flight from Imphal to Dimapur was cancelled, and upon seeing the situation for himself, sent orders that the remainder of the company now making their way to Kanglatongbi were to halt at Imphal, where they moved into defensive positions at Whale Box. They were to wait there because it was thought they might be needed to help evacuate the Lion Box at some time over the next few days. Next to arrive was a detachment from 36 Section of 864 ME Company from their position in Trout Box, to augment the hundred or so men of the HQ and Workshop Sections, already in position on the perimeter. Captain Matthew Cork Revell, the OC of 36 Section, and his men only had a short time to acquaint themselves with their dispositions as they manned the perimeter defences. Captain Revell's trusted driver and batman of two years, Driver Bert Kadwill, was fortunate not to have been with him, as he would have been normally. He was hospitalised

Captain Matthew Revell, OC 36 Section 864 ME Company Royal Engineers, and Driver Bert Kadwill.

that morning and missed the ensuing action, as did Lance Corporal Welsh, who went down with dysentery at around the same time.

Further alterations and movements were made during the afternoon to 517 AW Company positions when more men from the 9th/12th Frontier Force Regiment of the Box Reserve took over from No. 3 Section on the western perimeter of Sector 1. They joined with their No. 4 Section in reserve behind Section Nos. 1 and 2. This allowed Major Henderson to free up enough men to begin evacuating the company stores to Imphal in preparation for the unit's impending move. Sector 4 was also bolstered at this time as its northern perimeter seemed vulnerable with little or no wire in places, and at around 13.00 hours, X Company of the Machine Gun Battalion of the 9th Jat Regiment began arriving in their unit transport. Major Bernard Marie Davies and his second in command, Captain Peter William Dron, liaised with the Box Commander as to where he would like their eight 3-inch mortars, and eight medium machine guns (MMGs) placed for best effect. It was decided that as this was mostly open ground, the MMGs and mortars would be given direct-fire tasks from along the track that formed the boundary between Sectors 4 and 1, and they began digging in. Despite this addition there was still not enough manpower to cover the full length of the perimeter, so another 100 Gurkhas from the Box Reserve were placed along the remainder of the track.

Also, during the afternoon, the company of Assam Rifles who should have arrived to reinforce the box the day before, finally arrived from Imphal, this time with the addition of their medical officer, Captain Phillip Weyman RAMC, in anticipation of casualties. Lieutenant Colonel Murray and his company were placed near to the new Box HQ as part of the Box Reserve, together with the two platoons of the 27th/5th Mahratta Light Infantry and a platoon of Gurkhas. This was a more central location within the box, enabling the quick reinforcement of any unit needing support, especially Sector 4, which seemed the most vulnerable to attack.

By this time, the tanks and their infantry support had carried out their tasks around the box as requested, and they were heading back to their harbour for the night at Sengmai. No sooner had they arrived when orders were received to return to Lion Box, because the Japanese were thought to be forming up again in the old depot area. Half of Squadron HQ Troop and 3 and 6 Troops, together with their covering party of a platoon of West Yorks, went back to Lion Box, where they proceeded along the road to the old depot. No enemy were seen, but in order to ensure the bashas in this area could not be used for cover, they were set on fire, with the Carbs and the West Yorks finally returning to Sengmai just as darkness began to fall.

At evening stand-to, the whole of Lion Box was on full alert. Despite the reinforcements arriving during the day to bolster the defences, the brunt of this work fell on the shoulders of the men from the 20 Rft Camp who were stretched to the limit, and they now held the whole of Sector 3 and large parts of Sector 4, also providing a large part of the Box Reserve. However, their section commanders were confident that they could hold their area providing that the units on their flanks did not give way. As the tanks and their infantry support 'drew stumps' for the day and trundled off into the dark, there were, no doubt, many of the defenders whose hearts sank at the thought of the long night still to come with the Japanese on the hills and in the jungle surrounding them.

Chapter Four

Good Friday

The evening of Thursday, 6 April had started quietly, but an air of nervous anticipation was running through the defenders of the box. The Box Commander, Lieutenant Colonel Wells-Cole, a soldier of thirty years' experience and fully aware of the importance of troop morale at this crucial time, sent copies of a personal congratulatory message to all sector commanders of the box and to 221 AOD, acknowledging he had received the message from IV Corps Commander Lieutenant General

A personal congratulatory message from Commander IV Corps Lieutenant General Scoones to Lion Box defenders.

Aerial photo taken by a drone of the north-western part of Lion Box, where a Japanese attack was launched at dawn on 7 April 1944.

Scoones late that afternoon. The message read: 'Following message received from IV Corps, please inform all units in your Sector. Congratulate all ranks on spirited and staunch defence of your Box. Confident you will continue hold this and kill enemy. Well done.' This would surely have buoyed up the troops knowing that all their efforts had been duly recognised at the very highest level of command.

The Japanese plans for the forthcoming night attack had been altered from the previous night's failed and aborted attempt to capture the box. This time the 11th Company would instead lead the attack commanded by the long-serving Lieutenant Ishikawa, accompanied by 3rd Battalion Commander Major Fukushima. To facilitate an unseen approach through the jungle, their start point would be further to the north of the old depot area, where their route would take them west before turning south and then east to their forming-up point, on the slopes of a hill overlooking the western perimeter of the box. This would avoid a repetition of Wednesday night's attack when their 12th Company were caught in a heavy bombardment as they formed up in the old depot area, breaking up their attack before it had a chance to develop as planned. In order for this manoeuvre to succeed in the dark, their route would need to be carefully and clearly marked, and during the day reconnaissance scouts had placed pieces of white paper on various landmarks and trees along the route, to act as markers in the dark. After leaving their heavy equipment behind, the advanced guard, under the command of 2nd Lieutenant Inahara, set off at about sunset with the remainder of the column of men heavily laden with ammunition following behind. However, once again movement in the jungle in the dark with large numbers of men was proving more difficult than the Japanese had anticipated. With such a long column of men moving, the slightest obstacle would hold up progress, causing those in front constantly having to wait to be caught up with before they could move on, while those behind waited for the blockage to clear.

At around 23.00 hours, a serious setback befell the Japanese column when a sudden and heavy downpour of rain caught them out, washing the paper markers away and leaving them virtually blind. Unable to advance for the time being, they waited like 'drowned rats' for the rain to stop, while Major Fukushima and Lieutenant Ishikawa conferred and made the decision to continue with the advance, even though they were falling behind schedule with a long way to go before reaching their destination. As the column slipped and slithered their way in the darkness on the hillside, they soon realised that at this rate of progress it would be daylight before they would be ready for an attack, but they pushed on regardless as best they could. Having now lost contact with their 11th Company and unaware of their progress, the remainder of the 3rd Battalion went ahead with the planned programme. They began their diversionary artillery bombardments and the probing of the defences all around the box.

The 864 ME Company were the first to be alerted of a Japanese presence on the perimeter when one of their booby trap bombs exploded at about 21.00 hours. At 23.00 hours, a barrage from two Japanese 75mm mountain guns, firing from the vicinity of Ekban Ekwan near to Piquet Hill, fell along the road on the southern perimeter, and also close to the HQ of Sector 1, which lasted for half an hour. At the same time, a mortar barrage fired from the old depot into the camp area of 58 Field Company wounded two sappers, while other bombs fell in Sector 3. This was followed up by several attempts to infiltrate the Sector 3 perimeter, but they were stopped by the alertness of the sentries, with Captain Baker and the box 3-inch mortar teams doing particularly good work again. Just before 02.00 hours on 7 April, ironically Good Friday, a movement was seen in front of 652 Mechanical Excavation (MEx) Company positions; there was a short period of firing at enemy patrol activity and again at 02.30 hours, while under the cover of a mortar barrage falling in this area of the sector, fired from the old depot. A mortar bomb scored a direct hit on the guardroom of 517 AW Company at around 03.00 hours, killing Sapper Hukam Singh and damaging some rifles. The location of these mortars was spotted by 864 ME Company and the Box Commander was informed, while Captain Baker requested a direct-fire barrage from the artillery on standby. Unfortunately, the 5.5 guns fell short and into the sector, with one shell exploding a few feet from the HQ. Captain Baker immediately ordered them to cease firing, and the 25-pounders near Sengmai took over the barrage, causing the Japanese mortar attack to break off when it was believed they were destroyed. Heavy rain, now accompanied by mist, added to the poor visibility for defender and attacker alike as they peered into the gloom.

The advanced elements of the Japanese 11th Company column had by this time arrived at their planned positions on the hillside where, in the distance, they could make out the dim lights of a camp within a clearing of the jungle. There, they waited for the remainder of the company to arrive before beginning their attack, as they were low in numbers being only about seventy men strong, including the battalion and company commanders Lieutenant Tanaka of the Machine Gun Company, 2nd Lieutenant Yamamoto, Lieutenant Asai, and the battalion adjutant, Lieutenant Takahata. Even though they did what they could to conceal themselves, Lieutenant Ishikawa was unhappy with the situation as it was dangerous, and he wanted to move on because it would not be too long before daylight. Major Fukushima then detailed Lieutenant Takahata to go back along their route to find the remaining men of the attack force and he, together with Lance Corporal Hirata, set off to act as guides for them and any stragglers. Having moved a considerable distance, and with the dawn now beginning to break, Lieutenant Takahata took the decision to return to Major Fukushima to tell him there was no one

Part of the nullah from where the Japanese launched their attack at dawn on 7 April 1944.

to be seen at all, despite their searches. The battalion commander decided to continue with the plan and advanced cautiously as they descended the slope into better cover, and also into the dried-up nullah, hiding under the vegetation growing over the side of the banks. Together, Major Fukushima and Lieutenant Ishikawa then set off on a reconnaissance mission of the camp, leaving their men concealed but in close proximity to the enemy. Lieutenant Takahata was jubilant, thinking what a great victory this would be for the battalion as he surveyed the view in front of the camp, with its many parked trucks and tents, apparently unguarded with the occupants still asleep. Upon their return, Major Fukushima and Lieutenant Ishikawa concluded that they did not have enough men to successfully attack the position, and once again, Lieutenant Takahata was sent back to gather whatever manpower he could, while Major Fukushima and his force waited in their positions for his return. With daylight almost upon them and still no sign of Lieutenant Takahata or anyone else, it became all too apparent that it would be suicide to remain in their present positions, waiting for reinforcements that might never arrive. Movements within the camp then alerted the Japanese that the occupants were now getting ready to man their defences, so, throwing caution to the wind, Major Fukushima ordered an all-out surprise attack with what troops he had to break into the defences as planned.

Sergeant John Rawson, 864 ME Company Royal Engineers, KIA 7 April 1944.

Just before 04.00 hours, a Japanese attempt to cross the nullah was spotted on the right flank of 652 MEx Company and was engaged by light machine-gun fire, killing two while the remainder withdrew. There was a quiet period before another attempt to cross the nullah was again frustrated by 652 MEx Company machine gunners, but just before 05.00 hours, there was a heavy and determined attack to penetrate the perimeter at the point where 652 MEx Company and 864 ME Company defences joined at a track, leading westwards into the hills from Sector 1. It was believed that the initial breakthrough may have been when a Japanese officer tricked an Indian sentry by giving a password in English, when, instead of being shot, he was challenged to 'Halt, halt'. The sentry was then shot, and grenades were thrown at 864 ME Company's No. 1 machine-gun post. It was at this time that one of the earliest British casualties occurred, when Sergeant John Dewar Rawson of 864 ME Company was shot as he ran to his position in one of the pillboxes of which he was in charge. Major Gray and two NCOs carried him to Captain Young's medical centre, but he died

A trench above the nullah on the 864 ME Company perimeter.

on the way there.[1] During this confusion, about twenty of the enemy were seen to have infiltrated into the sector heading towards 302 GPT Company positions, and the sector HQ and the Box Commander were immediately informed. Heavy and continuous firing broke out all along this section of the perimeter as the Japanese used many hand grenades, directing their mortars on the machine-gun posts, in front of which Japanese dead bodies were piling up as they attempted to climb the steep banks of the nullah. The 652 MEx Company machine-gun post nearest the breakthrough counted nine dead and 864 ME Company's nearest post counted seven.

Lieutenant Takahata had been searching for some time along the route back, when he heard the sounds of battle coming from the direction from

1. Although Sergeant Rawson was one of the first casualties taken to the medical aid post of 864 ME Company, his body was not recovered or positively identified for burial in the Imphal Cemetery after the action. Because of his time served overseas (six years) in the Western Desert and India, he was shortly due for repatriation to the UK. Interestingly, Sergeant Rawson is commemorated on the CWGC list as being with 2 Field Company RE at the time of his death. This unit was part of the Chindit expedition so why he was with 864 ME Company is unknown.

The author's son exploring the nullah below 864 ME Company defences, where Lieutenant Takahata lay.

where he had left his comrades. Realising that for whatever reason, the company must be attacking the camp by the sound of explosions and machine-gun fire, he ran back as fast as he could to their positions. Reaching there, he could see no signs of the company except for one soldier lying face down in a hollow. Lieutenant Takahata crawled over to this man, who explained to him the situation of how they had been ordered to attack, but they were being pinned down by heavy fire from a pillbox on their left. Carefully glancing up at the top of the nullah 40 yards away, Lieutenant Takahata could see that the Bren guns of 864 ME Company were now pointing eastwards and firing in the direction of those Japanese who had already broken through the defences. He later wrote:

From the left I heard someone shout my name. It was Lt Asai. He had with him about four or five other soldiers. Perhaps his voice brought me to my senses, but I suddenly heard excited voices from the pillbox to the left followed by a sudden burst of fire in my direction. There were two or three people in the pillbox. The intense gunfire was concentrated on me. Dust clouds rose from the earth and bullets cracked against stones. I threw myself down on the ground and pretended to be dead. I could not move a muscle.

Despite being low in numbers for the attack, Major Fukushima's plan had worked, and the perimeter defences were momentarily overwhelmed and disorganised. The 302 GPT Company was taken completely by surprise as the Japanese now ran amok in their camp, causing a large number of casualties. The same move as before was used to trick those sentries in their trenches to stand up when a Japanese officer gave a password, spoken in Urdu this time. It was mooted at the time that there were some INA troops present as well, causing further confusion for the Indian sepoys, with some still on their charpoys, and were bayoneted where they rested. Enraged upon seeing his men being killed, Major Greenberry

Major Leslie Greenberry, OC 302 GPT Company RIASC.

desperately led a charge at the Japanese, almost single-handedly, with only just a handful of BORs in support. Rushing headlong, firing his Sten gun from the hip, Major Greenberry was seriously wounded in both thighs, left leg and right arm, falling to the ground, from where he was dragged away to safety and taken to the box advanced dressing station before eventually being evacuated to 19 Casualty Clearing Station.

For the next several hours, Sector 1 was the scene of some very confused and heavy fighting as the defenders on the perimeter sought to repel those Japanese attempting to enter the sector, ejecting those who had entered. The Japanese, in turn, sought to consolidate their gains, at the same time desperately trying to break through to the main road as planned.

When news of the breakthrough came, all the personnel of the Sector 1 HQ immediately ran to the cover of their trenches, from where it was just possible to see in the gloom some of the enemy making their way into 302 GPT Company lines. Others had passed through and were heading towards the position of the reserve platoon of 58 Field Company. Lieutenant Colonel

Peacock, the sector commander, then ordered his second in command, Major Jocelyn William Maxim Alexander, to run to the reserve platoon and organise a bayonet charge to push the Japanese out of 302 GPT Company lines, before they broke through to the main road. Captain Joseph Ross Severn, the adjutant of CRE 671 MEx Company, was still manning the telephone in the sector HQ as the bullets whizzed and cracked around him. He phoned through to the Box Commander asking for reinforcements to be sent up as Lieutenant Colonel Peacock

Lieutenant Keith Dormer, 671 MEx Company Indian Engineers.

was now being attacked, and together with Lieutenant Keith Frederick Dormer, the unit transport officer, was defending his HQ under fire. To emphasise the urgency, Captain Severn ran to the Ordnance Depot at around 06.00 for immediate help, but by this time Major Boyd and his mobile patrol from the Ordnance Depot had already been ordered to give assistance, and they had left their positions near the Box HQ and promptly headed towards the sound of firing. As the situation was unclear, Lieutenant Colonel Wells-Cole decided not to commit all of Major Boyd's patrol at this time for fear of reinforcements being required elsewhere on the perimeter of the box, so only Major Boyd and Lieutenant Buckingham, together with Conductor French and six BORs, took up positions around the Engineers' HQ to give assistance. With the commitment of the sector's reserve from 58 Field Company, this left the sector with no spare troops, so a further request was sent to the Box Commander for another 200 reinforcements to be sent up. As there were no reinforcements of this amount available, a party of around fifty Assam Rifles would be dispatched, but Lieutenant Colonel Wells-Cole was still reluctant to commit all of his reserves, as the situation was still very fluid and confused.

Upon arriving at 58 Field Company's lines, Major Alexander and Major Pearce organised a bayonet party to be led by them, with another led by Captain Walsh. By this time sentries in 58 Field Company's defences spotted a number of Japanese making their way towards their cookhouse area and opened fire, killing three, with one of the engineers being shot and killed at the same time. The acting company sergeant major accounted for four more of the enemy in the cookhouse area before being wounded in the leg himself, while another was killed by an NCO. The two bayonet parties quickly moved forward to halt the Japanese advance from reaching the main road. Six Japanese were killed by the party led by Majors Pearce and Alexander, with Major

Corporal Edward Robinson, 58 Field Company Royal Engineers, KIA 7 April 1944.

Pearce accounting for three of the dead, shot with his Tommy gun. This counterattack caused some of the Japanese to retire while others returned fire, pinning down Major Pearce and his party in a small nullah near to the rear of 864 ME Company's positions, where a sapper was killed.

Private Mitchell, one of the six men from B Company 1st Seaforth Highlanders attached to 221 AOD, remembered that at about 05.30 they were awoken by their sentry, Private Kirby, who had heard some Japanese shouting, and were immediately stood-to. A few moments later, Captain Duckworth arrived, explaining that the Japanese had broken through on the Engineers' front, and that Major Boyd had called for reinforcements who were to join him there. Captain Duckworth then led them and ten men of his platoon from the Ordnance to the area of the breakthrough, but the Seaforths had arrived too far to the right, Private Mitchell later recalled:

> Captain Duckworth called to the BORs to come left to re-join Major Boyd but Sergeant Campbell and three of us were ahead and had already spotted some enemy to our front. Sergeant Campbell carried on with the three of us to where the enemy had been seen amongst some vehicles and tentage. Sergeant Campbell went forward and saw a party of Engineers pinned to the ground by enemy fire. We opened fire on the enemy over the heads of

the Engineers while Sergeant Campbell shouted to them to get up and go forward, but nothing happened. Major Pearce was also urging the Engineers to go forward. Sergeant Campbell turned to us and said, 'Come on lads, we'll have to show 'em. Spread out in a line.' We went forward and some of the Engineers followed. The party cleared some open ground, and the enemy were seen to be running back and Sergeant Campbell shot four of the enemy with a burst from his Bren gun, firing from the hip.

The party of the Seaforths with a few engineers moved on towards some bashas with Sergeant Campbell leading the way. He passed word back for the engineers to search through the bashas to flush out any Japanese, while he and the other Seaforths would bypass the bashas and catch the enemy on the other side. As they approached the bashas alongside a line of scrub jungle, Sergeant Campbell spotted a Chinese civilian crouching in a ditch and signalled for him to come forward. He approached hesitatingly, talking loudly with excitement and fear. He was passed to Private Mitchell, who searched him and

Lance Sergeant David Campbell, 1st Seaforth Highlanders, attached 221 AOD, KIA 7 April 1944.

placed him under the guard of the engineers, who explained that the Chinese man was one of the thirty or so civilian mechanics attached to 864 ME Company, and there were others hiding nearby as well. The party moved off again and as Sergeant Campbell rounded the end of the scrub there was a burst of firing, with both Sergeant Campbell and the enemy firing simultaneously. Sergeant Campbell staggered back towards Private Mitchell just 5 yards behind him, saying, 'Watch yourself, Mitch, they're around here and they've got me.' He then took another step forward and fell into a nullah, where he died. Private Silk of the Seaforths was wounded at this time. Major Pearce now arrived at the scene where the Japanese soldier wounded by Sergeant Campbell was lying. He ordered that he should be finished off and one of the engineers shot him before the bayonet party resumed their task, though somewhat reluctantly, until Major Pearce reassured them.

With the confusion of a running battle, any direct support by Captain Baker and his box mortar teams was very difficult, and the best they managed was to target the Japanese mortars hiding in the jungle, and who were still causing casualties. When known Japanese positions were located within the box, they were heavily engaged and harassed by the mortars of Major Davies's X Company 9th Jats as well as Captain Baker's teams. Sapper Ray Lewis of 58 Field Company had a lucky escape from almost certain death when a mortar bomb exploded near him. He was one of Lieutenant Mellor's party who were trying to draw fire from a Japanese sniper hidden near one of the engineers' bulldozers. He had been kneeling down receiving instructions from Lieutenant Mellor and just as they stood up a mortar bomb exploded nearby, peppering Sapper Lewis with shrapnel in his pelvis and legs. Had he still been kneeling, this shrapnel would have hit

Major Jo Alexander, CRE 671 MEx Company Indian Engineers.

him in the head and chest. He was then evacuated by two Seaforth men and two Gurkhas carrying him on a groundsheet to an awaiting jeep, which transported him away for medical treatment, while the Gurkhas gave him the thumbs-up sign. Another who also had a lucky escape was Major Alexander of 671 MEx Company, who had been giving orders to two sappers beside a slit trench. A mortar bomb exploded beside them and blasted all three into the trench, where the heavily concussed Major Alexander lay underneath the two dead sappers until he was eventually recovered sometime later.[2]

Major Pearce and his men now moved cautiously through the long grass towards 671 MEx Company's position to the west, killing another one of their enemies on the way. Unaware, they passed by a Japanese sniper hidden in the grass who opened fire from behind them. A sapper was killed and

---

2. Major Alexander remained at duty despite his concussion and at this time was still recovering from a bout of malaria after returning from Broadway airfield with the Chindits behind the Japanese lines. As a technical major he had been sent to oversee the work of the bulldozers constructing the vital runway there.

130   Box of Lions

Major Pearce wounded in the right shoulder. Three other sappers were also wounded, with one dying of his wounds later in hospital. Captain Walsh and his small party then moved forward to the left of Major Pearce's party to support them, killing a number of Japanese with hand grenades as they hid in trenches, but they too became pinned down by snipers. The enemy attempts to break through on 864 ME Company's front were being held, enabling Major Gray to put together a small party of his company to go to the assistance of 58 Field Company's stalled counterattack. They and their company medical officer, Captain Young,

Corporal Harry William Lewis, 864 ME Company Royal Engineers, KIA 7 April 1944.

moved out from their defences and crawled along the small nullah in which the two bayonet parties of 58 Field Company were pinned down and taking heavy casualties. The Japanese were now laying down accurate fire, and Captain Walsh and two BORs were killed, all being shot in the head. Captain Young, tending the wounded, was having a difficult time as the casualties mounted. When Major Gray was shot in the shoulder, Captain Young was grateful for his refusal to be evacuated because he was still able to continue organising his men, keeping the situation under control. Lieutenant Mellor and twelve BORs of 58 Field Company now moved round to the left, pushing the enemy back as they then took up positions around the sector HQ alongside the Ordnance mobile patrol, and eventually up to the perimeter of the box.

Further Japanese infiltration was also taking place behind the areas held by 652 MEx Company to the west of the Dak Bungalow, where some of 221 AOD defences were situated. Havildar Basant Singh, a clerk by trade, had spotted a group of the

Lance Corporal William Warrillow, KIA 7 April 1944.

Captain Charles Phillip Walsh, 58 Field
Company Royal Engineers, KIA 7 April 1944.

Captain Henry Adams Young RAMC,
medical officer 864 ME Company.

Driver Reginald Corbyn, 58 Field Company
Royal Engineers, KIA 7 April 1944.

Sapper Ronald Golding, 58 Field Company
Royal Engineers, KIA 7 April 1944.

enemy making their way through the tall grass from his position, and in order to obtain a clear field of fire he coolly stood up on top of his bunker with his Bren gun. Regardless of his personal danger, Havildar Basant Singh remained in this exposed position for over fifteen minutes firing from the shoulder, stopping any further advance by the Japanese in this direction after killing an unknown number of the enemy. Other troops of the Ordnance Corps were also heavily engaged, though not with the enemy. Private Parsons, the depot's librarian, found himself administering first aid to the many wounded now coming in and giving assistance with their evacuation, while two Havildar clerks manned the depot telephone exchange. Housed in a small hut with no protection from bombardment or small arms fire, these two NCOs had been at their posts for the last three nights, remaining cheerful throughout. Further Ordnance IORs led by Captain Jadvev and Lieutenant Shamsha Brar arrived, intending to bolster those already in position around the stores area. With the situation now stabilised around the Sector 1 HQ, Major Boyd, together with Lieutenant Buckingham and their mobile patrol, then moved to the area on the perimeter being held by the machine-gun posts of 652 MEx Company, where Captain Duckworth had already arrived. Although there had been no other officers in this position until the company second in command arrived, a considerable number of enemy casualties had been inflicted by the sappers, and it was believed there were twenty to thirty dead and wounded in this area, with more having dropped into the nullah and into the jungle. Despite this excellent work, a serious situation had developed for a while as the Japanese were now in the rear of their defences threatening to cut them off. Captain Knight ordered that the company reserves were to be placed to counter this problem, but they found difficulty in shooting at the enemy with automatic fire for fear of hitting their own men within the sector, especially those of 302 GPT Company. When the fighting here eased off, Captain Duckworth and his men were left in charge, supporting the

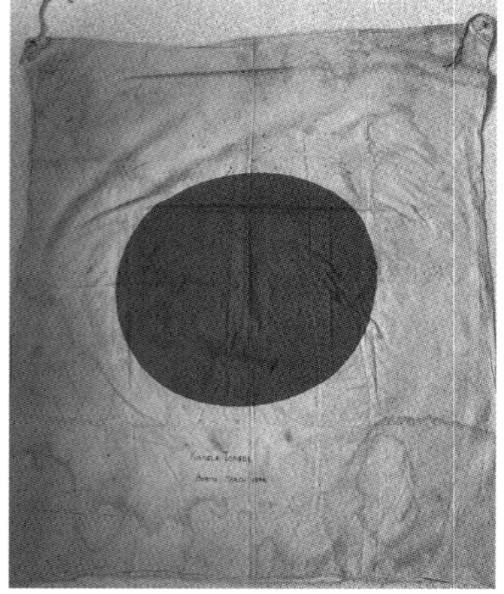

A Japanese flag picked up from the battlefield by Lieutenant Dennis Buckingham.

tired defenders of this position and helping cover any infiltration at their rear, while Major Boyd and Lieutenant Buckingham left to go in search of further reinforcements, gathering up the scattered members of the mobile patrol, some still fighting in other parts of the sector.

While Lieutenant Takahata lay in the nullah hardly daring to move, his mind wandered off to other times before being jolted back into reality, when he remembered that he still had with him his unit's code book, later writing:

> Wait a minute, I've got the code book. It will be disastrous if the enemy get their hands on this. Even if I die, I've got to make sure that I hide this. I know, I'll bury it beneath my chest, and I'll die on top of it. When our army comes to pick up our bodies someone will hopefully find it then. These were my thoughts as I started to dig a hole beneath my chest with my hands. As it was sandy soil in the riverbed it wasn't difficult to make some kind of hole. Keeping an eye on the enemy in the pillbox I extracted the code book from where it was hidden in a map attached to my waist. Laboriously, I lowered it into the hole and then managed to cover it with sand. I breathed a sigh of relief and then urinated. As my body was still chilled from the previous night's rain, and the lower half of my body had felt as heavy as lead since the soaking, this at least made me feel a little better.

The sounds of battle continued while Lieutenant Takahata waited for Lieutenant Asai to finish digging the hole for him to shelter in, but by now the cries and crackle of gunfire were joined by heavier explosions and the sound of heavy engines. Raising his head a little, Lieutenant Takahata could now see the gun turret of a tank appearing above the top of the nullah before the body of the tank came into view, making the ground shudder as it moved along the edge, later writing:

> Looking up at a tank from a distance of thirty to forty metres made it appear strangely large, and with the dirty pale green colour inspired an overpowering feeling of dread. The roof (the commander's hatch) of the tank opened, and an enemy soldier appeared from within and calmly lit a cigarette. He spoke with a loud voice with a soldier in the pillbox, and then all of a sudden extended his left arm.[3] At that moment both the tank's machine guns and

---

3. This could have been Lieutenant Cole, who was later killed in action 8/6/1944 with three other members of his crew when their tank was destroyed. They had been attacking 'Isaac', a large Japanese bunker complex at Modbung, which had overlooked Lion Box.

those in the pillbox started firing in unison and the earth began to tremble again as the tank moved inexorably forward. I could hear repeatedly the sound of voices shouting, hand grenades exploding, and guns being fired from inside the enemy camp. Two or three times tanks appeared only to then disappear again.

After passing several small groups of marching troops and loaded vehicles heading south along the road to Sengmai, two tanks of 5 Troop and their platoon from B Company West Yorks finally arrived at the Box HQ at 06.20, ready for their usual daily instructions, only to be met by a very irate Box Commander. It had been assumed that the Carbs and their infantry escort would arrive in strength at first light ready to give assistance. Lieutenant Colonel Wells-Cole let them know in no uncertain terms that they were late, and to get themselves up to Sector 1 immediately and do something. Duly chastised (through no fault of the men themselves), the tanks and infantry moved off, but it was almost 07.00 by the time they were organised and into action. Arriving at the Dak Bungalow the column turned left off the main road and along the track leading to the admin commandant's old position, halting while the infantry alighted from their transport and formed themselves up ready. Not being too sure of the dispositions of the defenders nor the location of the sector HQ, nor indeed that of the enemy incursions, Lieutenant Cole, 5 Troop Commander commanding 'Cirencester', moved his tanks to where he thought they would be of most use near to the Japanese breakthrough where he could hear firing.[4] The movement of the tanks behind the positions of 528 AW Company on the northern perimeter caused even more confusion for those sappers holding the line, for not only were they facing the enemy to their front, but to their rear the Japanese were continuing their infiltration. Lieutenant Cole and his tanks now reached 864 ME Company lines, where again considerable disorganisation of the defences was caused by their presence, and that of the infantry as they engaged the enemy within this part of the sector. After contacting 864 ME Company officers, the platoon commander of the West Yorks informed Lieutenant Cole that the Japanese were in the nullah below the perimeter, and that the two

---

4. It was customary for the tanks of 'C' Squadron to name their tanks after cities or towns in the UK that began with the letter 'C'.

machine-gun posts of the sappers positioned there needed relieving. These sappers manning the defences had been in continuous action, firing for more than three hours, and were exhausted. Spraying the area with machine-gun fire, the tanks of Lieutenant Cole and his troop corporal, Corporal Leslie Albert James Akerman, commanding 'Clydebank', moved into the nullah, where they proceeded to where the two pillboxes were. Both tanks then climbed up to the north bank, where they began to cover the evacuation of No. 1 post. The sappers manning the pillbox and adjacent trenches were ordered to leave their positions in ones and twos and not bunched up. The pillbox was quickly evacuated

Lance Corporal Thomas Payne, 864 ME Company Royal Engineers, KIA 7 April 1944.

before it was destroyed by the tanks, preventing its use by the enemy.

Now satisfied that this was a full-scale attack centred on the north-west corner of the box, Lieutenant Colonel Wells-Cole now committed more reinforcements from the Box Reserve, as well as requesting further reinforcements of tanks and infantry from Sengmai. At around 06.45, the remainder of B Company West Yorks together with 6 and 7 Troops and half of HQ Troop were finally ordered out of their positions to support Lion Box. Arriving at the Box HQ at about 08.30, the tanks parked by the left-hand side of the road under some trees while the infantry found cover nearby as they awaited their orders and the arrival of their commanders, who were not far behind. Such was the seriousness of the situation, the CO of 2 West Yorks, Lieutenant Colonel Gerald Hilary (Munshie) Cree and the OC of C Squadron, Captain Ian Morgan, also came to take control, but just as their Bren gun carrier arrived, they came under Japanese 75mm artillery bombardment from near Ekban Ekwan. The Japanese artillery spotters posted on Piquet Hill had seen the arrival of these reinforcements and were able to bring down accurate fire on them. Before they had the chance to move off, the tank of 7 Troop commander Lieutenant Rowe-Wilson was hit and put out of action. The driver of the tank, Trooper Connolly, had been casually watching a party of West Yorks hastily digging in for protection just in front of him, when there was a loud explosion to the rear of his tank, and the infantry immediately took to their legs and scattered before another shell crashed into their partly dug trench. Within seconds, another shell

Lieutenant Colonel Gerald 'Munshie' Cree, CO 2nd West Yorkshire Regiment.

burst on the 75mm gun sponson of the tank, damaging a track connector and buckling the steel plate into the shape of a boil, sending fragments of metal flying around the inside of the tank. There were shouts over the intercom of 'MOVE, MOVE! For Christ's sake move.' Trooper Connolly immediately engaged reverse gear and pulled back just in time before another shell exploded exactly where the tank had stood a few seconds previously, which would have proved disastrous. Although it had been a glancing blow, the tank had considerable damage, enough to warrant it being pulled out of the battle until repairs to the track had been completed. The tank's wireless had also been put out of action and would need replacing. The squadron commander, Captain Morgan, gave permission for the tank to retire to wait for the arrival of the fitters from the Squadron Light Aid Detachment, with replacement track blocks and another radio. The sergeant major's tank from HQ Troop was sent as a replacement for 7 Troop when the half squadron moved up to the north-west corner of the box.[5]

Trooper Connolly now carefully nursed the tank back along the main road to be clear of any more shelling, hoping the track would hold together a bit

---

5. This was to be the first of many battle 'wounds' for Trooper Connolly's tank named 'Clacton'. The coming weeks would see much heavier battle damage inflicted upon it.

7 Troop leader Lieutenant Rowe Wilson (standing middle) and his crew with their Lee tank being repaired by IEME fitters: standing left, Trooper Connolly (driver); kneeling with a Thompson machine gun, Trooper Lynn (wireless operator); standing right, Trooper Carter (37mm gun loader); sitting on turret, Trooper French (75mm gunner), Trooper Butler (37mm gunner); other crew member, Trooper Blunson (75mm loader).

longer, but after a mile or so it finally gave out. The crew then dismounted and hurriedly began dismantling the smashed track ready for the fitters to complete their work. At this time, some of the non-combatants of the garrison and followers in the box had started being evacuated. They came pouring down the road like a crowd leaving at the end of a football match, carrying as much kit as they could hold. Seeing that Trooper Connolly's tank was facing south towards Imphal, some of these men thought they would cadge a ride, and fights broke out as they jostled for space on the rear of the tank before a stop was put to this ill-discipline, allowing the repairs to continue. When the work of the Indian Electrical and Mechanical Engineer fitters was finally completed, the squadron commander was informed the tank was ready and was then ordered to rejoin 7 Troop with all possible haste. Having already 'shaken hands with the Devil' once that day, the tank crew entered Kanglatongbi, where Trooper Connolly saw all the signs of battle from his driver's hatch, as huts were burning and ambulances were rushing about as the casualties mounted, accompanied all the time by the distant crackle of small arms fire and the thud of artillery and mortar rounds exploding. They soon made their way to Sector 1, where they contacted their supporting infantry and joined the fray.

When this shelling near the Box HQ stopped, a conference was held when Lieutenant Colonel Wells-Cole explained the situation to Lieutenant Colonel Cree and his B Company commander, Major Dunlop, and Captain Morgan. Because his box defenders had been in heavy action with very little rest, Lieutenant Colonel Wells-Cole felt that they could not reasonably be expected to hold out for another night and recommended that they should come out that day before dark. Lieutenant Colonel Cree had orders that on no account was he to allow his battalion to get themselves into a static defence of the box and therefore he now needed clear orders about what to do next. He informed his HQ at 9 Brigade of Lieutenant Colonel Wells-Cole's recommendation. This was passed on to 5 Division, where it was eventually approved and the wheels set in motion for the complete evacuation of Lion Box.

Lieutenant Colonel Peacock at Sector 1 HQ was then informed of the plans to hold the line and stem the flow of enemy incursion, while clearing them from the north-west corner of the box. The units on the perimeter there

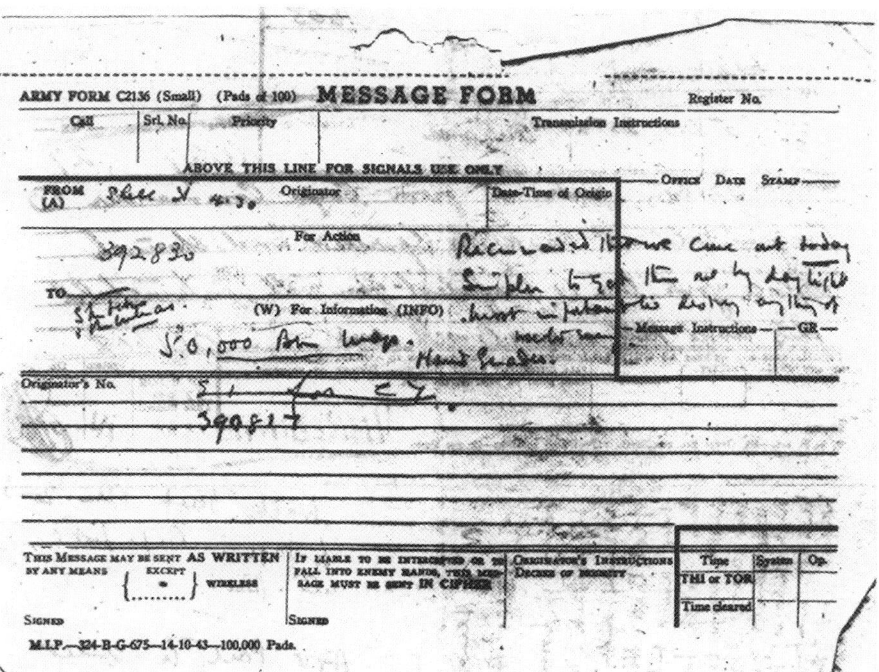

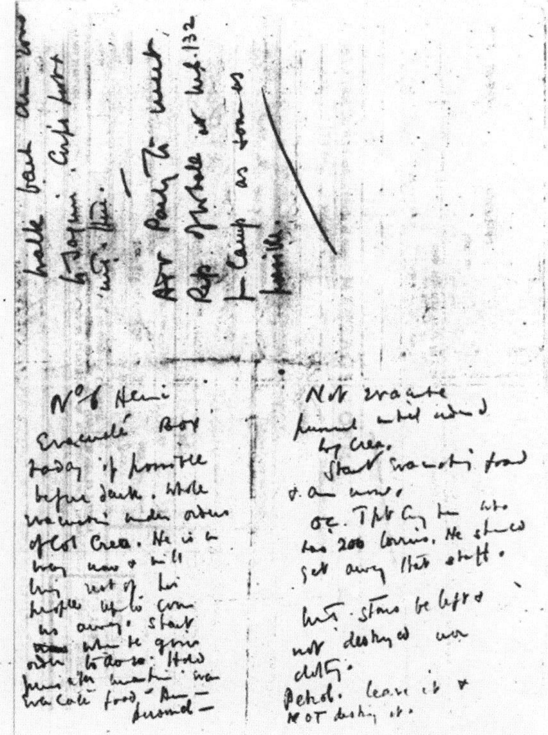

Box Commander's battle notes.

would then be relieved, as they had been in constant action now for many hours; the men were becoming tired, especially as they had had little rest for at least three days. Once cleared, the Carbs and West Yorks were ordered to form and hold a defensive line running roughly diagonally through the sector from the northern roadblock on the main road across to where the breakthrough had occurred. Further infantry reinforcements would be sent to bolster them at the same time, allowing other units within the box to prepare themselves to move. Lieutenant Cole and his tanks, already fighting in the sector, now came under Captain Morgan's command, but owing to the tanks being widely spread and out of view of each other in the thick scrub jungle, it was difficult to co-ordinate their moves. As such, it was therefore decided that all six tanks would mark their positions by the firing of a Verey signal light individually as they set about their task. Guides from the sector HQ were also sent to help the tanks, and the West Yorks positioned themselves for their best use. An abandoned truck, which was thought to be a Japanese position that had been causing problems for the engineers, was pointed out to one of 7 Troop's tanks, and two rounds of 75mm high explosive destroyed the position, where seven bodies were counted.

As Major Boyd gathered up his fragmented mobile patrol, news arrived that Conductor Ronald Wright Parker and his party were presently attempting to rescue another wounded BOR, sheltering in a large basha in which a Japanese machine-gun crew had set up a post. Coming under heavy fire from the enemy machine gun, Conductor Parker, together with a BOR and two IORs from the Ordnance, were forced back. A second attempt was made by Conductor Parker with the help of Major Boyd and

Conductor Ronald Wright Parker, 221 AOD.

Captain Duckworth after the tanks and infantry had arrived. Under the direction of Major Boyd, the two tanks from Lieutenant Cole's 5 Troop and some of the West Yorks covered Conductor Parker and his small group as he succeeded in retaking the basha, rescuing the wounded engineer BOR and recovering the bodies of two other BORs. The bodies of the three Japanese killed by Conductor Parker were strapped to one of the tanks and taken back, while the other tank and their infantry escort were placed in defence by Major Boyd with Lieutenant Buckingham left in command. Another small group of Major Boyd's mobile patrol were also in close action, with another Japanese machine-gun post giving trouble in this area near to the 302 GPT Company lines. Conductor Slaney and Corporal Chapman together with two BORs attacked and silenced the post with hand grenades. Upon inspection, the bodies of nine Japanese soldiers with one officer were found nearby. His body was searched and stripped of papers, which were sent back to HQ. In a further search of the area, they found the bodies of six bayoneted sepoys from 302 GPT Company killed during the initial breakthrough.

Though not part of the Ordnance mobile patrol itself, Havildar Basant Singh, not content with just manning his bunker, actively sought out an enemy machine-gun post that had been reported to him as causing problems on the Ordnance front. Together with two BORs and an IOR, he led this group as they engaged and destroyed this position, killing three more of the enemy. It was noted that his bearing set a good example to all ranks throughout the day's action.

The infantry reinforcements sent by the Box Commander now began to arrive at about 09.00 from their previous defensive positions, to take over the defences of the

Driver Matthew Rawes, 864 ME Company Royal Engineers, KIA 7 April 1944.

engineers on the perimeter. About 100 Mahrattas and Gurkhas of the Box Reserve, commanded by Lieutenant Sparkes-Calcutt, and other officers from 20 Reinforcement Camp were escorted by 7 Troop tanks and deployed on the flanks of 528 AW Company to stabilise the situation, because the enemy had infiltrated behind their lines and those of 864 ME Company. This assistance was a great relief for 864 ME Company sappers as they moved off from their positions after taking many casualties. Guides were provided by this company who led the infantry to the perimeter defences, which they took over. After the successful evacuation of their No. 1 machine-gun post it was now time to clear No. 2 post under the cover of the tanks of 5 Troop. As the sappers prepared to leave the pillbox it was hit by a Japanese mortar bomb, injuring three. At first the Carbs were accused by the engineers of destroying the pillbox before the occupants had cleared it, but the fact that no tank was firing at the time was corroborated by the supporting infantry. A corporal from 864 ME Company was given a few choice words from a tank commander having climbed up and banged on the turret to attract his attention. He was told that in future he was to use the telephone placed in a box at the rear of the tank if he needed to contact the commander. The corporal was fortunate not to have been shot by mistake, because the Japanese would climb on the tanks in an attempt to place sticky mines or drop grenades inside. The full company of 4th Assam Rifles, led by Lieutenat Colonel Murray, was now detailed to relieve 652 MEx Company, instead of just the fifty riflemen as promised earlier. 652 MEx Company, who had also borne the brunt of the Japanese attack, had become disorganised as the enemy had also moved behind them. By about 09.00, the Assam Rifles had completed taking over the positions, quickly restoring the line on this vital part of the sector and allowing 652 MEx Company to retire and rest. This movement also released Captain Duckworth and his section, enabling them to rejoin Major Boyd again.

With all of his Box Reserves now committed to Sector 1 defence, Lieutenant Colonel Wells-Cole now called upon the Sector 3 Reserve to take on the role of Box Reserve in case of enemy attacks elsewhere, whilst their attention was being focused to the north-west, where the heavy fighting continued. 'Thank goodness for the tanks,' remarked Lieutenant Colonel Wells-Cole to Captain Charles at the Box HQ as the Carabiniers were, by now, causing large numbers of casualties as the Japanese attacks and their infiltration began to stall. Despite having no anti-tank weapons other than grenades and sticky bombs, the Japanese infantry attacks against the tanks were ferocious, and although trained to support each other, the tanks had great difficulty dealing with them, even with their infantry support. Trooper Connolly remembered that at one point the main guns could not be depressed low enough as the Japanese milled around his tank and the Browning machine guns fitted on the bow were red hot as he steered the tank in the direction of their attacks, later noting, 'We were killing the Japanese in large numbers but this did not stop the onslaught, they did not know the meaning of fear.'

The 6 Troop leader, Lieutenant Scott-Dickins, had manoeuvred his tank carefully to give himself an excellent field of fire of about 200 yards along the bed of the nullah on the western perimeter, and a while later, he spotted a group of Japanese troops in single file led by an officer heading south. Unaware of the tank's presence, they continued forward until Lieutenant Scott-Dickins ordered the tank's Browning machine guns to open fire, and the enemy were brought down in their tracks. When the dust had settled, Lieutenant Scott-Dickins could see no movement and gave instructions for his covering party of the West Yorks to check out the dead. The infantry proceeded cautiously, prodding each body with their bayonets, when amazingly, the Japanese officer leading the group, now lying face down, jumped up and threw a grenade in the direction of the nearest infantryman, who instinctively threw himself to the ground and rolled away. This then allowed a clear burst of fire from the tank's machine gun to finish off the officer. The bodies were quickly searched and amongst the officer's possessions were visiting cards printed in English giving his name and rank, and his address as New Delhi – obviously an optimistic person.

Orders were then received from the Box HQ for Lieutenant Scott-Dickins to bring in the dead and severely wounded for intelligence purposes, and they were loaded and strapped onto the engine decks of two of his tanks, accompanied by some infantry. A grisly business at the best of times, made worse now by the bloodied bodies being covered in flies, and upon starting up the tanks' engines, hundreds were drawn into the cooling fan in the turret and the hull before being expelled into the engine compartment. This brought cries of disgust from the crews as they headed back to the

HQ, where the dead and dying were quickly and unceremoniously booted off from the back of the tanks. Obviously beyond medical help and of no use for interrogation, the wounded Japanese were ordered to be dispatched by whatever means. After this brief respite, the two tanks returned to the location of their supporting infantry, where they remained on standby and were not involved in any further action that day, until they later covered the evacuation of the box.

The deadly game of cat and mouse continued in Sector 1, while the tanks and infantry sought out and destroyed the enemy infiltrators hiding wherever they could. Every basha, tent and abandoned vehicle was checked by the men of the West Yorks, as well as all the trenches and gullies that ran through the sector. They went in with the points of bayonets to winkle out the stubborn Japanese. The tanks, firing high-explosive rounds, caused many casualties, including the Japanese battalion commander, Major Fukushima, who was seriously wounded in the shoulder by shrapnel and rescued from the bottom of a trench by his men. Others were not as fortunate. Lieutenant Tanaka, the Machine Gun Company commander, and Lieutenant Yamamoto were both killed by a direct hit from one of the tanks' guns, while the 11th Company commander, Lieutenant Ishikawa, and ten of his men were killed in the area near the Sector 1 HQ. Other Japanese attackers almost made it as far as the main road before being stopped. Second Lieutenant Inahara at the head of the initial breakthrough was shot in the left thigh, and he died along with three others accompanying him. The resourceful Lieutenant Sawai had a narrow escape after being shot in the thigh when he buried himself with sand as he lay in a trench, and he was lucky not to have been crushed by the tanks as they manoeuvred themselves around the battlefield.

Despite their successes in containing the situation, the West Yorks, however, did not have things all their own way during the fighting, sustaining seven wounded casualties as the Japanese put up stiff resistance. The Carbs fared better because of their armoured protection, but the crews still had a most uncomfortable and exhausting time while they were battened down. The heat and acrid stench of burnt cordite and high-octane fuel dried the mouth and throat and together with the roaring engine, chattering machine guns and the blast from the main guns, produced an unpleasant cocktail. To add further to their discomfort, the crew also had to contend with the need of bodily functions while being confined to their posts for several hours. Some, if not all, were suffering with intestinal problems as well, with only the use of an empty 75mm shell case as a receptacle. Trooper Connolly remembered feeling as though his head was twice its size because of the constant crackle of the intercom and the shouted orders. The tank commander could at least get some fresh air, but at the expense of exposing himself to danger as he peered from out of his hatch. This was the case when enemy troops began infiltrating between 6 and 7 Troops. The 7 Troop reported shots from 6 Troop falling dangerously close to them and their infantry support, so they were ordered to use hand grenades instead, which entailed the tank commander standing in his turret to throw them. One of the tanks managed to manoeuvre beside a trench where the commander dropped a grenade, killing one Japanese while the tank tracks crushed another.

By 10.00 hours, the situation became more stabilised, and it was noticed that any Japanese outside the perimeter were digging in for their protection, while the fresh defenders ensured there would be no further breaches into the box. Indian other rank prisoners were seen to be used by the Japanese for digging their positions at the point of a bayonet. Some of these IORs were captured sepoys from the 15th/11th Sikh Regiment who had been taken prisoner on the night of 2/3 April when their positions on the Mapao Ridge, a few miles away, were attacked by a strong force of Japanese.[6]

By now, Lieutenant Takahata, still lying out of sight in the nullah, had noticed that firing in the camp area had subsided, and that the pillbox covering him 40 yards away was now unmanned. Taking this opportunity, Lieutenant Takahata jumped up and sprinted across to Lieutenant Asai and joined him in the hole he and his men had been digging. Huddled together with knees touching shoulders, the two Japanese officers pondered their situation and what they should do next.

---

6. All those Sikhs taken prisoner managed to escape during the confusion of the fighting and aftermath at Lion Box. One escapee reported that he had been used to recover the dead bodies of the Japanese, helping bring in thirty himself during the night of 7/8 April. He estimated that about forty Japanese casualties were attributable to the West Yorks and tanks, while another fifty were caused by air strikes. None of these figures can be confirmed.

Chapter Five

The Evacuation

As the infantry from the West Yorks and Assam Rifles now took over control from Major Boyd, he and his patrol cautiously made their way back to the Ordnance Depot because there were still isolated pockets of resistance and other Japanese in hiding within the sector. Along their way news came in that other members of the Ordnance mobile patrol had become casualties, and that Sergeant Campbell had been killed and Private Mark James Lawton of the South Lancashire Regiment was lying wounded in a nullah. Lieutenant Buckingham and Conductor Parker with two BORs set out to find the spot when they came across Private Mitchell, still in his position near to where Sergeant Campbell's body was lying.[1] Private Mitchell was able to explain to Lieutenant Buckingham what had happened and, though he did not say how Private Lawton was wounded, he knew where he was lying, still being covered by enemy snipers and grenade dischargers. The party set off to recover Private Lawton but came under fire themselves and took cover while these Japanese were dealt with and the area cleared. Eventually, Private Lawton was evacuated to the advanced dressing

---

1. Private Lawton had been a pre-war regular soldier in the South Lancashire Regiment and was called up for service again in 1939. A veteran of the Dunkirk fighting and evacuations, he also served in Madagascar and India until an eye injury caused his medical downgrading. After passing trade tests for the Ordnance Corps, he was then permanently posted to 221 AOD in November 1943. In mid-March 1944, he found himself in hot water and was deprived of his lance corporal rank by Lieutenant Colonel Cunningham for an unspecified misdemeanour. At the time of his death during the fighting at Lion Box, Private Lawton was still under open arrest awaiting his trial. Earlier in his service, Private Lawton had been employed as a nursing orderly in his battalion. An officer's testimonial describes him as being 'so pleasant mannered', doing his duties extremely well, which appeared to suit him. Did this cost him his life as he went to aid others?

   Official casualty reports state that Sergeant Campbell died of wounds, which would suggest he received some sort of medical attention before his death. Whether a medic attended to him before he died in the nullah or upon his admission at a medical facility is unknown. Private Mitchell stated that Sergeant Campbell died immediately, but he could have been mistaken.

station, where he succumbed to his wounds sometime later. Private Mitchell then gathered up Sergeant Campbell's Bren gun and Private Silk's Thompson machine gun with all their ammunition and returned to the depot in the back of an ambulance.

Away from the heavy fighting in Sector 1 things had been very tense all around the box perimeter, as Japanese diversionary tactics and shelling kept the defenders very busy and on full alert. In Sector 2, 440 Quarrying Company received orders from the Box Commander to send out a fighting patrol from their positions, because there had been reports of Japanese snipers in the nullah between them and Sector

Private Mark Lawton, South Lancashire Regiment attached 221 AOD, KIA 7 April 1944.

3. Captain Upfold with a jemadar and ten IORs went out and made a thorough search but no snipers were found, despite some having been heard by the sentries of the neighbouring unit. There were, however, many dead bodies found outside 440 Quarrying Company's perimeter, but it was unclear whether they had been 'bagged' by the sappers' fire or by the box mortars.

Back at the Ordnance Depot, Lieutenant Colonel Cunningham and his men were making themselves ready to resume their task of shifting the stores, but they had been held back as the Box Commander had stopped any movement of the trucks while the firing and the threat of enemy infiltration continued there. Captain Bhattacharyya of 1341 Pioneer Company had marched his men to the depot at about 07.30 hours in anticipation of work, only to be told that he must place them under cover and wait until further orders, while Major Hubbard and fifty lorries, arriving at 08.30, were halted at the box southern roadblock. Lieutenant Colonel Field in conjunction with the Box Commander now decided that this was the time to move out his 99 Mobile Workshop Company Group, who had been placed on standby to leave at short notice by him the previous day. With their vehicles moving off at two-minute intervals starting at 09.00 hours, this unit was soon clear of the box, meeting up with Lieutenant Colonel Kelly along the road to Imphal, from where he had just reconnoitred their new position and arranged their guides. Major Madden and 921 Garrison Engineers Workshop Section also moved out at this time.

As the heaviest of the fighting subsided, permission was given to resume loading and all ranks of the Pioneer, Transport and Ordnance groups swung into action with even greater zeal, and even though there was still considerable firing, this did not seem to worry the men unduly. At about 10.30 hours, Lieutenant Colonel Cunningham was summoned to the Box HQ, where he received his instructions for the evacuation of 221 AOD. All loading of the depot's stores by them was to finish at 11.00 when their labour and transport support would be taken away, just leaving them with their unit transport and any running vehicles within the Vehicle Reserve Group with which to clear their own unit rations, ammunition and kit. This would then free up manpower and transportation for those other units in the box who would need help to load their stores and equipment ready for their eventual evacuation. A further 700 or 800 tons of stores were evacuated during this period and although there were still large amounts of ordnance stores left behind, there were to be no demolitions of them as it was thought they would be of no tactical use to the enemy. There were also about twenty non-runners from the VRG that were left behind and these vehicles were then immobilised, rendering them useless. By 11.30, most of the Ordnance Corps defenders on the depot perimeter had been replaced by infantry reinforcements and were allowed to re-join the rest of the depot personnel as they began their final packing up. The QM of 221 AOD had by now already loaded and cleared all his rations and the fifteen days' reserve, together with all the reserve ammunition for the unit as these were the main priority for evacuation. Upon his return from Imphal, he was ordered to collect as much remaining essential mess stores and equipment as possible in the time available before retiring. All of the men's personal kit was loaded but, despite their hard work, it was estimated that 80 per cent of their equipment was left as well as all tentage and stationery. With only one truck being made available for its removal, the loss of his hard-gained stationery was a particularly bitter disappointment to the chief clerk, who had spent months accumulating a good stock.

With their work at the depot now finished, 1341 Pioneer Company were then detailed to report to the location of Transport Control Point 11, where large amounts of rations had been placed by other units and were needing to be loaded onto the trucks of 43 GPT Company and sent to Imphal. Captain Bhattacharyya met Captain Spence of L of C Labour there and was informed that his company would be moving to Imphal that evening, but only after all the food rations had been cleared from the box. The next task for 1330 Pioneer Company was the loading and clearing of 298 Field Supply Depot a few hundred yards away, which would take them most of the rest of the day to complete. This Pioneer unit had also been heavily committed at this time, and they performed their tasks well despite this being their first taste of being under fire. Captain Berry, the OC of 298 FSD, then sent the Box Commander an urgent message asking if he still required the balance of the fifteen days' reserve ration to remain within the box. If so, would he send someone to take it over because 298 FSD had been ordered out and would soon be moving. Unbeknown to Captain Berry at the time, the orders to evacuate the whole box had yet to be given, but when they finally came through he then made arrangements for these rations to be moved with him as a priority.

When direct telephone contact with the box and 5 Division HQ had been re-established after an earlier breakage that morning, Lieutenant Colonel Wells-Cole received a call from them at 11.30 hours giving orders for the complete evacuation of Lion Box, and at midday, Lieutenant Colonel Wells-Cole summoned all the sector commanders to the Box HQ for a planning conference to explain how a phased evacuation of the remainder of the entire box would work. This was to be completed by 17.30 hours that day, and it was emphasised that no stores of any value to the Japanese would be left and all food, arms and ammunition would take priority over any movement of personnel. With the understanding that there were still considerable amounts of other stores to be moved as well, anything unable to be cleared in the allotted time available was to be left and not destroyed because the evacuation could not be delayed. This included clothing, MT stores and POL (petrol, oil, lubricants) stocks. Extra transport would be available for those units whose own unit transport was insufficient to move the large amounts of stores and equipment they held. The 20 Rft Camp was allotted 100 lorries for the removal of all their equipment and personnel, and a further 200 lorries were to be sent to 298 FSD. Despite the small number of personnel within the canteen group, it held considerable foodstuffs and supplies and was to have twelve lorries sent for its removal. The whole box now became a hive of activity as the personnel began gathering up their belongings, such as they were, ready to load on the trucks while the administrative and clerical staff gathered up their papers and records, destroying any sensitive material lest it should fall into enemy hands during the move. To a man, the relief of knowing they would soon be moving to a place of safety must have been immense as the events and strain of the past few weeks had begun to take their toll ... their ordeal was not over yet, though.

By 14.30 hours, 221 AOD had left the depot area and were clear of the box, with the lucky ones riding in trucks while others marched until they were met by other transport along the road to ferry them to Imphal. A small rear party was left behind in the depot, clearing anything of importance that had been overlooked during the packing up. Attention was now turned to the evacuation of the Engineer units who were not in the line at this time. Because they had with them large amounts of heavy equipment that would take valuable time and lots of manpower to move, it was decided that most of it should be abandoned. Also, much of their equipment had been left in their old camp areas, where it was still under fire from the enemy situated outside the perimeter. 864 ME Company left two earthmovers, two Federal transporters, their workshop lorry, rations and all office equipment and records. The greatest loss to the men was probably that of their personal kits and tents, which would mean a few uncomfortable days until they were re-equipped. The 652 MEx Company were in the same predicament and lost three Federal trailers, one of which was badly damaged by shellfire. A D8 bulldozer, under repair and immobile, was left and a functioning D4 bulldozer was also left as there was concern that this slow-moving machine could block the road during this vital period. These two units together with HQ 671 MEx Company less their officers, C Section 70 Mobile Workshop and other small contingents were put on standby to be ready to move by 13.00, when 302 GPT Company would evacuate them and themselves too, and they were to be clear by 14.00 hours. Because there was very little equipment and stores left in these companies' possession, they were soon ready and began evacuating in good time as the operation was working well and according to plan.

The main Imphal–Kohima road south of Kanglatongbi was now a busy highway as the operation to evacuate Lion Box gathered pace. Hundreds of lorry movements in both directions were made as the composite 43 GPT Company, now running with twice their normal complement of trucks, shuttled back and forth. In addition to all these vehicles there were also large groups of troops marching, carrying as much equipment as possible, while waiting their turn to be ferried by the trucks of 242 GPT Company from Sengmai to their next destination. In amongst all these movements were the ambulances evacuating the casualties of the morning's fighting back to Imphal and the hospitals thereabouts. The 89 Indian General Hospital at Khamarol had only been opened five days earlier and received forty-four wounded patients and three dead bodies for burial in the Imphal Cemetery, which was being established in Dewlahland. More casualties were taken to 41 and 87 IGH and also to 19 Casualty Clearing Station.[2]

With the move of 221 AOD successfully carried out, albeit having to leave some stores, attention was now focused on the two largest remaining units, the FSD and 20 Rft Camp, to clear their large stocks, while the smaller units such as 11 TCP, the canteen, medical staging section and S&T Kangla Ops were soon packed and taken away. The small contingent of No. 1 MT Regiment had been sent on their way by Major Mackenzie, who was now having a last look around their position before following them out when he spotted Padre Brock kicking away on the starter of his Harley-Davidson motorcycle. Because he was obviously having difficulties in starting it, Major Mackenzie told him to leave it, as it had probably been hit again, and to get in his car. Padre Brock shouted above the din and commotion, 'No, Sir. I can't see any holes anywhere, and I can't leave it as I borrowed it from a friend.' Major Mackenzie yelled back to him, 'Get in. I can't leave you here.' Padre Brock still declined his offer, saying, 'No, you pull out. I'll

---

2. Many other casualties would never leave Kanglatongbi despite the best efforts of their comrades and the medics. Some of the British dead who were buried in battlefield graves near where they died were never recovered by the Graves Registration Units, while others were unable to be buried at the time because they lay in areas where fighting continued during the evacuation. The remains of some of the latter were found and buried when Kanglatongbi was finally retaken in May, but many of the Indian dead had to be left and were not cremated at the time, as per their religious rites. Their remains, if found, would have been collected later for cremation by the GRUs.

catch you up.' With this, he gave a last desperate and hefty kick, and the ageing motorcycle spluttered into life and, jumping on, Padre Brock slithered over the paddy fields and onto the road. Major Mackenzie followed and could see Padre Brock's white head bobbing along several vehicles in front as they slowly made good their escape. A few miles further along the road, Major Mackenzie came across Padre Brock sitting on the side of the road and stopped to ask if there was a problem. Padre Brock explained that the bike had just died on him and would no longer start. Hailing a passing lorry, the broken-down motorcycle was manhandled onto it with the instruction for it to be taken to one of the Workshop Sections in Imphal. Although extremely exhausted himself, Major Mackenzie, driving along with Padre Brock sitting beside him, could now see that the day's events had taken a toll even on this remarkable man.

With the plan for withdrawal devised by Lieutenant Colonel Wells-Cole and his staff working well, it was now time to move to the next phase of the operation. At 14.00 hours, the Box Commander, Lieutenant Colonel Wells-Cole, resumed his command of 20 Rft Camp after handing over command of Lion Box to Lieutenant Colonel Cree of the West Yorks who, after conferring with his company commanders and others, was now satisfied that his plans to cover the evacuation were ready to be carried out. All those units still manning the perimeter defences of the box then came under his command and, together with the West Yorks and tanks of the Carbs, would oversee their withdrawal in a careful and organised manner when the box defences would gradually collapse inwards from the north-west and withdraw southwards. Those engineers still on the perimeter with their infantry support, 58 Field Company, 528 AW Company, 440 Quarrying Company and the Company of 8 Sikh Engineering Battalion, would be relieved and would then start to withdraw at 15.00 and be clear by 16.00. The 517 AW Company, still being supported by the Frontier Force Regiment personnel from 20 Rft Camp, would be the last of the engineers to retire at 17.00, by which time all the other units within the box should have completed their move. The 440 Quarrying Company had to abandon their personal kits as these had been left in the area where there was still fighting but, in any case, there was insufficient transport to carry them, having only been allocated four lorries. Once on the main road, some of these men jumped onto passing vehicles if there was enough room and became separated. Eleven men were reported as missing because of this. Various other small Engineer detachments and units moved out at this time. Each of those units ordered to remain would come under the command of a designated officer who would then report directly to Lieutenant Colonel Cree and would become part of the box rearguard. This rearguard comprised the following: the box mortar team from 28 Jungle Field Regiment and the artillery spotters, together with the Assam Rifles and the Mahratta Light Infantry, commanded

Major Norman Chubb, 19th Hyderabad Regiment, attached 20 Rft Camp.

by Lieutenant Sparkes-Calcutt from 20 Rft Camp; the Sector 4 Defence Company (137 GPT Company and a detachment of 90 GPT Company), commanded by Major Lavell; Company of 8 Sikh Engineering Battalion and 440 Quarrying Company (until they were both relieved by the West Yorks); the Jat Regiment (mortars and MMGs) and Sections 1 to 6 of 20 Rft Camp under the command of Major Chubb, also from 20 Rft Camp.[3] The remaining two sections and headquarters of 20 Rft Camp in Sector 3 were now very busy helping the pioneers load their stores and the large quantity of ammunition they held, and once loaded would travel out with these trucks as well.

Watching all this hectic activity from the jungle where they were hiding were the few survivors of the Japanese 11th Company who had led the attack. Feeling helpless, with the element of surprise now long passed and unable to do anything further other than dig in and watch, they waited as the rest of their attacking formations finally arrived. Knowing it would be madness to attempt any further attacks in daylight, especially with the defenders now on full alert, and with enemy reinforcements and heavy armour arriving, the

---

3. Major Chubb would later describe this duty as being 'the longest hour of my life!' as he waited for orders to retire.

Japanese had to content themselves with sniping from concealed positions with harassing mortar and artillery fire.

With reports of further numbers of enemy troops arriving in the area, a reconnaissance sortie from No. 1 Squadron Indian Air Force was requested. An earlier sortie in the morning by the squadron was sent to Kangpokpi to investigate reports that the Japanese were using the former position of 20 Rft Camp at milestone 110 as a base. The old British roadblock there was seen to have been reinforced with bricks or dried mud, and on the way back to his base the pilot reported seeing two bashas on fire at Kanglatongbi and plenty of MT on the road to the south, but no enemy seen. Another sortie in the morning, this time flown by 28 Squadron RAF, could see no signs of the Japanese on the hillside overlooking the box from where the original attack was launched, though a possible gun emplacement was spotted near milestone 116. This second sortie of Hurricanes from 1 Squadron IAF was flown by Flying Officers Amber and Cheena, who took off from Imphal at 15.20 hours and were tasked to pay particular attention to the high ground west of the box, and the deep nullah along the western perimeter. Because of the topography, the aircraft were unable to fly sufficiently low enough for the pilots to see to the bottom of the steep-sided nullah and no positive identifications could be made. The flight returned to Imphal, landing at 15.55 hours, and reported seeing a large fire caused by burning petrol drums.

At around 15.30 hours, the Japanese began a bombardment of the road to the south of the box

Lieutenant Colonel Henry MacLaurin (Skinner's Horse pre-war).

Lieutenant Colonel Henry MacLaurin, MBE, Skinner's Horse attached HQ 5 Division, KIA 7 April 1944.

Lieutenant Colonel MacLaurin's original grave at the Imphal Cemetery.

and the area where the loading of trucks in Sectors 3 and 4 was the busiest. The Japanese artillery spotters up on Picquet Hill were again very accurate with the co-ordinates given to the 75mm gun crews at Ekban Ekwan, when this shelling claimed the life of the highest ranked soldier killed during the

One of a series of cartoons drawn by Lieutenant Colonel MacLaurin, MBE.

fighting at Lion Box. Two officers from 5 Division together with Lieutenant Colonel Field, Lieutenant Colonel Kelly and other officers were directing traffic and clearing congestion at the junction of the main road near to the Box HQ and TCP 11 when a barrage of about six shells was fired, with one landing on the road amongst them, killing Lieutenant Colonel Henry Normand MacLaurin, MBE of The Skinner's Horse (Indian Armoured Corps). He was the Assistant Adjutant Quartermaster General of 5 Division HQ. Major Archibald Percy Harrington of the Royal Artillery was the Deputy Assistant Adjutant General accompanying Lieutenant Colonel MacLaurin and was standing beside him when the shell exploded, and apart from being shaken up, was miraculously unscathed. This was a severe blow to the 5th Division as Lieutenant Colonel MacLaurin was a long-serving and much respected and liked senior officer.[4]

This barrage of mortars and 75mm shells caused several casualties and great alarm to the loading parties and drivers at the field supply depot, who were now being directly targeted. This was further compounded when an ordnance officer told the pioneers to 'Bhago' (run away) and during the resulting chaos some of them bolted and became mixed in with other non-combatant units who were marching out, and they were not seen again. The reluctance of those marching out to leave the road and make their way along the side caused tailbacks of vehicles, much to the frustration of the drivers, now eager to leave the area. A few lorries left the area immediately being only half loaded and, in some cases, completely empty. Other lorry drivers were detailed to return to the box after unloading at Imphal, and were then unable to return to those units who were still waiting with their stores and equipment ready to load and evacuate. By now, 1341 Pioneer Company had

---

4. Lieutenant Colonel Henry Normand MacLaurin, MBE, was a long-serving pre-war soldier who had joined The Skinner's Horse of the Indian Army in 1929 after being commissioned in the Territorial Army Scouts in 1927. He served on the North-West Frontier Province and on garrison duties throughout India with The Skinner's Horse, and in 1937 was awarded the MBE. He was posted as a staff officer to 5 Indian Division and became the AAQMG when the division was in Baghdad. An accomplished Scottish dancer and piper of note, he was often seen marching in camp as he practised playing his pipes. Among his many talents was his keen eye as a caricature artist. Just six days after celebrating his fortieth birthday, Henry became the highest ranked soldier to be killed at Kanglatongbi, and fittingly, a piper from the nearby Seaforth Highlanders played at his funeral at the Imphal Cemetery. He was also awarded a Mention in Despatches for his services, which was gazetted after his death.

completed their work and were waiting with their baggage by the main road for transport to take them to Ferret Box at Imphal, but they were caught up in this bombardment and confusion. Captain Bhattacharyya, who had already had difficulties in arranging transport for their move, was told by one of the transport officers not to be impatient as his men became restless. With the situation now looking bleak for any transport to turn up, Captain Bhattacharyya gathered up what men of his scattered unit that he could find and set them off marching to Imphal with orders for them to rendezvous with him at milestone 127.

The 20 Rft Camp was another unit that lost half of its men's personal kit and other stores including tents when the last twenty lorries detailed for this did not arrive. The small amount of food rations left behind were polluted with petrol, and any ammunition that could not be carried by the men themselves was destroyed before Sections 7 and 8 marched out to Sengmai, where they boarded trucks to Imphal.

The POL reserve dump of the L of C transport units in the B park area of Sector 4 was hit during this bombardment, which spread fire over a very large area as barrels of fuel and other combustibles exploded and were sent flying high into the air while a huge pall of black acrid smoke rose over the whole box. This seemed to frighten the Indian troops who were clearing the dump more than anything else that the Japanese had thrown at them. Some vehicles parked behind 517 AW Company in Sector 1 were hit by mortars and set on fire, adding to the smoke. Satisfied that their bombardment had had the desired effect, there was now a pause while the Japanese artillery and mortars were replenished and moved location as a precaution against any counter battery fire.

The Engineer units who were on the perimeter to the north began their steady withdrawal at 15.00, covered by the West Yorks and the Assam Rifles, and were clear of the box before the shelling had begun. There had been no running or signs of panic, and though the enemy were very close, they made no attempts to follow up or rush the perimeter, nor the roadblock being manned by the platoon from 58 Field Company. As per Lieutenant Colonel Cree's plans, the tanks and the West Yorks had by then placed themselves into position to cover these withdrawals, with 5 Troop under the command of A Company to the east of the main road in Sector 2, and 6 Troop and their support platoon from C Company now under the command of B Company to the west in Sector 1. The tanks of 7 Troop and HQ Troop were held in reserve at the Box HQ in case they needed to be called on to give assistance, with 3 Troop under the command of Lieutenant Kenneth Alan Boadle being sent up from Sengmai as further reinforcement and placed under command of C Company. A further reserve from D Company West Yorks were placed near to a bridge halfway between Sengmai and Kanglatongbi and were to cover the evacuation in this area of open plain.

At the field supply depot, the situation was quickly restored and the remaining stores and transport cleared from the area, allowing Lieutenant Colonels Field and Kelly to have a final look around their former B Park positions within Sector 4. A few pioneers were found still hiding in trenches after the confusion during the bombardment and were sent to the main road to make their own way to Sengmai, while Lieutenant Colonel Kelly then set off himself to organise the onward transportation of those troops who were there waiting. Lieutenant Colonel Field then joined Major Levell at the defences of Sector 4, where 137 GPT Company and others of the Defence Company were still holding the line, awaiting their orders to withdraw. During the day, when news came through that 137 GPT Company were to be part of the rearguard, Lieutenant Bird realised that when orders would eventually come for them to retire, there would be very little time or opportunity to gather their personal belongings. He therefore arranged for his batman to collect all of his belongings and place them in a tin trunk that he had had with him since his time in India. This was then placed in a trench next to his basha and covered with tin sheets and earth, while Lieutenant Bird took careful compass bearings with the intention of retrieving it at a later opportunity.

At around 16.30 hours, Captain Bhattacharyya returned to his unit's old camp area in Sector 3 in a desperate search for his missing men and was immediately fired upon. Diving for cover, he carried on with his search of the trenches and managed to locate one of his pioneers and sent him off to the main road. After reporting to Major Sinclair, the Sector 3 commander, and explaining his reason for his presence there, Captain Bhattacharyya then resumed looking for any stragglers in the now empty FSD area and recovered four more. Marching back to Sengmai for transport, Captain

Bhattacharyya eventually arrived at milestone 127, but he could only muster 65 men waiting there for him from a strength of over 300, the rest being scattered amongst the several thousand troops making their way to Imphal.

It was now the turn of 517 AW Company and their support from 9/12 FFR to begin their withdrawal from their positions on the western perimeter, and at 16.45 hours Lieutenant Colonel Peacock arrived to oversee this. The Japanese, still in their positions on the hill slopes overlooking this side of the perimeter, were watching this steady withdrawal of forces from the box, decided to seize their chance of a final breakthrough and, thinking that all the defences were unmanned, began advancing. Major Henderson and his men were alerted of this and rallied themselves, opening fire as they came under attack to their front and flanks. Completely surprised by the ferocity of the defender's fire, the Japanese were beaten back into the jungle again after sustaining heavy casualties. This prompt and effective action prevented a serious threat arising because those of the box rearguard, still in position to the north of this attempted breakthrough, would then have had enemy forces behind them as well, preventing their withdrawal.

Lieutenant Takahata, still sitting in his hastily dug shelter in the nullah in front of 864 ME Company's former positions, looked up at the black smoke from the burning fuel of the reserve dump rising into the air above the rim of the nullah. The sound of engines and voices gradually receded and after a while were replaced by the faint sounds of gunfire coming from the south as his comrades made their last attempt to breach the defences further along the line. As the sun began to dip down over the high hills to the west, Lieutenant Takahata could now hear the sounds of aircraft engines approaching again, but this time the air was suddenly rent with deafeningly violent explosions.

After ensuring that this final attack was beaten off and the area secured, 517 AW Company and the Frontier Force Rifles then quickly made their way across the fields to the main road and marched off to Sengmai. Because of this brief engagement, and until he was satisfied that it no longer posed a threat, Lieutenant Colonel Cree had held up the progress and movement from the northern end of the box along the road and the rearguard remained in place. The Defence Company in Sector 4 were then instructed to leave their perimeter positions at 17.00 hours, and Major Levell began organising this while the tanks and rearguard resumed their slow movements along the road. Having heard all the previous heavy firing on their immediate right flank, the men were keen to move away, worried that the Japanese could be on their heels at any moment. The A Section of 137 GPT Company, commanded by Lieutenant Symington, being closest to the main road were soon out and away along with the HQ Section. Lieutenant Swailes and his B Section on the box southern boundary directed his men to cross the nullah to their front and move south before heading east and onto the main road, and once they were all clear he joined them after scrambling over the chest-high barbed wire in his haste to get away. It was not until next day that Lieutenant Swailes realised just how much he had injured himself on the barbed wire with cuts and scratches all over his body. Once they arrived at Sengmai, they were eventually evacuated in the vehicles of 135 GPT Company, who had also been pressed into the shuttle service.

Lieutenant Bird, commanding C and D Sections on the western perimeter, gave instructions to his leading VCO and havildars to move south across the nullah and the paddy fields before turning left to get onto the main road. Upon seeing in the distance that the road was heavily congested, Lieutenant Bird decided that he would instead send his men on a longer southerly route cross-country to avoid this problem while he brought up the rear. Some of the men from A and B Sections were mixed in with Lieutenant Bird's C and D Sections, when they also decided to avoid the congestion on the road and joined in their trek for a while but, unbeknown to anyone, they became separated in the thick scrub jungle and ended up being lost on the hills to the west. Lieutenant Bird remembered that all was going well until there were screams of '*Dushmen! Dushmen!*' (enemy) and upon catching up with his men came across one of the younger sepoys who had become caught on the low branches of a small tree. Unhitching the straps of his backpack, Lieutenant Bird quietly assured the frightened lad that there were no enemy present, and even if there were, they would catch him first as he was at the rear. This prompt action by Lieutenant Bird no doubt saved a lot of panic, though it may have been at this time that the men from A and B Sections became separated. Having now gathered up the rest of C and D Sections, Lieutenant Bird commandeered three empty trucks, loaded his men onto them and set off to Imphal.

Those in another small group who became lost in this area at the same time were from the Kangla Ops of the L of C transport. Captain Peter Edmund Deverall of the RIASC and thirty-six men under his command also decided to bypass the congestion on the road, and after clearing the large southern nullah, made their way nearer to the base of the high hills to the west. Fortunately, watching this exodus unfolding from his nearby hilltop village, the headman, Tuluwa Hkambi, saw his friends Captain Deverall and Subedar Bansi Lall and went to their aid, and for the next few hours guided them to safety as he directed them to Imphal. Shaking hands and saluting each other, Captain Deverall and Tuluwa Hkambi parted, never to see each other again.[5]

A small 'bombing party' from 20 Rft Camp was now organised and sent to hunt out any Japanese still hiding in trenches and claimed several enemy casualties, though had they had more grenades it was believed this party could have inflicted further casualties. With the tanks now clear and their infantry escorts making their way out of the box, it was found that some of the rearguard sections from 20 Rft Camp had not been given the order to retire from Sector 3, and watching the tanks and escorts disappear, some of the men, unsure of what was happening, began drifting down to the sector HQ from their positions. It was then that disaster struck when the Hurribombers (Hurricanes) of 60 Squadron RAF came over, bombing and strafing the whole area by mistake.

---

5. After the war, Captain Deverall recounted the extraordinary tale of how he and his orderly, Subedar Lall, climbed the high hills to the west of Kanglatongbi to visit Tuluwa Hkambi's village, which was in the midst of a smallpox outbreak towards the end of 1943. After doing what they could for the stricken villagers, they returned next day with their unit medical officer who was able to administer medical assistance and vaccinations. Though there were further deaths, thankfully contained to just one particular basha, the disease did not spread to the other villagers and three weeks later, a message was received informing Captain Deverall of this and an invitation given to attend a community thanksgiving feast. Sometime later, the three honoured guests sat down together with the village elders and leaders while the rest of the community sat around their compound perimeter softly chanting and playing a violin-like instrument. Quantities of the local brew called *zu* were offered and drunk, followed by helpings of their speciality dish of *kutta aloo aur sabse* (dog, potato and vegetables) served in bone bowls. Mutual expressions of respect were exchanged, despite the language difficulties, no doubt helped by the linguistic abilities of Captain Deverall. Early next day, the three foreign soldiers returned to their camp, surely with tales to tell of their new friendships and unique experience. Though Captain Deverall and Tuluwa Hkambi never met again they both knew that faith, trust and mutual respect would make them friends forever.

Peter Deverall returned to India to work after the war with his family and finally came home in 1954.

The earlier reconnaissance flight sent to milestone 110 had identified an enemy presence there and 113 Squadron RAF, based at Tulihal, were ordered to send two flights of five aircraft to bomb and strafe the old site of the reinforcement camp. The first flight, led by Flying Officer Seitz, successfully dropped their 250-pound bombs on the target, setting one basha alight. The second flight, led by Flight Lieutenant Rolls, only managed to place four bombs on target with the rest being slight overshoots and all aircraft were safely back at base by 17.35 hours. A follow-up attack on the same target was given to 60 Squadron RAF based at Silchar, but now operating out of Palel airfield. The first flight of six Mk II C Hurribombers took off at 16.50 hours led by Flight Lieutenant Busbridge. With him were Flying Officers Duncan and Rutherford and Flight Sergeants Polak, Bambridge and Davies. Upon nearing Kanglatongbi just after 17.00 hours and seeing smoke still rising from the burning POL reserve and bashas, the flight went into attack, not realising that their intended target was a further 8 miles to the north.[6] The box was now subjected to intense aerial bombardment as the six aircraft dropped all of their bombs on target and came around to strafe the area with their 20mm cannons. Gunner Betteridge of 20 Rft Camp remembered how 'all hell was let loose' as he and his companions frantically waved their rifles above their heads and to their sides in a vain attempt to attract the pilot's attention to this mistake. The tanks, unable to contact the aircraft because they were on different radio frequencies, were powerless to do anything and Trooper Connolly remembered being frightened out of his life as the Hurribombers came in low over them, firing their cannons.[7]

The attacks finally broke off after quite some time and left in their wake many casualties from the rearguard, including the Assam Rifles and some of the Mahrattas who were killed when their truck was hit and caught fire,

6. In mitigation, it can be argued this was the first time that 60 Squadron had flown any sorties north of Imphal and therefore were not familiar with the area. The squadron had only been fitted with bomb racks to their aircraft two weeks previously for their role as fighter-bombers.

7. Lieutenant Colonel Cree of the West Yorks was also caught up in this attack, later commenting that it was caused by aircraft from the Indian Air Force flown by Sikh pilots. He even gathered up some of the empty 20mm cannon cases from the aircraft machine guns as evidence when he put in an official complaint about this incident. His accusations can now be disproved because there were no aircraft from the IAF flying at this time. The confusion may have come about by the reconnaissance flight flown by No. 1 Squadron IAF earlier in the afternoon who had already been back at their base for over an hour before the first attack by 60 Squadron had begun.

along with some other vehicles. A group of engineers from 517 AW Company, marching along the main road, were attacked and lost one man killed and several others wounded. Another victim of this tragedy of war was Private William John Howard of 2nd Battalion The Border Regiment who had been attached to 20 Rft Camp since December 1943. A pre-war regular soldier, Private Howard was a popular and reliable man who was used by Captain Ewing and Company Sergeant Major Johnson of No. 1 Section as their runner and had been held back from his posting to the Border Regiment because of this.[8]

Private William Howard, 2nd Border Regiment attached 20 Rft Camp, KIA 7 April 1944.

He had been waiting for orders from Captain Ewing at the sector HQ (possibly for the order to withdraw) when the RAF began strafing, and was hit by a cannon shell and seriously wounded. CSM Johnson was still holding his position when he was informed of this and immediately ran to where Private Howard was, where he found Corporal Packer and two others present. Upon reaching his stricken man, CSM Johnson could see that he was still alive but beyond medical help, with no hope of moving him. There were no medics or medical facilities thereabouts because the 14th Light Field Ambulance ADS and all the day's wounded had gone by this time and

---

8. Private Howard enlisted into the Loyal Regiment in 1937 and went to France as part of the Guards Brigade on the outbreak of the Second World War, where he was posted as missing during the Dunkirk evacuations. Eventually arriving back in the UK, he was posted to the Reconnaissance Corps before being transferred back to the Loyal Regiment. In 1942, Private Howard found himself in Ceylon with the King's Own Royal Regiment until his posting to the Border Regiment. In a letter to Private Howard's widow, Winnie, written a week later, Captain Ewing wrote: 'You have lost a husband that loves you and baby dearly, and I have lost a cheerful companion. Just before he went off, he and I were in the Battle HQ. I had one bottle of beer left which we split and talked of our families. He was so looking forward to seeing the baby he had never seen after the war, but the Good Lord willed otherwise. He had very little private property as we all had to leave with what we could carry. I am sending these on to you. My deepest sympathies are with you and baby.'

this group from 20 Rft Camp were among the last troops left in the box. CSM Johnson made the decision to end Private Howard's suffering and shot him. He died in CSM Johnson's arms. Captain Charles, the adjutant of 20 Rft Camp, remembered how CSM Johnson later reported to him and gave an account of what had happened in a clear and proper manner despite obviously being upset. Captain Charles said, 'Sergeant Major, you are a very brave man.' Neither could say anything more.

Captain Ewing arrived at the scene a few moments later and while still being sniped at from the jungle and hills, urgently began organising the withdrawal of his men because it was feared the Japanese would soon be upon them. There was also fear of further air attacks. Gunner Betteridge remembered being one of those last to leave: 'I was starting with malaria, and some kind chaps dumped a Bren gun on me complete with four full magazines and a spare barrel. This was in addition to my full kit, rifle, a hundred rounds [of ammunition] and tin-hat, which was quite a load.' Coming out onto the main road, Gunner Betteridge saw the body of the man whom he described as being the man who had volunteered to be their dispatch rider leaning against the bank leading to the supply depot.[9]

Gunner Betteridge now found himself becoming weaker and gradually being left behind, so he decided to lighten his load by dumping his large pack and tin helmet. A little further along the road he came across another straggler from 20 Rft Camp who had just been shot in the leg by a Japanese sniper. Struggling along together, they eventually came to where the tanks had halted, and where a Bren gun carrier was being used to pick up the wounded. Gunner Betteridge said, 'I got this chap into the carrier and thought a Bren gun carrier without a Bren gun wasn't right, so I gave them mine, much against the Medical Corps driver's wishes.' Carrying on with his trek, he found a group of men from 20 Rft Camp resting in a field and joined them. One of these men was severely shell-shocked and began shooting at him, probably thinking he was Japanese. Someone quickly knocked him out with a rifle butt, and he was taken to hospital while the other men then boarded the

---

9. It is quite possible that this may have been the body of Private Howard that had been left because there had been no time for a burial. His body was never recovered.

transport waiting to take them away.[10] Private Ronald Read, a reinforcement for 2 Border Regiment, was a survivor of the so-called 'friendly fire' incident by the RAF, but sadly his luck ran out two months later in another incident when a faulty mortar bomb dropped short amongst a group of Border men, fatally wounding him and killing several others.

By this time, the second flight of six Hurribombers from 60 Squadron tasked with attacking milestone 110 were already airborne having taken off at 17.10 hours. It is not clear if they too mistook Kanglatongbi for Keithelmanbi, or whether during mid-flight they were given new orders to attack Lion Box to hold back the advancing Japanese, but at about 17.30 hours, Flight Lieutenant Butler led his flight of Flight Sergeant Taylor, Flying Officer McClymont, Flight Sergeant Woodhouse, Flying Officer Johnson and Flight Sergeant Greyvensteyn, and once again the box was heavily bombarded. The overall damage of the combined attacks with twenty-four 250-pound bombs was considerable, with twelve huts and other large buildings on fire and others badly damaged. Transport and tents were heavily strafed before the aircraft made off south following the main road, by now cleared of all movement. This last attack caused no British or Indian casualties, but the Japanese were believed to have taken several more while they took cover wherever they could, as the RAF pressed home their attacks.

Except for the crackle of the burning huts and bamboo, there was now silence as Lieutenant Takahata spotted Lieutenant Miyazawa slowly coming towards him leading a swarm of his men. He wrote:

Absorbed by this, I climbed the steep riverbank, and setting foot in the encampment, took a sharp intake of breath and came to an abrupt halt. What a terrible sight …! The corpses of my comrades were burnt black. They were scattered over almost the entire ground area, smoke still rising from them. This must have been the smoke that we had spotted just prior to the enemy's retreat. Those who had lain seriously wounded had been trampled on by the

---

10. Another story about how stress affected men in these circumstances was recounted by CSM Johnson. A group of men from 20 Rft Camp had been playing cards when a fight broke out, and during the melee a shot was fired. Alerted by this shot, CSM Johnson arrived and broke up the fight, resorting to using his fists and boots to separate those involved. When the dust had settled, a man was found to have had a bullet wound through his hand and was taken to get medical attention. Upon further investigation, this man was then placed under arrest for the offence of a self-inflicted wound and was later placed before a court martial.

enemy's tanks and, you could call it merciless cruelty or even the devil's work, gasoline had been poured around and set alight. My body cramped up and tears began to flow. It was difficult to distinguish one of my comrades from another as their clothing had been burnt, and their bodies were covered with black blisters. I had to lower my eyes from this scene.[11]

The Japanese then began consolidating their positions before it became too dark. The machine gun company and artillery platoon were ordered to secure the main road and began building a strong barricade on the bridge over the Dak Bungalow nullah made from oil drums, packing cases and other materials scavenged from the now derelict Ordnance Depot. This barricade was then covered by carefully positioned machine-gun emplacements while the remaining forces began the grisly task of collecting and burying their dead. Lieutenant Takahata vividly remembered:

> With the thought of enshrining their remains at the Yasuka Shrine, we cut off a thumb or some small part of our comrades. Completing this task was like a bad nightmare as the corpses of many of our comrades were grotesque, such had been the manner of their death, and it was difficult to lift them. Those corpses that could be lifted, about sixty-eight, were piled up into a large hole, like a small mountain, and dazed, I just about managed to keep standing until the job was finished. There was no end to my regret of this terrible outcome. No, there was to be no boasting of a great military success.

As both attacker and defender licked their wounds it was evident that the Japanese had underestimated their enemy, and from here onwards would be on their back foot despite their fanatical and dogged resistance. It was here at Lion Box that a hard lesson was learned by the Japanese Imperial Army, that even normally non-fighting British and Indian troops, when motivated and properly led by good officers, could take them on and give as 'good as they got'. With the battles of Nungshigum, Red Hill and Kanglatongbi, their aspirations to capture Imphal had reached its high-water mark, and their much-vaunted 'March on Delhi' eventually turned into a rout of epic proportions.

---

11. Lieutenant Takahata was mistaken in his belief that fuel had been deliberately set on fire. It was from the POL dump that was hit during the Japanese bombardment.

Chapter Six

The Aftermath

As darkness fell, the heavy artillery at Sengmai now began a harassing fire programme to keep the Japanese heads down in Kanglatongbi, ensuring they would have as little rest as possible. This bombardment would also prevent any follow-up of the evacuation even though the Japanese 3rd Battalion 60th Regiment had had a very heavy knock with the taking of Kanglatongbi. They were in no condition to exploit their gains at that time, but the defences at Sengmai were still on high alert for any enemy movements.

The Military Police were now extremely busy along the main road and at Imphal as they sought to identify each man and unit from Lion Box, ensuring they were sent to the correct destination. There would be very little sleep that night for these exhausted men who now found themselves scattered all around the Imphal area, as they began digging their new defensive positions. The task for their officers was now to ensure that all their men were accounted for and were properly fed, sheltered and re-equipped ready to continue their work. This would take time to complete, and in some cases many days. There was an immediate concern for those caught up in the air attack, and others who were thought to be wounded or found themselves separated in Kanglatongbi during the confusion in the latter stages of the evacuation. Gunner Douglas, one of the artillery signallers from D Troop 522 Battery 4 Field Regiment, was one of those wounded men who fortunately had been evacuated to hospital, but several riflemen from the Assam Rifles thought to be wounded were still missing. After dark, at about 19.30 hours, Major Hayter and Lieutenant George Bazely Scurfield left the 4th Assam Rifles' position in Imphal to search for these missing men along the main road to Lion Box, though none could be found. These riflemen were part of the V (Viper) Force operations and were experts in moving and living in the jungle and, depending on the severity of any wounds, could well have found shelter and assistance locally.[1] Lieutenant Scurfield, together with a handful of his V Force men, had recently been deployed on patrols behind enemy lines in the area of Kanglatongbi, carefully reconnoitring the Japanese positions, and sent back vital information to 5 Division. Their work continued for several weeks after the evacuation, going as far north as Kangpokpi, while 5 Division gradually cleared the main road of Japanese resistance. Lieutenant Scurfield described how he would go out on patrol to the wrecked remains of the Ordnance Depot, noting, 'I would encounter the great, blown-up bodies of our recently killed, the flesh grey and distended, the bodies shrouded in a blanket of flies and smelling the sour-sweet smell of death and decomposition.'[2]

Amongst these bodies were some of the men that Captain Bhattacharyya had desperately been searching for and who had been caught up in the Japanese bombardment of the loading parties. His search continued for several days as nominal roles of the missing were issued to other Pioneer units nearby. The Military Police contacted medical units and the 51 Rest Camp, these being the most likely places the men would be found. The 137 GPT Company also had a lot of missing men. After many stoppages en route, Lieutenant Bird finally arrived with C and D Sections at their new location on the side of Sentinel Hill overlooking the Tulihal airfield, just south of Imphal, at 03.00 hours on 8 April, and they settled in for the remainder of the night. He was awakened by Major Levell, who seemed surprised to see him and asked if he had any missing men. Lieutenant Bird was able to confirm that all his men were present and accounted for. Major Levell then informed him that a preliminary check had revealed that about 150 men and 12 vehicles of the L of C Road Transport were unaccounted for as a result of the action at Lion Box. The A and B Sections of the company

---

1. The war diary for the Assam Rifles states that two were wounded in the box before the evacuation. One was killed and four wounded with two more missing, believed killed during the air attack, but no record of any deaths can be found for 4AR on the CWGC list.

2. Lieutenant Scurfield of the Royal Artillery had been a V Force operative with 3 V Ops, living in the jungle for many months, patrolling both banks of the Chindwin River looking for signs of Japanese movements, ready to give advance warning of any build-up of troops for the anticipated invasion. Once the invasion began, Lieutenant Scurfield escaped back to Imphal after he had to shoot two of his wounded riflemen who were unable to walk out. He also remembered how, in all of his time in Burma, he was often in more danger from his own planes than from those of the enemy.

had sixty-five men missing, but he was hopeful more would turn up in the coming days once things had settled down.

The evening of 14 April brought tragic news of the remaining missing men from 137 GPT Company, now numbering twenty-five as others had re-joined the unit over the previous days. On a routine patrol in the hills around the Kanglatongbi area, Gurkhas had come across a weak, wounded and dazed sepoy wandering in the jungle and he was taken to their officer for interrogation. Unable to fully answer any questions due to his weakened condition, Sepoy Muhammad Khan of 137 GPT Company was sent to 87 IGH for treatment, before recounting the fate of his fellow sepoys from A and B Sections.

During the evacuation of the box, Havildar Sardar Ali and his group became separated when they decided to make their way to the hills to avoid the congestion on the main road, with the enemy who they feared were not far behind them. Climbing the hills to the west of the road to get their bearings, this group became lost in the jungle, where they wandered about until on the third day, they found themselves surrounded by a party of about fifty Japanese soldiers, and despite being well armed with rifles and two Bren guns, they were disarmed and taken prisoner without offering any resistance at all. With their hands bound behind their backs, they were marched to a well-concealed Japanese camp near a small village for interrogation. Sepoy Khan and Havildar Sardar Ali motioned to the rest of the group not to say anything while they were being questioned by a Sikh JIF officer, but Sepoy Yaqub Khan broke down and said he would tell him what he wanted to know. This sepoy was then led away to where Sepoy Kahn assumed he must have told his inquisitors that they were drivers from a transport company who had been in Kanglatongbi, because the Japanese, upon hearing this, became infuriated and began beating their prisoners badly, as no doubt they felt humiliated that it was these men who had helped thwart them for three days. That night, the captives remained bound together and received further beatings with rifle butts to keep them awake, and they were denied any water, despite their pleas.

Just before dawn the next day, the Japanese took their prisoners a little way out from their camp and, untying their bonds, began bayonetting them in cold blood. Sepoy Muhammad Khan was wounded seven times and rolled down the side of the khud and into the small nullah that ran at the bottom. Here, he was able to take a much-needed drink of water before setting off to hide and rest in the jungle. A while later, he heard the sounds of someone searching for him, but he remained still until they had passed and then made good his escape. Despite hearing their screams while he was in the nullah, Sepoy Khan was unable to say whether any of the other prisoners had also been able to escape, but he presumed they had all been killed during this typical Japanese atrocity.[3]

Lieutenant Jack Swailes, the officer commanding some of these men, remembered how upon hearing this news he felt sorrow for the families of these men back home in India for their loss (in most cases now deprived of their breadwinner) but could not feel sympathy for those who had foolishly disobeyed their orders and had given themselves up without firing a shot in their own defence.

The 137 GPT Company continued their presence at Sentinel Hill, providing valuable patrols around the defensive perimeter and airfield throughout the remainder of April, often coming under air attack until they were flown out of Imphal to Comilla on 5 May. This move came as no surprise to them, because as a GPT unit with no transport to use, this was another drain on already depleting resources. Lieutenant Swailes recounted:

> At midnight on the 4th the OC called us up to his office and told us he had just received orders for us to be on the Imphal airstrip at 07.00 hours. We spent the rest of the night packing up, and transport duly arrived at 05.15 hours. We were all on the strip by 07.00 and then ensued a long weary day in scorching sunshine with no shade. The first plane available for us left at 10.30 hours with the OC and part of HQ. The next left at about 11.30 and then three arrived together at about 14.00 hours. Murray [Lieutenant Symington] went on one of those and the rest of us gave up hope of any more that day. However, four came in between 17.15 and 18.00 hours. I went in the last of my Section's planes and we left at 17.30. The plane was a DC3 with a crew of five Americans. The trip was a very smooth one except the last five minutes of the Lushai Hills which were enough for me and up came

---

3. The CWGC lists state that thirteen men from 137 GPT Company died on 10 April 1944 and eleven on 1 July 1944. Quite how this later date of deaths was established is unknown. All these men were listed as missing in action on 137 GPT Company's casualty list dated 13 April 1944.

the lunch I had had at 51 Rest Camp. We touched down at Tandani about eight miles from Comilla. I had a dickens of a job to get transport as there was no one to receive me and by 22.00 hours I had 118 men on the strip. However, we finally got them all to 23 Rft Camp and I was accommodated at HQ Mess for the night. Next morning I went in search of the Major and Murray and found them in the No. 3 Mess to which I transferred my kit. Khan and Dickie [Captain Khan and Lieutenant Bird] arrived in with the rest of the Company about 16.00 hours. The full night's sleep which followed was a tremendous joy.

This night's sleep would have been the first full night in many weeks for Lieutenant Swailes. The duties of an officer meant that sleep would always be at a premium and when, for a short period, Major Lavell ordered that section commanders should check their men every two hours, this reduced further what sleep was possible. Lieutenant Swailes recorded:

I have just got in from the first patrol I have had to do and coming in at the end of the night of checking the positions leaves one pretty fagged out. I picked the best six men from the Section, and we went out through A Section's wire at 04.45 hours. The next half hour was the worst as it was dark, and we had to go a mile through deserted bashas and compounds with small, cultivated plots between them. There was plenty of cover, of course, but that also meant plenty of cover for the Jap. After about ten minutes a shot from a Sten gun rang out, which shook me for a moment. It must have come from our piquets on the hills by mistake, no doubt!

Another, more mundane entry from his diary gives an idea of the stress these men had been under:

This morning, I went into Imphal by motorcycle to get some ointment for 'dhobi-itch'. The road is so awful that the effect on my tender rear was probably calculated to neutralize any good the ointment may do. The MO at 41 IGH said they are pretty busy, rushed with battle casualties. The airstrip presented a busy appearance, there were no less than ten transports on the ground loading up casualties. Somehow the sight of these planes landing and taking off all day lessens the uncomfortable feeling one would otherwise have of being cut off. We have been isolated for three weeks, but somehow one doesn't feel any nervous strain, or not much anyway. Of course, one's nerves do tend to be on edge but have improved a lot since the Kanglatongbi withdrawal. One tends to jump at a bang and little things wake one suddenly at night. One has an ear open for a shot the whole time, but that is only to be expected.[4]

When the Siege of Imphal was lifted, 137 GPT Company resumed their L of C transport role and moved back to Kanglatongbi on 25 June. Lieutenant Ralph Bird remembered:

Late that evening my convoy eventually arrived at our old 137 GPT site. Apparently, some Japanese were still wandering around and after having posted sentries for the night and stand-to next morning I could see the devastation left with all the burnt-out vehicles and skeletons lying around. My basha had been burnt to the ground and in order to find my tin trunk that had been buried I started to probe the ground with a long steel rod but sorry to say I couldn't find it and the trunk is still at the bottom of the trench in Kanglatongbi.

*　　*　　*

As the battles raged along the ever-shrinking Imphal perimeter, so the casualties rose. Some of the more fortunate wounded men could be receiving medical attention within minutes whilst others, in more isolated positions, waited for days, enduring a nightmare journey back to the overflowing hospitals in Imphal. It was here that Padre Brock now found himself assisting the nursing staff as well as giving his much-appreciated spiritual guidance to their patients after his refusal to leave the area. Padre Brock had been the honoured guest (and somewhat of a mascot) of No. 1 MT Regiment since the middle of March, spending much of his time with Major Mackenzie, forming a close bond. Now, at the beginning of May, it was time for No. 1 MT Regiment and others from the L of C transport operations to be flown out of Imphal like thousands of others, and Padre Brock was left looking for new billets. He recalled:

It would have been a pleasant personal experience to have stayed with the British Major but just at this time a call came from one of the hospitals.

___

4. Lieutenant Swailes was later promoted to major (Deputy Assistant Adjutant General) with the Army Legal Department as a prosecutor at GHQ in Delhi and took part in the trials of INA officers who had been accused of ill-treatment or atrocities during the war.

That was a genuine challenge. The sick and wounded British soldiers in these seventeen wards were desperately in need of a friend. They needed a man who could sit down at the foot of their bed, give them the news and talk over the things in which they were interested … at first the ordinary things of life and then, when confidence has been established, about the more intimate affairs, even the heart-breaking tragedies that form even the heaviest burden of the soldier far from home. At times there was almost a clinging attitude. The fact that I was not officially connected to the army seemed to add to the spirit of response. I gave them news, I conducted religious services, I tried to do anything a friend would do but I wore no official insignia. The lack of official designation kept our relationships from seeming professional.

This generous humanitarian work by Padre Brock did not go unnoticed and made him many friends. He gained a lasting respect from all ranks, one of whom commented: 'Padre, these boys respect you far more than you think. You didn't have to stay here but you did because you wanted to help. They think a lot of you for that.'

Still under canvas, Padre Brock now found himself in different surroundings on the 'dismal mudflat' at the end of the Imphal Main runway, where 41 IGH had set up camp. Thinking this would be a place of healing and a sanctuary from war, Padre Brock learnt that just a few days before his arrival the hospital was machine-gunned during a Japanese air raid. This was still very much on the front line. His immediate neighbour was a unit of heavy anti-aircraft artillery protecting the vital airfield, with one artillery piece being concealed just 75 yards from his tent. Here, the weeks of the siege passed by as Padre Brock carried on with his work while the continuous flow of wounded men arrived and departed, flown out to other hospitals in the rear areas of India.

Within four days of the main road being reopened in June, Padre Brock returned to his Mission compound at Kangpokpi, noting:

I knew that the buildings had been used as a headquarters for the enemy until the dive-bombers had drove them into the jungle. I had been told that there was probably very little left where we had a station for four hundred people. Imagine the anxiety with which I watched as I rounded the turn in the road from which the station could be seen and the joy of seeing the main buildings nestling on the hillside … damaged but still there.

Expecting to find the compound deserted, Padre Brock was surprised to see it was now occupied by a large number of troops from the British 2 Division who had fought their way down from Kohima. Guards had been posted, and he was warned not to wander far unarmed, as there were still Japanese stragglers in the vicinity. Surveying the damage, he could see it was considerable but repairable. There were two large craters caused by aerial bombs dropped near to the church, the blast that had rattled all the plaster loose from the walls and ceiling. There were gaping holes where windows and doors had been, together with others in the corrugated tin roof, making a sorry spectacle. Further bomb craters dotted about the compound bore testament to the RAF's attacks to dislodge the Japanese. Moving on, Padre Brock came to his bungalow, now peppered with bullet holes. He counted forty-three in the roof of the veranda and a further sixty-eight in the back room.[5]

Despite being surrounded by so much destruction, Padre Brock's spirits were lifted when he held the first church service upon his return. He wrote:

> It was impressive and, in its own way, had a special message for us. The room itself bristled with rifles and sub-machine guns leaning against the seats by the side of the men or resting nearby and gave a suggestion of the seriousness of the situation through which we had passed. Yet the seats that had not been taken away were filled to capacity and the men listened with intense attention as we talked of the God on whom we can depend in times of trial.

The Japanese invasion had had dire consequences for Padre Brock's flock as well as the countless others living in the hills. With their food stores plundered by the starving Japanese troops, and unable to plant that year's full rice crops, or any crop other than a few pumpkins, the future was looking bleak. The disruption to their lives also meant that even basic items such as clothing were in short supply, and with the approaching cold weather

---

5. Because of financial constraints and other priorities, it was not until 1949 that the repairs to the mission were started and a further year of construction work before completion and the reopening of the station. It had been hoped to commemorate the fiftieth anniversary of the coming of the first missionaries in 1896, but this was put back to 1948 because of the conditions left by the Japanese invasion. However, 10,000 Manipuri Christians gathered there, some travelling six days, and despite reminders of the old ways of headhunting still being on display just half a mile away, a joyous event was held.

would mean a further hardship. The Indian Government were aware of this and were planning to alleviate the situation, but the wheels of government turned slowly, too slowly for Padre Brock. Bearing in mind that 'the Lord helps those who help themselves', Padre Brock began his personal efforts ensuring that those in need would have whatever assistance he could obtain.

Before Major Mackenzie had been flown out of Imphal, he came across Padre Brock leading a very bedraggled and hungry-looking mule one day, whom he described as 'another one of my assistants'. He went on to explain to the major that he had been scouring the jungle and rounding up those mules that the Japanese hadn't eaten and had abandoned as they fled from the victorious XIV Army. His intention was that when he had sufficient supplies, he would use these mules to deliver the much-needed supplies to those in the remote hills, noting:

> At that time, I had several thousand rupees in my hand … money given in relief [by the American Baptist Foreign Mission Society]. Ordinarily, this would have seemed a large amount but in view of the desperate needs of thousands it seemed so inadequate that I was tempted to think much as the disciple thought as he looked at the five loaves and two small fish; tempted to say, 'What are these among so many?'

Because of the close associations Padre Brock had with the Army, he decided to approach them for help. Meeting with the Kangla Admin Commandant, Major Scanes, Padre Brock asked if it were possible to purchase any used clothing with the grant money he had been given. Major Scanes's answer was rather non-committal, saying he would see what could be done, and for him to come back for an answer in a few days. Leaving the meeting feeling a bit discouraged, Padre Brock nevertheless returned the following week to an answer from Major Scanes that far exceeded his hopes. Upon discussions with the Ordnance Corps about Padre Brock's needs, it was decided that Lieutenant Colonel Boyd (newly promoted from major), the Chief Ordnance Officer of 221 AOD, would supply all the clothing, and that Major Scanes would provide the transport with which to haul the load. In all, twelve truckloads of condemned battledress, blankets and sacks of rice were sent, of which only one was paid for by Padre Brock. About 1,500 miles was covered by these trucks over very tough terrain, often no more than a jungle track, but it was still not enough as many of the more isolated villages could not be reached at all by wheeled transport. Again, the military came to Padre Brock's assistance when it was arranged with higher authorities that, such was the seriousness of the threat of famine, airdrops were needed. Two DC3 transport planes were used to drop supplies to a central point from which they could be distributed while another half load was dropped near to the Burma border.[6]

Padre Brock's decision and determination to stay in the area after the Japanese invasion in March had proved to be a wise one, because not only was he able to provide for his flock's immediate needs, but their long-term ones as well. This became apparent to him when visits to various villages became almost a series of ovations, albeit pitiful ones given the conditions in which these people found themselves. The people were extremely grateful and tended to be exaggerated far beyond what Padre Brock felt he deserved. He later wrote:

Padre Earl Ernest Brock and his wife, Rosa, in their latter days after retiring from missionary work.

6. This is in contrast to all the accusations of deliberate British neglect during the Bengal famine of 1943.

The most touching came from a smaller gathering which was in the area we had been visiting when the enemy came. These people had been hit hardest of all. Though this group represented about one sixth of the people in the invaded territory, they suffered so severely that we had to pour in five truckloads of clothing and blankets to meet even the most desperate needs. Yet they felt they needed to give me something. Barefoot men, who still did not have enough to keep themselves warm, got together to present me with a specially woven tribal blanket. And in the presentation ceremony they had but little to say except, 'He stayed with us. The Japanese nearly got him.' It had paid. Staying had paid.

Padre Brock continued with his missionary work in Manipur, and when his wife Rosa joined him later after the war had finished, their efforts were concentrated in the Ukhrul area of Manipur, where the church membership rose to over 10,000 such was their success. They retired in 1955 and returned to the USA.

*   *   *

The 221 Advanced Ordnance Depot was now placed in Lobster Box within the Keep area of Imphal. After a few days of settling in and placing their tents on the hillside, they were informed that they would be taking over from 52 Ordnance Field Depot, including all their stores. On 12 April, this order was changed to the exact opposite, and 221 AOD would now be flown out to Jorhat, where they would take over an Ordnance Field Depot there. A number of officers and men were then attached to 52 OFD to assist in the running of the depot.[7] A further detail from 221 would remain at Imphal under the command of Major Boyd and were to proceed to their former site at Kanglatongbi, when the situation permitted, to retrieve certain important stores abandoned during the evacuation on 7 April. In the meantime, before being flown out, a special ammunition detail was formed from specifically chosen officers, warrant officers and men, to move ammunition under the cover of darkness to a new camouflaged site on the surrounding hills. Waiting

---

7. Havildar Dulip Singh Rathore was one of those who stayed behind during the siege. In commemoration of his many years of service to the IAOC, a gateway at the Corps HQ at Jabalpur is named after him.

for just the light of the waning moon to help, this party, for two nights, laboured in silence and secrecy as many tons of ammunition were relocated and safely stored. On 23 April, the whole complement of 221 AOD were paraded in front of the Director Ordnance Services of 11th Army Group, Brigadier Herbert Morris, CIE, OBE, who was on a visit to IV Corps, and he was accompanied by Brigadier Brian Pennefather-Evans, OBE, the DDOS 14th Army. Here the unit was inspected and addressed by Brigadier Morris who, in glowing terms, commended them for their magnificent efforts and conduct during the period of the action at Kanglatongbi.[8] The following day, the first tranche of over 200 officers and men arrived at Jorhat, with the remaining two parties arriving over the next two days. The special detachment of twenty-seven officers and men under the command of Major Boyd were left behind to retrieve important stores items from the old depot site, and they were in a state of frustration because the situation at Kanglatongbi was still unclear. After waiting for several days, Major Boyd went to meet the commander of 63 Indian Infantry Brigade, controlling the area, who explained to him that the Japanese were still in the vicinity in strength and were holding a strong roadblock on the bridge over the Dak Bungalow nullah, and it would be at least three days before there was any possibility of entering the depot. With this further setback, Major Boyd contacted the DDOS IV Corps on 1 May for instructions and to see when they would be flown out to join the rest of 221 AOD. He was informed that they would be leaving on 5 or 6 May, and that he was now being promoted to lieutenant colonel and was to take over command of 221 AOD from Lieutenant Colonel Cunningham, who would be taking command of 226 AOD at Dimapur. Leaving Captain Fitzgibbon in command of the detachment, Lieutenant Colonel Boyd finally arrived at 221 AOD's location

Captain Paul Fitzgibbon, Punjab Regiment attached 221 AOD.

---

8. A few months later, Brigadier Morris was made Aide-de-Camp to HM The King.

and took up his duties on 7 May, and a few days later, Lieutenant Colonel Boyd's award of the Military Cross for his conduct during the fighting at Lion Box was approved by General Gifford. The special detachment flew out of Imphal without getting their special stores from Kanglatongbi, though when it was finally retaken on 23 May, over 200 lorry loads of stores were retrieved during the following few days and sent to 52 OFD, in what was now the 'Keep Ordnance Depot'.

At the end of July, Lieutenant Colonel Boyd was recalled to Imphal to oversee the siting of a new depot to be built for 221 AOD at milestone 130 on the Imphal–Dimapur road. In conjunction with engineers and Major Scanes, now the Keep Administration Commandant, blueprints were drawn up and work commenced, while various elements of 221 AOD gradually moved in when their particular area was completed, and they continued with the work there. In March 1945, the depot was closed down when the personnel were withdrawn to Bokakhat in India, to undergo training in advance of Operation Zipper, and in May 1945, Lieutenant Colonel Boyd left 221 AOD and was posted to the DDOS HQ 14th Army and took up his position there.

*　*　*

After meeting their guides from IV Corps at milestone 132, the senior officers from 20 Reinforcement Camp were taken to their new location in Whale Box about 2 miles south of the Imphal Main runway, adjacent to Imphal itself. Here they began organising their dispositions, acquainting themselves with the area and the other occupants of the box. Defensive positions and air raid shelters were dug, and patrol boundaries laid out as the permanent staff resumed their work with the reinforcements. Working closely with 43 GPT Company and other transport units ferrying men to and from both Imphal and Tulihal airfields, 20 Rft Camp was soon up and running at a very busy pace as the reinforcements poured in, and the wounded and surplus mouths were evacuated. Understandably, very little further training of the reinforcements was possible at this time, with the main priority being to ensure any reinforcements were fully equipped and arriving at their unit when required. This situation continued for several weeks while the Imphal battles raged but it became apparent that this work could be done further back in India, especially when it would save supplies having to be airlifted into Imphal, while rations for the besieged garrison were cut once again at this time. On 14 May, 20 Rft Camp began to be flown out of Imphal to Comilla and then transported to the Mainamati Ridge, where they joined with several other reinforcement camps already there. Over the next few days, nearly 900 men were airlifted out from Imphal. The vital work of these camps continued until June 1945, when a complete overhaul of the reinforcement system was made in light of the proposed invasion of Malaya and the next phase of the campaign. Lieutenant Colonel Wells-Cole was now repatriated and Lieutenant Colonel Gerald Macnamara took over command, and CSM Johnson was promoted to regimental sergeant major, when 20 Rft Camp became No. 2 Forward Army Reinforcement Holding Unit. It was based in Pollachi near Cochin in readiness to join Operation Zipper, but with the dropping of the atomic bombs on Hiroshima and Nagasaki, the war ended before the invasion took place and 2 FARHU then became part of the RAPWI (Returned Allied Prisoners of War and Internees) operations.

*　*　*

The GREF Engineer units who bore the brunt of the fighting now found themselves dispersed in various boxes around the Keep area. Major Henderson's 517 AW Company were directed to Prawn Box and arrived there in small parties throughout the night, while 528 AW Company were sent to GREF Box at Bishenpur, where other GREF units had come from Tiddim earlier and had assembled. Next to them was the 440 Quarrying Company who had several more men missing who had become separated during the journey from Kanglatongbi. A search of adjacent units produced fourteen men, but despite Captain Upfold's best efforts, eleven were still missing when the unit was flown out to Comilla ten days later. The remaining units initially went to Hare Box but were then sent to Trout Box at milestone 129, where they then formed their own box, called Crab Box. At this time the old position of 864 ME Company's workshop and stores at Sengmai was cleared of all heavy plant and spare parts that had been left behind when they moved to Lion Box, and IV Corps now gave orders that the engineers

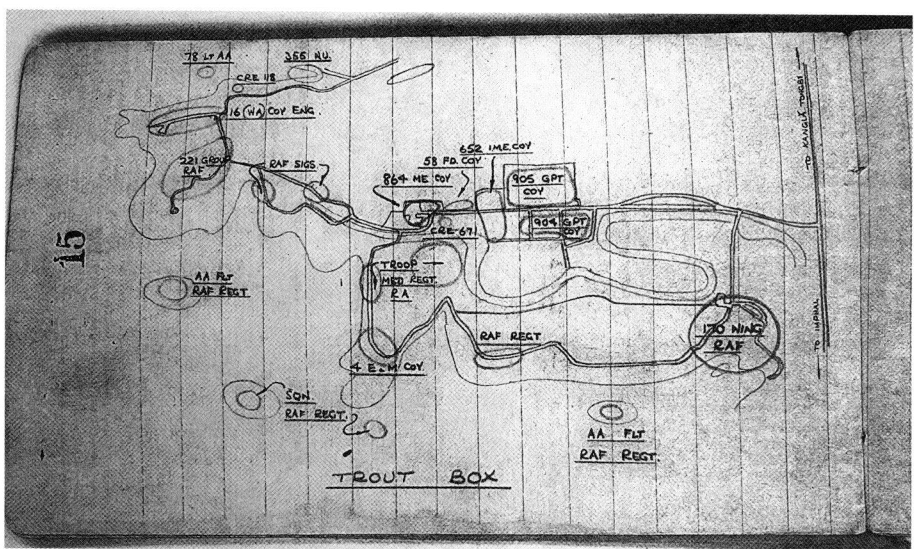

Trout Box in the Imphal Keep, to where some of the Engineer units from Lion Box were evacuated, April 1944.

were to continue work on several projects around the Keep. This included the building of bridges at various river crossings, while others were engaged in drainage work and shingling the network of roads within the Keep. Despite having the unenviable honour of taking the most casualties in the fighting (thirty-seven killed and wounded), 58 Field Company were still fully committed to their work as they manned the stone crushers at various quarry sites, until 442 Quarrying Company relieved them. The Hamilton bridge over the Imphal Turel near to the Keep was completed by 58 Field Company on 13 May, and two days later they were flown out to Shillong via Jorhat. The 864 ME Company continued with the building of the new fighter airstrip at right angles to the end of the Imphal Main runway, before being flown out from there to Dhanbad and Asansol in Bihar at the beginning of June. The sections of the unit were split up at various locations to opencast coal mines to aid the Indian war effort. In October, large numbers of sappers from 58 Field Company went to help with this, and to learn how to handle the various machines in preparation for their change of role to a Mechanical Equipment company in November. This was to be a very different life compared to what the sappers had been used to for the past two years, where, instead of living in tents in the steaming jungle, they were at one point

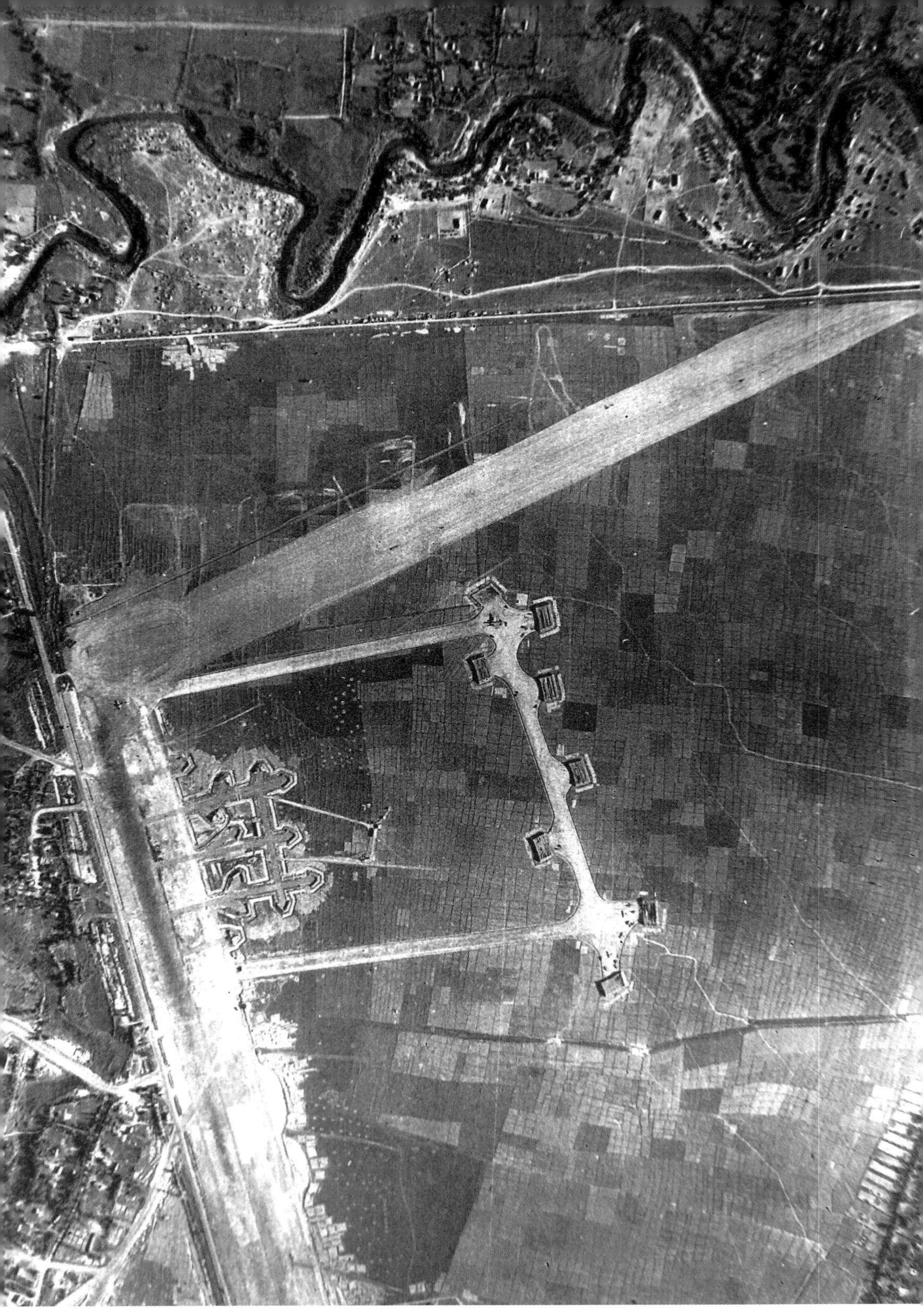

Imphal Main airfield and the dry weather fighter airstrip built by 864 ME Company Royal Engineers.

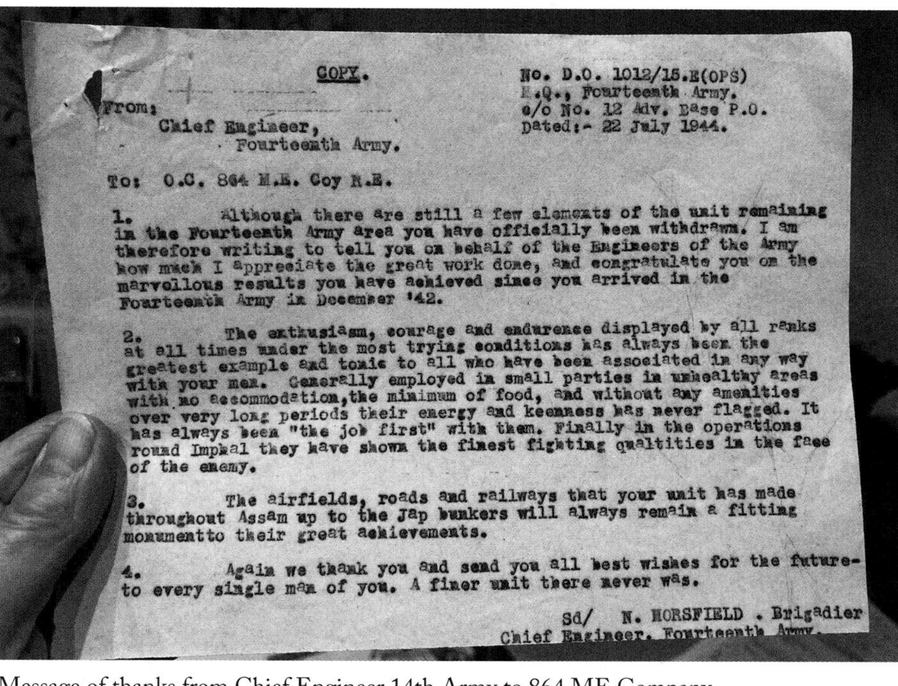

Message of thanks from Chief Engineer 14th Army to 864 ME Company.

COPY.

D.O.1012/15.E.(OPS).
H.Q.Fourteenth Army,
C/o.No.12.A.B.P.O.,
Dated. 22 July 1944.

From:- Chief Engineer,
       Fourteenth Army.

To:- O.C. 864.M.E.Coy.R.E.

1.   Although there are still a few elements of the Unit remaining in the
Fourteenth Army Area you have officially been withdrawn. I am therefore
writing to tell you on behalf of the Engineers of the Army how much I
appreciate the great work done, and congratulate you on the marvellous
results you have achieved since you arrived in the Fourteenth Army in
December '42.

2.   The enthusiasm, courage and endurance displayed by all ranks at all times
under the most trying conditions has always been the greatest example and
tonic to all who have been associated in any way with your men. Generally
employed in small parties in unhealthy areas with no accomodation, the
minimum of food, and without any amenities over very long periods their
energy and keenness has never flagged. It has always been "the job First"
with them. Finally in the operations round Imphal they have shown the
finest fighting qualities in the face of the enemy.

3.   The airfields, roads and railways that your Unit has made throughout
Assam up to the Jap bunkers will always remain a fitting monument to
their great achievements.

4.   Again we thank you and send you all best wishes for the future - to every
single man of you. A finer Unit there never was.

                         Signed. N. HORSFIELD.
                              Brigadier,
        Chief Engineer,Fourteenth Army.

Note of thanks to 864 ME Company from Brigadier Horsfield, Chief Engineer XIVth Army.

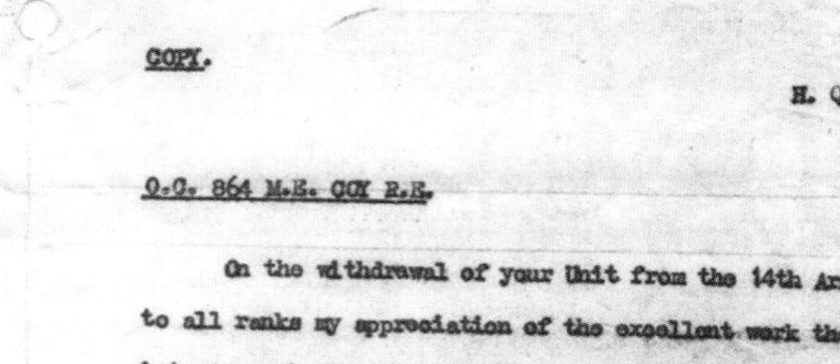

General Slim's message of thanks to 864 ME Company.

housed in American-made air-conditioned huts. Lance Corporal Welsh thought this was the life of luxury. Over 1.25 million tons of coal were extracted by 36 Section from the coal seam at Teetulmuri before 864 ME Company sailed for home on 28 November 1945.

At the beginning of May, Lieutenant Colonel Peacock, the CRE of 671 MEx Company and former commander of Sectors 1 and 2 Lion Box, was posted away and his second in command, Major Alexander, took over as CRE and commander of Crab Box as well. For the next two months, Major Alexander oversaw the workings of his group until the beginning of July, when

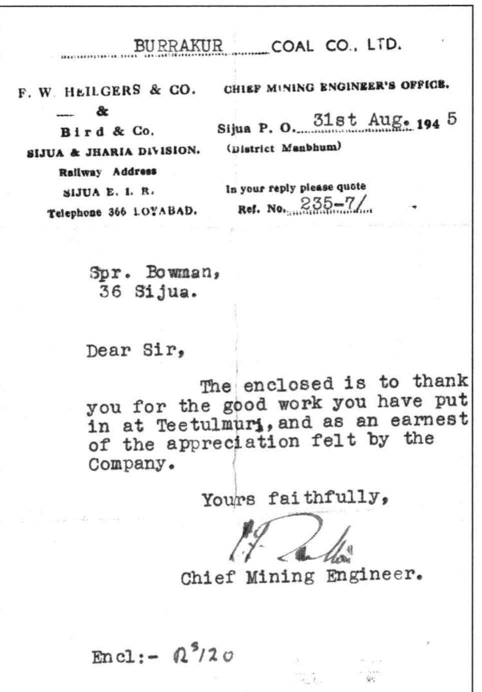

Chitty from Burrakur Coal Company to Sapper Miff Bowman, 864 ME Company, thanking him for his work in the coalfields, paying him 120 rupees.

Major Gray, the former OC of 864 ME Company, now promoted to lieutenant colonel, took over command from him. Lieutenant Colonel Gray's return to duty after recovering from his shoulder wound received during the fighting on 7 April was met with a certain amount of disappointment by Major Alexander, because had he returned just a few days later, then it would have meant that Major Alexander would have gained his colonelcy due to the time he spent as acting CRE.[9] One of the first duties undertaken by Lieutenant Colonel Gray was to visit the battlefield graves of three of his men from 864 ME Company killed at Kanglatongbi. It would be

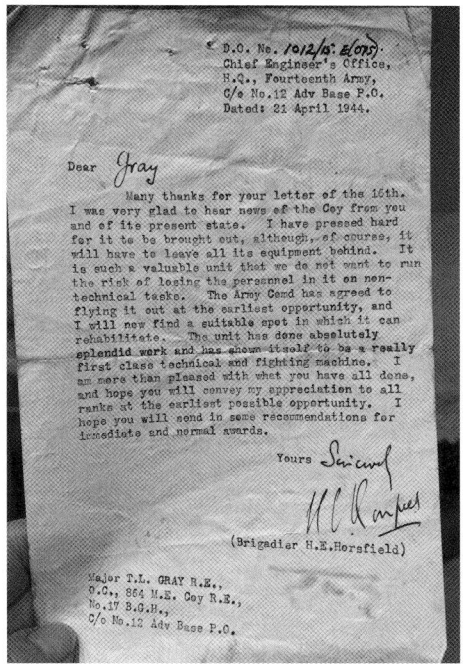

D.O. No. 1012/15: E(Ops).
Chief Engineer's Office,
H.Q., Fourteenth Army,
C/o No.12 Adv Base P.O.
Dated: 21 April 1944.

Dear *Gray*

Many thanks for your letter of the 16th. I was very glad to hear news of the Coy from you and of its present state. I have pressed hard for it to be brought out, although, of course, it will have to leave all its equipment behind. It is such a valuable unit that we do not want to run the risk of losing the personnel in it on non-technical tasks. The Army Comd has agreed to flying it out at the earliest opportunity, and I will now find a suitable spot in which it can rehabilitate. The unit has done absolutely splendid work and has shown itself to be a really first class technical and fighting machine. I am more than pleased with what you have all done, and hope you will convey my appreciation to all ranks at the earliest possible opportunity. I hope you will send in some recommendations for immediate and normal awards.

Yours *Sincerely*

[signature]

(Brigadier H.E.Horsfield)

Major T.L. GRAY R.E.,
O.C., 864 M.E. Coy R.E.,
No.17 B.G.H.,
C/o No.12 Adv Base P.O.

Chief Engineer note to Major Gray regarding 864 ME Company's performance and withdrawal from the front line.

another five months before the Graves Recovery Units would collect their remains and place them in the Imphal Cemetery alongside the others who were killed.

*   *   *

The patrolling and probing by the infantry of the Japanese-held areas began almost immediately after the evacuation of the Lion Box, while Lieutenant Scurfield and his V Force riflemen then moved deeper behind the lines as far north as Kangpokpi. The C Squadron of the Carabiniers and their Lee tanks joined with their infantry escorts from the West Yorks and Gurkhas of 63 Brigade based at Sengmai. On some of these patrols, several fierce skirmishes took place as they tried to break the two roadblocks built within

---

9. A year later, almost to the day, on 10 April 1945 Lieutenant Colonel Gray, now a staff officer, was wounded again when he and another officer driving a jeep were ambushed by a party of Japanese near Meiktila in Burma.

Engineers and infantry clearing a Japanese roadblock on the Dak Bungalow bridge, with Picquet Hill in the background.

The Japanese roadblock at the Dak Bungalow bridge, Lion Box, being inspected for booby traps by engineers.

The Japanese roadblock at the Dak Bungalow bridge 1944, in comparison with 2015.

the box. As well as the block on the Dak Bungalow bridge, which was cleared by engineers then subsequently rebuilt by the enemy, the Japanese had utilised the old British roadblock on the northern perimeter of the box, which proved to be a more difficult nut to crack because of the strong

West Yorks, Gurkhas and Carbs crossing the Imphal Turel, heading west to Lion Box in the treeline, 23 April 1944.

Lee tanks of the 3rd Carbiniers and 2nd West Yorks enter the old Sector 3 of Lion Box, 23 April 1944.

Japanese defences overlooking the area. This situation continued for quite some time and Trooper Connolly remembered how they would 'mix it' with the Japanese almost daily. As they moved along the road into position, Trooper Connolly remembered how the stench from the rotting corpse of one of those killed during the RAF attack alerted the crew to close down the hatches and prepare to be engaged by the enemy. This routine carried on for one time too many, and on 24 April, the Japanese were prepared and waiting for them and during a heavy response from the Japanese artillery, Lieutenant Rowe-Wilson's tank was hit nine times, putting out of action both main guns and seriously wounding Troopers Blunson and Butler.

The terrain hereabouts on either side of the road was not suited for the tanks to outflank the roadblock and the Japanese positions, so it fell to the infantry to take the lead, supported wherever possible by the tanks of the Carbs and also the Indian 7th Cavalry. With the monsoon season almost upon them, the raising of the siege became more important because the flying-in of crucial supplies for the garrison of Imphal would be seriously affected by the weather conditions. The urgency of the retaking of Kanglatongbi and the push northwards along the Imphal–Dimapur road was impressed upon the commanders of 5 Division by GHQ in India, who were unaware of the actual conditions these men on the ground were living and fighting under, and why it was taking so long to make any headway. In May, 123 Brigade of 5 Division moved to Kanglatongbi and the troops of the Suffolks, Dogras and Punjabis began engaging with the Japanese in their strong fortifications at key points along the road northwards. The hill feature named Pyramid on the west of the road overlooking the original site of 221 AOD was taken after some fierce fighting by the Suffolks, sustaining many casualties in this attack. This bypassed the strong roadblock that had caused so many problems, enabling them to move forward to the next Japanese strongpoint at Zebra. It was not all bad news for the Suffolks, for at this time they were positioned within the old Ordnance Depot and able to replenish their stocks of clothing and footwear and other equipment from the abandoned supplies. Permission was granted for limited replenishment, but large amounts of stores were pilfered despite the efforts of guards posted to stop this. Other units passing through also helped themselves, West Yorks included, and these units probably looted far more stores than the Japanese Army, who had originally captured the depot. However, the one thing that was not pilfered was the large numbers of gas masks, which, for whatever reason, were found strewn about the area.[10]

To the east of the road, the dominating Kanglatongbi Ridge and Point 3813 were finally retaken on 20 May by the King's Own Scottish Borderers and Gurkha Rifles, after a magnificent feat of arms by the 1/11 Sikh Regiment. For five days, the Japanese troops dug in along the top of the ridge in strong bunker positions, and held up the Jocks of the KOSBs. An unseen night march through the jungle between the Japanese defences to the east of the road near the roadblock and the Imphal Turel allowed the Sikhs to sneak through this gap and outflank the Japanese on the Kanglatongbi Ridge and so position themselves to their rear at Ekban Ekwan. For the next few days, the Sikhs beat off numerous counterattacks by the Japanese, with high casualties on both sides, until the Japanese finally melted away from the ridge to reform on the next set of hills to the north.

Kanglatongbi was finally cleared of the Japanese on 23 May, enabling stores and equipment to be salvaged. Those entering the depot were met

---

10. The British soldier is renowned for taking advantage of any surplus 'buckshee' kit. It always was, and probably still is a valuable bartering commodity.

by a scene of dereliction, with overgrown and burnt-out vehicles and huts, with abandoned equipment lying everywhere as the jungle began to reclaim its own. One eyewitness described it as being 'literally a dump, with a very forlorn and depressing atmosphere with burnt-out vehicles and huts and putrid bodies lying everywhere. One will always remember the stench of death that hung over this depot.' Major Alexander, the acting CRE of 671 MEx Company, and a party of engineers went to the old positions of the engineers to retrieve what plant and equipment they could. It was noted that it had been untouched by the Japanese but had been badly damaged by shell and gunfire. Large parties of pioneers and Ordnance personnel were dispatched at the same time to the depot, where once again it was a hive of activity while as much equipment and stores as possible were gathered and transported to Imphal for salvage.

The advance up both sides of the main road continued at a snail's pace as the monsoon now slowed progress, making life even more miserable for those men feeling the effects of the reduction in their rations, and those suffering with various tropical ailments sapping their strength, especially dysentery and malaria. Life was no better for the Japanese, and in fact was much worse as their supply lines collapsed, leaving them to scavenge for whatever they could. Despite all these hardships, both sides doggedly stuck to their tasks. After they lost more men at Zebra, the Suffolks now changed position to the east of the road after the West Yorks relieved them. At the

Some of the artefacts found on Isaac during an expedition in 2014, including a 75mm solid shot projectile from a Lee tank.

beginning of June, the hill features of George and Harry were taken, leaving the large Japanese bunker complex on Isaac to be cleared. The tanks of the Carabiniers C Squadron, who had already taken part in capturing the previous hills, now found great difficulty in climbing the steep gradients required to make it to the top of Isaac. This difficulty was made worse by the heavy rains, so the Indian Sappers of 74 Field Company were then instructed to build an access ramp across the saddle between Harry and Isaac made from logs cut from nearby trees, and together with the help from a bulldozer started to get the tanks into position. Having already made several attempts, Lieutenant Cole and his 5 Troop tanks supported by HQ Troop still found the going difficult, and after briefly managing to engage some Japanese bunkers, slid down the side of the khud, losing a track in the process. Another tank slid over the khud and had to be abandoned. Because Lieutenant Cole's tank engine seemed to have insufficient power to climb the gradient it was decided that he would swap tanks with one from HQ Troop whose engine was better and to try again. Whether Lieutenant Cole took over command of this HQ Troop tank with its usual crew or he took his own crew with him remains unknown, but they managed to negotiate the slope and made their way to the top of the bunker complex. As the tank began to make its way westwards along the ridge, tremendous firing broke out and the tank was struck twice on the front with what appeared to have been an anti-tank rifle firing a hollow charge grenade and the hull was penetrated once, which started a fire inside. There was a bit of confusion as the Suffolks reported a large explosion and a white cloud of smoke coming from the rear of the tank. It was thought that a 75mm gun firing from a position called Isaac's Nose on the reverse slope further along the ridge had been the cause.[11]

Coming to an abrupt halt, the tank began 'brewing up' right next to two Japanese bunkers, and when the crew began to bail out, they became easy targets, with Trooper Chic Henderson being cut down near the back of the tank; he was later found dead with his Thompson machine gun lying beside him. Trooper Barker escaped unhurt and assisted the badly burnt Lance

---

11. Photos taken of the tank show that it was halted facing towards Isaac's Nose and therefore could not have been hit on the rear from there. No damage can be seen on the rear of the tank, which would have been considerable if hit with a 75mm shell. It is possible that what the Suffolks saw was a shell explode close to the side of the tank near the rear.

Lieutenant Cole's destroyed Lee tank at Isaac.

Corporal Jenkins and Trooper Nevols to get clear. The remaining crew members were less fortunate and were either killed in the initial strike or were shot and fell back into the hull when they tried to get out. Lieutenant Cole, Trooper Mountney and Trooper Mulvey all perished in the hull of the tank as the fire took hold. These men died within sight of Lion Box, where they had fought just two months previously because Isaac overlooked the whole of Kanglatongbi.[12]

More British and Indian lives were lost as the stubborn and fanatical Japanese soldiers

Trooper Harry Mountney, 3rd Carabiniers, KIA 8 June 1944 while attacking Japanese positions on Isaac.

---

12. In 2019, a party of British and local Manipuris from the Imphal Campaign Foundation went on an expedition to the battle site and uncovered large numbers of artefacts from the fighting. Among these were solid shot projectiles used by the tanks for bunker busting, a Japanese bayonet and an unexploded British hand grenade, which no doubt was last touched by one of the Suffolks. Fourteen poppy crosses were placed there in commemoration of the four Carabiniers and ten Suffolks who lost their lives on that hill.

Milestone 112 area: 1. Octopus feature; 2. Driffield; 3. Liver.

fought to the death on almost every hill as 5 Division relentlessly pushed them back northwards. When the weather permitted, RAF Hurribombers were used to pound the defences before the infantry moved in with the bayonet, to winkle out those of the enemy still putting up resistance. Gradually, the milestones and Japanese-defended hills were ticked off the list one by one, milestone 116 Zebra, milestone 115 Dot and Dash, milestone 114 Pip, Squeak and Wilfred. At milestone 112 Driffield, the bridge across a nullah had been blown up, and a roadblock of felled trees covered by a powerful Japanese position on Octopus to the west of the road was holding up progress. On 15 June, the plan to clear Octopus was put into operation with the Jat

Regiment supporting by attacking the hill Liver to the east of the road, while the West Yorks were to make a long flanking movement to the west and come in from the north behind the Japanese positions. Support from the 7th Cavalry Stuart tanks would be from the road and the low-lying ground to the east of the road. The Octopus feature was within the old positions of 20 and 25 Rft Camps at Lynx Box and Leopard Box where, back in March, strong and well-positioned defences were dug as per IV Corps' instructions. When the boxes were closed down, and before the occupants moved out, these defences were hurriedly destroyed or rendered useless to the enemy. However, it was believed that the Japanese had refurbished some of them during the interim three months, and they now occupied them and others in strength. Because of the pressures being applied to get the road open quickly, there was insufficient time given for reconnaissance and intelligence gathering, and D Company were unsure of how far west the Japanese defences extended. This proved disastrous, for when the West Yorks began their movements, they found themselves being attacked from their left flank, and withdrawing south, they were then heavily engaged from three directions when they encountered the enemy rear positions covering Driffield as well. From a strength of seventy-seven, only forty-seven men made their way back to the start point, and of these, twenty were wounded.[13]

Having learnt a severe lesson, the next few days were spent in reconnaissance of the complete area and plans were made to take Octopus and positions as far north as the northern perimeter of the old Lynx Box. The 1/17 Dogra Regiment of 123 Brigade had now joined with 9 Indian Brigade and had taken a westerly route in the foothills of Mount Koubru, and by nightfall on 21 June were in position on high ground just north of Lynx Box at milestone 110, ready to establish a roadblock at milestone 109. By this time, 9 Brigade had launched the attack and through the day, the Jats had taken the high ground to the east of the road while the Punjabis had cleared the enemy positions to the north of Octopus. The West Yorks followed up a

---

13. Lieutenant Bird of 137 GPT Company recalled seeing a wooden plaque with the names of those killed branded on it near the road at milestone 112 when passing by as he returned to Kanglatongbi after the siege was lifted. His attention was particularly drawn because the West Yorkshire Regiment was the regiment he originally enlisted with before taking a commission in the RIASC. It is believed that the wooden plaque was eventually replaced by one of carved stone and was placed at a small temple just a few yards from the main road.

heavy mortar and artillery bombardment on Octopus with patrols but were again frustrated by enemy fire from other bunker positions. A further heavy concentration of artillery fire was put down during the evening, and by 06.30 hours on 22 June, the Punjabis reported that Octopus and the areas to the north in the former location of 20 Rft Camp were now clear of the enemy, who had withdrawn during the night after losing an estimated fifty-five dead during the course of this action. The Dogras now began their move forward and were advised to keep a lookout for patrols from the Lancashire Fusiliers of 2 Division, who by now had pushed on south from Kangpokpi. However, it was patrols from the 2 Durham Light Infantry that the outlying Dogras first encountered at about 10.30 hours, near to milestone 109. The armoured support from C Squadron Carabiniers and 7 Cavalry now made their way along the road while the engineers cleared any booby traps from the roadblocks. Just as the lead tank of Lieutenant Rowe Wilson's 7 Troop was about to smash through the block at Burton Bridge at milestone 110,

Troops from 2 British Division and 5 Indian Division meeting at milestone 109, 22 June 1944.

the tank commander noticed unexploded mortar bombs and 37mm shells hidden amongst the rocks, and the engineers were called forward to deal with this while the Carbs parked up and waited. When the sappers finally gave the all-clear for the Carbs to proceed, and just as they were making ready to move, a column of the 7 Cavalry came roaring through past them and headed on up the road. At milestone 109, they came to a halt at about 11.00 hours when they met up with 149 Regiment Royal Armoured Corps and other troops from 2 Division. Official photos of this important event were taken as the men of the two divisions shook hands and congratulated each other on this magnificent achievement.

In 2018, a large stone monolith to commemorate this event was placed within a few yards of the actual meeting place. Designed and commissioned by members of the Second World War Imphal Campaign Foundation, this monument records the valour of those men from the Indian 5th Division and the British 2nd Division who fought and gave their lives to open the Dimapur–Imphal road in April to June 1944. Within a few hours, the men and trucks of the RIASC once again began hauling supplies from Dimapur along the road to Imphal. The three-month-long Siege of Imphal was over.

Appendix One

Casualties Lion Box

The accurate recording of casualties immediately after the confusion of battle is no easy task and searching these records and casualties many years later is not much easier, especially with such a diverse composition of units being present in this case.

Because of the volume and make-up of some of the units involved at Lion Box, i.e. some being only sections or platoons or even individuals from larger units, it is almost impossible to tell if a certain casualty was actually present there or elsewhere during the actions between 29 March and 10 April 1944, the period covered by this book. (The exception to these dates being for those who died of wounds later, and the eleven prisoner of war sepoys from 137 GPT Company, officially recorded as dying on 1 July 1944, who, with little doubt, were killed on 10 April 1944 at the same time as the thirteen other prisoners from 137 GPT Company.)

An example of how difficult it is to determine a man's whereabouts, 20 Reinforcement Camp comprised men awaiting posting to the various units of 20 Indian Division, adding to the confusion whether they were at Lion Box or already serving with their unit. The case of Private William Howard of the 2nd Border Regiment (as officially recorded) is a good example of this and if it were not for the in-depth research taken it is unlikely anyone would have known that he was killed at Kanglatongbi fighting with 20 Reinforcement Camp. He never had the chance to join the unit to which he had been posted. The permanent staff of the camp were on attachment, being drawn from various other units of the British and Indian armies also making it very difficult to be sure of their presence. The 221 AOD had a considerable number of attached personal fighting with them as well. Another difficulty with identification was the problem of men being from the larger corps such as Indian Engineers, Pioneer Corps or Royal Indian Army Service Corps not having their precise unit recorded on documentation.

Searching through unit war diaries, the Commonwealth War Graves Commission (CWGC) records and official British Casualty Lists of the time has not quite produced a definitive list of British casualties, but probably one that comes very close and shows the ferocity of the engagement by the numbers involved. Sadly, the same cannot be said for the Indian casualties as no official lists of the wounded for them are extant or, perhaps, are buried and forgotten in some dusty archive in India (possibly in Jhansi, where 2nd Echelon records were held). The CWGC records, of course, only contain the details of those killed, and war diaries vary so much in the details given that these cannot be wholly relied upon by themselves. Another factor in confirming how these men died, i.e. killed in action, died of wounds, died (of disease or from an accident) can be found on the official casualty lists whereas the CWGC lists only state that all 'Died'. To be recorded as 'died of wounds', a casualty was deemed to have received some medical treatment or had been admitted to a medical unit prior to their demise.

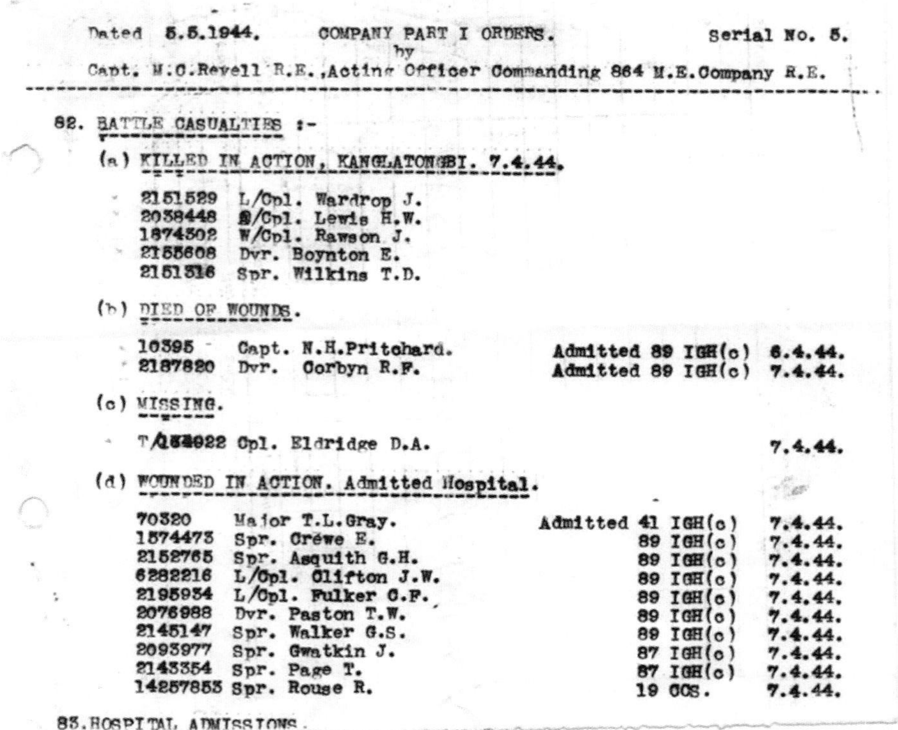

Dated 5.5.1944.   COMPANY PART I ORDERS.   Serial No. 5.
                               by
Capt. M.C.Revell R.E.,Acting Officer Commanding 864 M.E.Company R.E.
----

82. BATTLE CASUALTIES :-

    (a) KILLED IN ACTION, KANGLATONGBI. 7.4.44.

        2151529   L/Cpl. Wardrop J.
        2038448   S/Cpl. Lewis H.W.
        1874302   W/Cpl. Rawson J.
        2155608   Dvr. Boynton E.
        2151316   Spr. Wilkins T.D.

    (b) DIED OF WOUNDS.

        10395   Capt. N.H.Pritchard.   Admitted 89 IGH(c) 6.4.44.
        2187820   Dvr. Corbyn R.F.   Admitted 89 IGH(c) 7.4.44.

    (c) MISSING.

        T/152022 Cpl. Eldridge D.A.   7.4.44.

    (d) WOUNDED IN ACTION. Admitted Hospital.

        70320   Major T.L.Gray.   Admitted 41 IGH(c) 7.4.44.
        1574473   Spr. Crewe E.   89 IGH(c) 7.4.44.
        2152765   Spr. Asquith G.H.   89 IGH(c) 7.4.44.
        6282216   L/Cpl. Clifton J.W.   89 IGH(c) 7.4.44.
        2195934   L/Cpl. Fulker C.F.   89 IGH(c) 7.4.44.
        2076988   Dvr. Paston T.W.   89 IGH(c) 7.4.44.
        2145147   Spr. Walker G.S.   89 IGH(c) 7.4.44.
        2093977   Spr. Gwatkin J.   87 IGH(c) 7.4.44.
        2143354   Spr. Page T.   87 IGH(c) 7.4.44.
        14257853 Spr. Rouse R.   19 CCS.   7.4.44.

    83. HOSPITAL ADMISSIONS.

Company Part One Orders, 864 ME Company Royal Engineers.

Using all the available documentation to try to verify each man's place on the casualty list, it has, in just a few cases, been necessary to resort to 'best guess', especially when a casualty has died of wounds at a later date. Again, British casualties can be confirmed but Indian ones are more difficult, mostly relying on the fact that they were either buried in the Imphal Indian Army Cemetery or commemorated on the Imphal Cremation Memorial near the medical facilities, closest to where the fighting had been. All other Indian casualties are commemorated on the Rangoon Memorial as either being cremated on the battlefield as per their religious beliefs, or as missing or unidentified.

The recording of the Japanese casualties was very difficult to ascertain with any certainty or accuracy, but what was gleaned from Japanese sources named seventy-four officers and men being killed in the actions at Kanglatongbi. Another source stated that approximately sixty-eight were buried on 7 April on the actual battlefield after the heavy fighting that day. This left six casualties (presumably buried elsewhere or missing) for the remainder of the three-day period of the action, which seems a very low figure given the reports of the fighting from British sources. No records of the wounded for this period could be found, but it is thought that numbers may have been at least as many as those killed or, most likely, considerably higher.

<u>LION BOX CASUALTY LIST</u>

<u>BRITISH ARMY UNITS</u>

<u>58 FIELD COMPANY ROYAL ENGINEERS</u>

2937187 SAPPER ADAMS A WOUNDED 7/4/1944[1]

6460689 LANCE SERGEANT ADAMS. HARVEY JOSEPH MAURICE AGE 27 DIED 5/4/1944 RANGOON MEMORIAL[2]

2137957 LANCE CORPORAL AMISS RT WOUNDED 7/4/1944

1871803 SERGEANT BEYNON DL WOUNDED 7/4/1944

1869268 SERGEANT BYE OJ WOUNDED 7/4/1944

2121909 SAPPER DAY WJ WOUNDED 7/4/1944[3]

2005663 SAPPER EBURY WH WOUNDED 7/4/1944

1940207 DRIVER FESSEY. RONALD AGE 31 DIED 5/4/1944 RANGOON MEMORIAL[4]

---

1. Discharged from service due to wounds 14/5/1945.
2. Previously reported missing, presumed killed.
3. Discharged from service due to wounds 14/9/1945.
4. Previously reported missing, presumed killed.

2010519 SAPPER FROST JA WOUNDED 7/4/1944

1873845 SAPPER GILES JCG WOUNDED 7/4/1944

2156223 SAPPER GOLDING. RONALD AGE 22 DIED 7/4/1944
IMPHAL WAR CEMETERY[5]

1872356 LANCE CORPORAL GREEN W WOUNDED 7/4/1944

1892730 SAPPER HAWLEY BB WOUNDED 7/4/1944

1901503 LANCE SERGEANT HERD. WILLIAM AGE 26 DIED 7/4/1944
IMPHAL WAR CEMETERY

2007444 DRIVER HERR. JOHN FREDERICK AGE 27 DIED 7/4/1944
IMPHAL WAR CEMETERY[6]

2130357 SAPPER HOWLETT. EDWARD THOMAS AGE 37 DIED 7/4/1944
IMPHAL WAR CEMETERY

2113122 SAPPER HYDE. FREDERICK WILLIAM AGE 24 DIED 20/4/1944
IMPHAL WAR CEMETERY[7]

2196366 SERGEANT JACKSON CN WOUNDED 7/4/1944[8]

1875928 SAPPER LEWIS RC WOUNDED 7/4/1944

1892722 SAPPER LUCAS H WOUNDED 5/4/1944

1901555 LANCE SERGEANT MCMILLAN N WOUNDED 7/4/1944[9]

2128190 LANCE CORPORAL PAYNE. THOMAS DOUGLAS FREDERICK
AGE 30 DIED 7/4/1944 IMPHAL WAR CEMETERY[10]

1892774 SAPPER PEACH JW WOUNDED 7/4/1944

181465 TEMPORARY MAJOR PEARCE LA WOUNDED 7/4/1944

2114983 SAPPER PEARCE RW WOUNDED 7/4/1944

1893637 DRIVER RAWES. MATTHEW AGE 30 DIED 7/4/1944
IMPHAL WAR CEMETERY

2191692 CORPORAL ROBINSON. EDWARD AGE 32 DIED 7/4/1944
IMPHAL WAR CEMETERY

1888297 SAPPER ROGERS. RAYMOND GEORGE AGE 29 DIED 7/4/1944
IMPHAL WAR CEMETERY

---

5. Originally buried in a battlefield grave 7/4/1944 and was recovered and reburied in Imphal Cemetery 13/2/1945 as unidentified. Finally identified 7/10/47. Sapper Golding's younger brother John was killed in June 1944 serving in France with the Royal Scots Greys.

6. Previously reported as missing, presumed killed, though was buried on the battlefield. Recovered and reburied in Imphal Cemetery 11/12/1944.

7. Died of wounds received (ruptured liver) 7/4/1944.

8. Discharged from service due to wounds 14/9/1945.

9. Discharged from service due to wounds 5/1/1945.

10. Originally buried in a battlefield grave 23/5/1944 and was recovered and reburied in Imphal Cemetery 11/12/1944. It is possible that Lance Corporal Payne's remains were found and first buried by British or Indian units when they took over positions in Kanglatongbi in May 1944. It maybe that he was either killed early during the fighting or later during the evacuation, when his body could not be recovered, being in enemy-held territory.

2122561 LANCE CORPORAL ROWE. EDWARD GEORGE ASHWORTH
AGE 28 DIED 5/4/1944 RANGOON MEMORIAL[11]

1892735 SAPPER STEVENS E WOUNDED 7/4/1944

2069340 SAPPER TAYLOR H WOUNDED 7/4/1944

2161009 SAPPER TURNER J WOUNDED 7/4/1944[12]

188987 SAPPER TURNER RA WOUNDED 7/4/1944

130876 CAPTAIN WALSH. CHARLES PHILLIP AGE 25 DIED 7/4/1944
IMPHAL WAR CEMETERY

2016645 LANCE CORPORAL WARRILLOW. WILLIAM THOMAS
AGE 28 DIED 7/4/1944 IMPHAL WAR CEMETERY[13]

1427732 DRIVER WINESTEIN JS WOUNDED 5/4/1944

2119450 LANCE CORPORAL WRIGHT. CHRISTOPHER REGINALD
AGE 28 DIED 5/4/1944 RANGOON MEMORIAL[14]

864 MECHANICAL EQUIPMENT COMPANY ROYAL ENGINEERS

2152765 SAPPER ASQUITH GH WOUNDED 7/4/1944

2158608 DRIVER BOYNTON. ERNEST AGE 20 DIED 7/4/1944 IMPHAL
WAR CEMETERY[15]

2187820 DRIVER CORBYN. REGINALD FRANK AGE 33 DIED 7/4/1944
IMPHAL WAR CEMETERY

1574473 SAPPER CREW E WOUNDED 7/4/1944

6282216 LANCE CORPORAL CLIFTON JW WOUNDED 7/4/1944

164922 CORPORAL ELDRIDGE. DONALD ALAN AGE 24 DIED 7/4/1944
IMPHAL WAR CEMETERY[16]

2195934 LANCE CORPORAL FULKER CF WOUNDED 7/4/1944

70320 MAJOR GRAY O.B.E. TL WOUNDED 7/4/1944

2093977 SAPPER GWATKIN J WOUNDED 7/4/1944

2038448 CORPORAL LEWIS. HARRY WILLIAM AGE 24 DIED 7/4/1944
IMPHAL WAR CEMETERY[17]

2143354 SAPPER PAGE T WOUNDED 7/4/1944

---

11. Previously reported as missing, presumed killed.
12. Discharged from service due to wounds 19/3/1945.
13. Died of wounds in 19 Casualty Clearing Station.
14. Previously reported as missing, presumed killed.
15. Battlefield burial recovered and reburied in Imphal Cemetery 11/12/1944.
16. Previously reported as missing, presumed missing but was buried on the battlefield 7/4/1944 and was recovered and reburied in Imphal Cemetery 11/12/1944.
17. Originally buried in a battlefield grave 22/5/1944 and was recovered and reburied in Imphal Cemetery 11/12/1944. It is possible that Corporal Lewis's remains were found and first buried by British or Indian units when they took over positions in Kanglatongbi in May 1944. It

2076988 DRIVER PASTON TW WOUNDED 7/4/1944

103950 CAPTAIN PRITCHARD. NORMAN HOLMES AGE 38 DIED
8/4/1944 IMPHAL WAR CEMETERY[18]

1874302 SERGEANT RAWSON. JOHN DEWAR AGE 24 DIED 7/4/1944
RANGOON MEMORIAL[19]

14257853 SAPPER ROUSE R WOUNDED 7/4/1944

2145147 SAPPER WALKER GS WOUNDED 7/4/1944

2151529 LANCE CORPORAL WARDROP. JAMES AGE 26 DIED 7/4/1944
IMPHAL WAR CEMETERY

2151316 SAPPER WILKINS. THOMAS DOWNES AGE 39 DIED 7/4/1944
RANGOON MEMORIAL

2nd BATTALION WEST YORKSHIRE REGIMENT

3856187 PRIVATE BROWN F WOUNDED 7/4/1944

4542220 SERGEANT DEXTER F WOUNDED 7/4/1944

14509540 PRIVATE GILL G WOUNDED 7/4/1944

3713446 PRIVATE JOHNSTON GH WOUNDED 7/4/1944

13102166 PRIVATE LAWSON. JOHN OWEN AGE 35 DIED 5/4/1944
RANGOON MEMORIAL

5116030 PRIVATE MORRIS WT WOUNDED 7/4/1944

4621665 LANCE CORPORAL PARADINE FJ WOUNDED 7/4/1944

4541292 CORPORAL PEARSON W WOUNDED 5/4/1944[20]

308939 LIEUTENANT POCOCK. ALFRED MEREDITH AGED 27
DIED 6/4/1944 RANGOON MEMORIAL[21]

14222850 PRIVATE WALKER. JOSEPH AGE 20 DIED 6/4/1944
RANGOON MEMORIAL[22]

4547305 PRIVATE WATSON CD WOUNDED 7/4/1944

---

may be that he was either killed early during the fighting or later during the evacuation when his body couldn't be recovered, being in enemy-held territory.

18. Died of wounds received 7/4/1944 in 89 IGH. Captain Pritchard's younger brother John was killed in action 8/7/1944 serving in France with the Royal Warwickshire Regiment.

19. On attachment from 2 Field Company Royal Engineers.

20. Corporal Pearson recovered from his wounds but died four months later after contracting scrub typhus.

21. Previously reported as missing presumed killed. On attachment from the Lincolnshire Regiment.

22. Previously reported as missing presumed killed.

<u>**522 BATTERY 4th FIELD REGIMENT ROYAL ARTILLERY**</u>

1085231 GUNNER DOUGLAS J W WOUNDED 7/4/1944

<u>**INDIAN ARMY UNITS**</u>

<u>**302 GENERAL PURPOSE TRANSPORT COMPANY ROYAL INDIAN ARMY SERVICE CORPS**</u>

MTN 842049 SEPOY ABDUL JABAR AGE 20 DIED 7/4/1944
RANGOON MEMORIAL

MTN 833741 SEPOY ABDUL RAHMAN AGE 22 DIED 7/4/1944
RANGOON MEMORIAL

MTN 953143 NAIK BALDEV SAHAI AGE 21 DIED 7/4/1944
RANGOON MEMORIAL

MTN 980541 SEPOY BHIRAM PAL AGE 24 DIED 7/4/1944
RANGOON MEMORIAL

MTN 978187 SEPOY CHIRAGH DIN AGE 20 DIED 7/4/1944
RANGOON MEMORIAL

MTN768309 SEPOY DAULAT SHAH AGE 18 DIED 7/4/1944
RANGOON MEMORIAL

MTN 819227 SEPOY GAJ RAJ SINGH AGE 32 DIED 7/4/1944
RANGOON MEMORIAL

130288 MAJOR GREENBERRY M.B.E. LW WOUNDED 7/4/1944

MTN 764249 COOK HAZARA SINGH AGE 37 DIED 7/4/1944
RANGOON MEMORIAL

MTN 778198 SEPOY HIDAYAT ULLAH AGE 25 DIED 7/4/1944
RANGOON MEMORIAL

MTN 962089 SEPOY ISHWARI DATT AGE 24 DIED 7/4/1944
RANGOON MEMORIAL

MTN 791144 SEPOY KHAN MIR AGE 28 DIED 7/4/1944
RANGOON MEMORIAL

MTN 977265 SEPOY KISHAN LAL AGE 28 DIED 7/4/1944
RANGOON MEMORIAL

MTN SEPOY MAHABIR AGE 19 DIED 7/4/1944
RANGOON MEMORIAL

MTN 736884 SEPOY MATHURA AGE 30 DIED 7/4/1944
RANGOON MEMORIAL

MTN 950803 NAIK MIAN GUL AGE 30 DIED 9/4/1944
IMPHAL INDIAN ARMY WAR CEMETERY

MTN 842337 SEPOY MOTI MIAN AGE 23 DIED 7/4/1944
RANGOON MEMORIAL

MTN 782277 SEPOY MOHAMMAD MUSTAFA AGE 23 DIED 7/4/1944
RANGOON MEMORIAL

MTN 980627 SEPOY MUNSHI AGE 24 DIED 7/4/1944
RANGOON MEMORIAL

MTN 749448 SEPOY PAHLAD AGE 20 DIED 7/4/1944
RANGOON MEMORIAL

MTN 980516 SEPOY PARSHADI AGE 30 DIED 7/4/1944
RANGOON MEMORIAL

MTN 832612 SEPOY RAM DEV RAM AGE 32 DIED 7/4/1944
RANGOON MEMORIAL

MTN 927599 HAVILDAR RAM SARAN DAS AGE 24 DIED 7/4/1944
RANGOON MEMORIAL

MTN 750633 SEPOY SHANKAR LAL AGE 28 DIED 7/4/1944
RANGOON MEMORIAL

MTN 980006 SEPOY SHEO SINGH AGE 24 DIED 7/4/1944
RANGOON MEMORIAL

MTN 980342 LANCE NAIK SOHAN LAL AGE 24 DIED 7/4/1944
RANGOON MEMORIAL

MTN 978871 SEPOY SUKHA RAM AGE 29 DIED 7/4/1944
RANGOON MEMORIAL

17 WOUNDED 7/4/1944

137 GENERAL PURPOSE TRANSPORT COMPANY ROYAL INDIAN ARMY SERVICE CORPS[23]

MTN 780428 SEPOY ABDUL HAKIM AGE 30 DIED 1/7/1944
RANGOON MEMORIAL

MTN 995324 SEPOY ABDUL KARIM AGE 28 DIED 1/7/1944
RANGOON MEMORIAL

MTN 779771 NAIK AIMAL KHAN AGE 20 DIED 10/4/1944
RANGOON MEMORIAL

MTN 779594 SEPOY AKRAM KHAN AGE 20 DIED 1/7/1944
RANGOON MEMORIAL

MTN 790991 SEPOY ALAM KHAN AGE 18 DIED 1/7/1944
RANGOON MEMORIAL

MTN 996459 SEPOY ALLAH DITTA AGE 19 DIED 1/7/1944
RANGOON MEMORIAL

---

23. These men were reported as missing by 137 GPT Company after the Lion Box evacuation and were later captured by the Japanese. Thirteen men were executed on 10/4/1944 and a further eleven men from this list of the missing are commemorated by the CWGC as all having died on 1/7/1944.

MTN 780799 SEPOY CHANAN MUHAMMAD DIED 1/7/1944
RANGOON MEMORIAL

MTN 779565 LANCE NAIK FIROZ KHAN AGE 19 DIED 10/4/1944
RANGOON MEMORIAL

MTN 779640 SEPOY GHAFUR DIED 10/4/1944
RANGOON MEMORIAL

MTN 974376 NAIK GHULAM SAYID AGE 21 DIED 1/7/1944
RANGOON MEMORIAL

MTN 768197 SEPOY MARDAN ALI AGE 28 DIED 10/4/1944
RANGOON MEMORIAL

MTN 780752 LANCE NAIK MUHAMMAD ANWAR AGE 20 DIED 1/7/1944
RANGOON MEMORIAL

MTN 780639 SEPOY MUHAMMAD ASGHAR AGE 25 DIED 10/4/1944
RANGOON MEMORIAL

MTN 780507 SEPOY MUHAMMAD FIROZ AGE 22 DIED 10/4/1944
RANGOON MEMORIAL

MTN 811799 SEPOY MUHAMMAD SADIQ DIED 10/4/1944
RANGOON MEMORIAL

MTN 983653 LANCE NAIK MUHAMMAD SHARIF AGE 22 DIED 1/7/1944
RANGOON MEMORIAL

MTN 779555 SEPOY NAWAZ KHAN AGE 28 DIED 1/7/1944
RANGOON MEMORIAL

MTN 779624 LANCE NAIK NUR MUHAMMAD AGE 23 DIED 1/7/1944
RANGOON MEMORIAL

MTN 779997 SEPOY NUR MUHAMMAD AGE 23 DIED 10/4/1944
RANGOON MEMORIAL

MTN 974269 SEPOY SAIN KHAN AGE 27 DIED 10/4/1944
RANGOON MEMORIAL

MTN 952393 HAVILDAR SARDAR ALI AGE 20 DIED 10/4/1944
RANGOON MEMORIAL

MTN 827853 SEPOY SHAKUR MUHAMMAD AGE 29 DIED 10/4/1944
RANGOON MEMORIAL

MTN 780728 LANCE NAIK WARIS KHAN AGE 18 DIED 10/4/1944
RANGOON MEMORIAL

MTN 780795 SEPOY YAQUB KHAN AGE 18 DIED 10/4/1944
RANGOON MEMORIAL

MTN 975131 SEPOY MOHD KHAN WOUNDED 10/4/1944
1 WOUNDED 29/3/1944

1341 COMPANY INDIAN PIONEER CORPS

28872 PIONEER BHIRAN PATRO AGE 18 DIED 7/4/1944
RANGOON MEMORIAL

272407 PIONEER BRIJ BASI BISWAS AGE 35 DIED 7/4/1944
RANGOON MEMORIAL

273576 PIONEER GAUR CHANDRA MURARI AGE 21 DIED 7/4/1944
RANGOON MEMORIAL

272392 PIONEER KASU DAS AGE 20, DIED 7/4/1944
RANGOON MEMORIAL

21262 PIONEER MADHAV DOURI AGE 24 DIED 7/4/1944
RANGOON MEMORIAL

272384 PIONEER MOTI RAM DAS AGE 23 DIED 7/4/1944
RANGOON MEMORIAL

21696 PIONEER SURESH CHANDRA DAS AGE 26 DIED 7/4/1944
RANGOON MEMORIAL

20 REINFORCEMENT CAMP

19660 RIFLEMAN CHANDRA BAHADUR KHATTRI AGE 32 DIED
7/4/1944 (3rd/1st KING GEORGE V's OWN GURKHA RIFLES (THE MALAUN
REGIMENT)) RANGOON MEMORIAL

3856363 PRIVATE HOWARD. WILLIAM JOHN AGE 25 DIED 7/4/1944
(2nd BORDER REGIMENT) RANGOON MEMORIAL[24]

19573/1 SEPOY MUHAMMAD SARWAR AGE 18 DIED 7/4/1944
(9th/12th FRONTIER FORCE REGIMENT) RANGOON MEMORIAL

20588 SEPOY MAWAZ KHAN AGE 21 DIED 5/4/1944 (9th/12th FRONTIER
FORCE REGIMENT) IMPHAL INDIAN ARMY CEMETERY

13003 SEPOY MARIMUTHU AGE 24 DIED 7/4/1944 (4th/3rd MADRAS
REGIMENT) RANGOON MEMORIAL

19710 RIFLEMAN TEK BAHADUR GHARTI AGE 30 DIED 7/4/1944
(3rd/1st KING GEORGE V's OWN GURKHA RIFLES (THE MALAUN
REGIMENT)) RANGOON MEMORIAL

1 WOUNDED 5/4/1944

1 WOUNDED 6/4/1944

528 ARTISAN WORKS COMPANY INDIAN ENGINEERS

93204 SAPPER BATTAN SAHA AGE 23 DIED 5/4/1944 IMPHAL
CREMATION MEMORIAL

---

24. On attachment from the 2nd Border Regiment.

94666 SAPPER BENGALI MISTRI AGE 20 DIED 5/4/1944
IMPHAL CREMATION MEMORIAL

E88779 SAPPER DURYAMAN AGE 27 DIED 7/4/1944
RANGOON MEMORIAL

E80518 HAVILDAR JAMIL HUSAIN AGE 21 DIED 9/4/1944
IMPHAL INDIAN ARMY CEMETERY

93203 SAPPER KESHWAR BHAGAT AGE 26 DIED 6/4/1944
IMPHAL CREMATION MEMORIAL

2 WOUNDED

46 GENERAL PURPOSE TRANSPORT COMPANY ROYAL INDIAN ARMY SERVICE CORPS

MTN 984870 SEPOY BHAGWAN DIN AGE 22 DIED 7/4/1944
RANGOON MEMORIAL

MTS 836275 SEPOY KUTTAN PILLAI DIED 7/4/1944
RANGOON MEMORIAL

MTS 984934 SEPOY RAMA GHARAT AGE 23 DIED 7/4/1944
RANGOON MEMORIAL

SR/206361 LANCE NAIK VELAYUDHAN NAIR AGE 19 DIED 9/4/1944
IMPHAL CREMATION MEMORIAL[25]

27th BATALLION 5th MAHRATTA LIGHT INFANTRY

8514 SEPOY BABU KATE AGE 49 DIED 7/4/1944
RANGOON MEMORIAL

26100 SEPOY SHIVA DHURI AGE 30 DIED 7/4/1944
RANGOON MEMORIAL

19499 SEPOY DATTU JAGTAP AGE 30 DIED 7/4/1944
RANGOON MEMORIAL

517 ARTISAN WORKS COMPANY INDIAN ENGINEERS

109 NAIK AMAR SINGH AGE 30 DIED 7/4/1944
RANGOON MEMORIAL

886526 SAPPER HUKAM SINGH AGE 27 DIED 7/4/1944
IMPHAL CREMATION MEMORIAL

82019 SAPPER SIKANDER SHAH DIED 8/4/1944
RANGOON MEMORIAL[26]

6 WOUNDED 7/4/1944

25. Died of wounds received 7/4/1944.
26. Reported Missing 7/4/1944.

<u>221 ADVANCED ORDNANCE DEPOT INDIAN ARMY ORDNANCE CORPS</u>

288287 LANCE SERGEANT CAMPBELL. DAVID ALEXANDER AGE 23 DIED 7/4/1944 (1st SEAFORTH HIGHLANDERS) IMPHAL WAR CEMETERY[27]

3650648 PRIVATE LAWTON. MARK JAMES AGE 32 DIED 7/4/1944 (2nd SOUTH LANCASHIRE REGIMENT) IMPHAL WAR CEMETERY[28]

6098645 PRIVATE SILK J WOUNDED 7/4/1944[29]

1 WOUNDED 5/4/1944

1 WOUNDED 7/4/1944

<u>43 GENERAL PURPOSE TRANSPORT COMPANY ROYAL INDIAN ARMY SERVICE CORPS</u>

MTN 807267 SEPOY SHIV RAJ AGE 23 DIED 31/3/1944 IMPHAL CREMATION MEMORIAL[30]

MTN 980693 NAIK SULTAN MUHAMMAD AGE 21 DIED 7/4/1944 RANGOON MEMORIAL

1 WOUNDED 7/4/1944

<u>323 BULK PETROL TRANSPORT COMPANY ROYAL INDIAN ARMY SERVICE CORPS</u>

MTN 826385 SEPOY PHUL KHAN AGE 21 DIED 29/3/1944 RANGOON MEMORIAL

1 DIED 7/4/1944[31]

<u>242 GENERAL PURPOSE TRANSPORT COMPANY ROYAL INDIAN ARMY SERVICE CORPS</u>

MTS 758874 SEPOY VIRAN AGE 27 DIED 29/3/1944 RANGOON MEMORIAL

1 WOUNDED

---

27. On attachment from the 1st Seaforth Highlanders.
28. Buried in a battlefield grave and reburied in Imphal Cemetery 11/12/1944.
29. On attachment from the 1st Seaforth Highlanders.
30. Accidentally shot while at morning stand-to. Another example of how unsafe the Sten gun was.
31. Not possible to positively identify exact unit of RIASC.

HEADQUARTERS 5th INDIAN DIVISION

IA/16 LIEUTENANT COLONEL MACLAURIN M.B.E. HENRY NORMAND AGE 40 DIED 7/4/1944 (1st DUKE OF YORK'S OWN CAVALRY (SKINNER'S HORSE)) IMPHAL WAR CEMETERY

652 MECHANICAL EXCAVATION COMPANY INDIAN ENGINEERS

102765 SAPPER TARA DATT AGE 18 DIED 7/4/1944
2 WOUNDED

X COMPANY MACHINE GUN BATTALION 9th JAT REGIMENT

10838 LANCE NAIK BHIM SINGH AGE 25 DIED 7/4/1944
RANGOON MEMORIAL
4 WOUNDED 7/4/1944

90 GENERAL PURPOSE TRANSPORT COMPANY ROYAL INDIAN ARMY SERVICE CORPS

969170 SEPOY APPA HIPPARAGE AGE 22 DIED 7/4/1944
RANGOON MEMORIAL

1330 COMPANY INDIAN PIONEER CORPS

319279 PIONEER DEO RAM PANDIT AGE 30 DIED 7/4/1944
RANGOON MEMORIAL
2 WOUNDED 7/4/1944

4th BATTALION ASSAM RIFLES

6 WOUNDED 7/4/1944[32]

1390 COMPANY INDIAN PIONEER CORPS

2 WOUNDED 5/4/1944

---

32. Unit war diary states one killed but only the 3rd Assam Rifles are on CWGC records.

<u>**1351 COMPANY INDIAN PIONEER CORPS**</u>

1 WOUNDED 4/4/1944

<u>**1391 COMPANY INDIAN PIONEER CORPS**</u>

1 WOUNDED 5/4/1944

<u>**167 GENERAL PURPOSE TRANSPORT COMPANY ROYAL INDIAN ARMY SERVICE CORPS**</u>

1 WOUNDED[33]

<u>**99 MOBILE WORKSHOP COMPANY INDIAN ELECTRICAL MECHANICAL ENGINEERS**</u>

WATER CARRIER MAJID WOUNDED 6/4/1944

<u>**8th SIKH BATTALION INDIAN ENGINEERS**</u>

1 WOUNDED 5/4/1944

<u>**440 QUARRYING COMPANY INDIAN ENGINEERS**</u>

1 WOUNDED 5/4/1944

* * *

BRITISH TROOPS 30 DIED 43 WOUNDED
INDIAN TROOPS 85 DIED 45 WOUNDED
<u>TOTAL</u> 115 DIED 88 WOUNDED

<u>**IMPERIAL JAPANESE ARMY CASUALTIES**</u>

T. ISHIKAWA (OFFICER), M. INAHARA (OFFICER), G. YAMAGUCHI (OFFICER), K. TANAKA (OFFICER), T. BABA (OFFICER), H. YAMAMOTO (OFFICER), K. MOTIZUKI, J. YOSHIMURA, M. GOTOH, S. ASHIDA, C. HASHIMOTO, M. SATOH, Y. JYAKUBO, T. ITIKI, S. OHABAYASHI,

---

33. Accidentally shot.

N. CHIAKI, T. TANIGUCHI, Y. TANIGAWA, Y. YAGI, H. IWASAKI,
Y. YAMAMOTO, C. TAKAYAMA, N. NISIHIKI, S. INOUYE, E. HASHIMOTO,
S. USHIJIMA, I. FUJII, M. TUJI, T. AKAI, H. ADACHI, Y. OGAWA, S. YMADA,
N. KASUDA, J. HIROSE, N. SASAKI, U. SHIMIZU, G. ISODA, H. NISHIMURA,
Y. USHIDA, M. ADACHI, K. IDE, K. NISHIMURA, T. OZAKI, E. MORISHITA,
Y. HIRATE, I. TADA, M. TAKAYA, T. OHE, K. NAGAI, T. TUJIMOTO, I. MORI,
T. SHIMIZU, J. HASHIDA, Y. HIRAKI, S. KOMORI, S. TAKAI, S. AND,
N. SASAMURA, S. NAKAGAWA, C. AKIDA, S. HIROTA, Y. NAKAGAWA,
S. OKUDA, I. KAMATA, M. FUJIWARA, S. TOHYAMA, F. NISHOIKA, F. SUE,
K. KOBAYASHI, Y. ASAHINA, S. IKEDA, T. YAMAMOTO, Y. NAKANO,
S. OHNISHI.
TOTAL: APPROXIMATELY 74 DIED, UNKNOWN NUMBER WOUNDED.[34]

---

34. Alternative Japanese figures suggest that 145 were killed in the Kanglatongbi area.

Appendix Two

Awards and Battle Honours, and Lack of Recognition

The awarding of medals and decorations has always been and probably always will be a contentious issue. For some people, a certain man is a hero, while for others, the same man was just doing his duty in the job for which he was trained. Whatever viewpoint is taken, one thing is agreed upon, namely, a person must be in the right place, at the right time and be 'seen' to have performed an act deserving of recognition or reward. It is human nature to feel valued and respected within a given peer group and the rewarding of deeds of heroism is an important aspect that binds all men and military units. Very few men go into battle with the intention of winning a medal. It is thrust upon them as they rise to the occasion. As with all battles, the one at Lion Box had its share of recognised acts of bravery and exceptional service. However, and without doubt, its share of acts that went unnoticed or unrecorded went unrewarded. Others had their deeds noted but still went unrewarded, such as, for example: the unnamed Indian sapper who stayed at his post throughout the night despite his serious wounds; Captain Young, a medical officer, crawling out under fire to tend the wounded; Sergeant Campbell's gallant Bren gun charge that no doubt thwarted further Japanese incursions into the box; CSM Johnson's mercy killing of his mortally wounded runner while under fire, described as a very brave act by his officer; Private Parsons, the ordnance librarian, tending the wounded; and the two unnamed ordnance havildar clerk/storemen who maintained the telephone exchange throughout the action despite being in an exposed position. Another who received no official recognition for his exceptional commitment is Padre Brock. Though certainly no military man, his work in supporting the troops, often under fire, during which time he shared all their fears and discomforts, was invaluable and none more so than when he attended the wounded and sick in hospital later during the siege.

There, Padre Brock not only served their spiritual needs but also tended to their personal needs and worries as only a friend and confidant can do. His dedication and compassion were all the more remarkable given the fact that he as a civilian did not have to be there, and he had actually turned down the offer of evacuation to a safer place in India several times.

All these individual acts and many more besides emphasise the lottery of receiving awards, but one appalling – and which this author believes to be a disgraceful – omission stands head and shoulders above the rest, and that is the lack of any official recognition whatsoever for the Box Commander, Lieutenant Colonel Victor Henry Wells-Cole, MC. Having successfully evacuated the entire personnel of Lynx Box (several thousand strong) into Lion Box through 8 miles of enemy-patrolled territory, without serious mishap or casualties, is in itself worthy of recognition let alone his command of the defence of Lion Box for six days, three of which were under constant heavy attack. Despite the inexperienced and disparate composition of his garrison, Lieutenant Colonel Wells-Cole controlled the successful defence and evacuation of the largest Ordnance Depot on the Imphal Plain. While a feat nowhere near on par with the famed and much written about Battle of the Admin Box in the Arakan a few weeks earlier, it is still one that could have gone horribly wrong and would have been very costly in terms of men and materials during this crucial period. In a letter written from General Sir Charles P. Deedes, KCB, CMG, DSO (Colonel of the Regiment, King's Own Yorkshire Light Infantry) to Lieutenant Colonel Wells-Cole just a month after the war had ended, he noted: 'You continuously had a most difficult task, and I had no idea what an untrained and unorganised party you had. You must have had an unpleasant hour when the Japs got into the R.E. Sector. **I think your superiors might have given you more credit for what you did.'**[1]

Another letter also written just after the war, by Lieutenant Colonel Wells-Cole's former adjutant, Major Andrew Charles, who had served with Wells-Cole for two and a half years, commented: 'He really has been treated badly both in the matter of promotion and his postings. I do think that when one compares his ability with other senior officers there is no doubt, he has missed his niche in the Army due to the extraordinary ideas of promotions adopted by the Army.'

---

1. Author's emphasis in bold.

In addition, Lieutenant Colonel Wells-Cole's vital work overseeing the change of role of the 7th Battalion King's Own Yorkshire Light Infantry to that of an armoured unit, 149 Regiment Royal Armoured Corps, who famously fought at Kohima, went unrecognised, as did his service as commanding officer of 20 Reinforcement Camp. For two years, he ensured that 20 Indian Division were always supplied with well-trained reinforcements of a calibre befitting this formidable formation. This author can only assume that he must have stepped on the toes of some senior officers somewhere along the line during his long career. It is ironic to think that he would have put forward the names of those he thought being worthy of recognition whilst receiving nothing himself.

The above in no way takes anything from the bravery and exceptional service of the following individual recipients whose deeds are a testament of the action at Lion Box and can be seen as a recognition of all those who served there at Lion Box Kanglatongbi.

CITATIONS AS PER THE *LONDON GAZETTE*

183594 W/S CAPTAIN. T/MAJOR JOHN PETER MACBRYDE BOYD, RAOC. 221 ADVANCED ORDNANCE DEPOT, INDIAN ARMY ORDNANCE CORPS

At Kanglatongbi on 7/4/44, this Officer displayed courage and leadership of an exceptionally high standard. At 05.30 hours when the Japanese infiltrated into the NW Sector of the perimeter, he organised and led a small party of about 15 WO's, Sergeants and LMC BORs of this unit against the enemy. He succeeded in driving the enemy back and re-establishing the position. Later, he drove back a second Japanese attack. He held the position under heavy fire, until relieved at 14.00 hours. Due to his example and leadership, he succeeded in preventing a very serious situation and inflicted heavy casualties on the enemy with proportionately small casualties to his own men. His courage, determination and energy were largely responsible for the high performance of his party.

Awarded MILITARY CROSS
London Gazette, 27/7/44

130130 2nd LT. W/S LT. T/CAPTAIN. ACTING MAJOR KEITH THORNTON D'AWRE BAKER, RA. 28 FIELD REGIMENT, ROYAL ARTILLERY

Throughout the period May 1944 to August 1944 A/Major K.T.D'A. Baker RA has been in command of and commanding a mortar battery. During operations the battery has been split up with troops and sections as many as 20 miles apart. His example of leadership and devotion to duty has been of the highest order. His efforts have been untiring in ensuring the closest co-operation with the other arms, continually visiting his battery's positions and the FDIs.

In particular at Kanglatongbi on the Kohima road, Major Baker's battery was hurriedly placed to defend an area held only by admin units. By his quick appreciation of the situation and deployment of his mortars, the position was held whilst stores were evacuated over a period of three days. Throughout this action the position was under considerable mortar and MG fire and Major Baker was a constant source of encouragement both to his own troops and the admin troops with whom he had to fight. His gallant actions here and throughout these operations contributed largely to the success achieved.

His ability to overcome difficulties under arduous conditions of climate and terrain and his example and work have been of the highest order.

Awarded MILITARY CROSS
London Gazette, 28/6/45
Mentioned in Despatches
London Gazette, 10/01/46

Captain Baker, MC's medals.

194585 W/CAPTAIN (T/MAJOR) ALEC CHARLES DUNLOP (W/E COMMISSION) 2nd BATTALION THE WEST YORKSHIRE REGIMENT

Since the commencement of the campaign Major Dunlop has been in command of a company which has taken a leading part in almost every action in which the battalion has been engaged. In the early stages he carried out a particularly gallant attack in Nyaungyaung, Arakan. Later during the defence of 7 Division Admin Box, his company was called on incessantly for counter attacks, patrols and action in cooperation with tanks, finally being reduced to the strength of one platoon. Latterly the company has done some very useful work in mopping-up operations in conjunction with tanks, and in the final evacuation in the face of the enemy in the Kanglatongbi (Imphal) Box. On all occasions Major Dunlop has shown a calm fearlessness and a complete grip of the situation. This, combined with his painstaking preliminary training and organisation of his company, has made all his operations successful, and his company, in spite of heavy losses, and wear and tear of six months fighting, has maintained a consistently high standard.

Awarded MILITARY CROSS

London Gazette, 8/2/45

10537437 W/S CONDUCTOR RONALD WRIGHT PARKER, RAOC. 221 ADVANCED ORDNANCE DEPOT, INDIAN ARMY ORDNANCE CORPS

Throughout the operation at Kanglatongbi between 29 March and 7 April 1944, Conductor R.W. Parker invariably showed exemplary courage and resource. He especially distinguished himself in action at Kanglatongbi on 7 April 1944. The enemy were attacking Lion Box and had penetrated into the Box on the western perimeter over-running an ME Coy and setting up an LMG post on 221 AOD perimeter.

During his patrol's counterattack, Conductor Parker, on his own initiative and in the face of heavy LMG fire, organised a party of one BOR and two IORs to attack a Japanese LMG post established in a basha and from which a BOR had shouted for help. Conductor Parker succeeded in retaking the basha thereby rescuing one wounded BOR and recovering the bodies of two dead BORs. Three Japanese ORs were killed by Conductor Parker's party in this action alone.

Awarded MILITARY MEDAL
London Gazette, 5/10/44

1196 W/S HAVILDAR/CLERK/STORES BASANT SINGH, IAOC. 221 ADVANCED ORDNANCE DEPOT, INDIAN ARMY ORDNANCE CORPS

At Kanglatongbi on 7/4/44, he displayed exemplary devotion to duty. He remained at his post from 01.30 hours to 14.00 hours when he was relieved. During this period, he was continually under heavy fire. When the Japanese infiltrated into the NW Sector of the perimeter, regardless of danger to himself, he stood on a pillbox and operated a Bren gun for over fifteen minutes. His action was largely instrumental in driving the Japanese back. Later, accompanied by two BORs and one IOR he led an attack against a Japanese MG post, which he knocked out, killing three Japanese. His bearing throughout the engagement was of a very high order and was an example to all ranks.

Awarded INDIAN DISTINGUISHED SERVICE MEDAL
London Gazette, 27/7/44

The following officer was awarded the Distinguished Service Order for his Meritorious and Distinguished Services during the Burma Campaign, which would also have included his involvement in the action at Lion Box Kanglatongbi.

30831 LIEUTENANT COLONEL GERALD HILARY 'MUNSHIE' CREE, 2nd BATTALION. WEST YORKSHIRE REGIMENT.

The following officers were awarded the Most Excellent Order of the British Empire for Gallant and Distinguished Services during the Burma Campaign, which would also have included their involvement in the action at Lion Box Kanglatongbi.

130288 LIEUTENANT COLONEL LESLIE WILLIAM GREENBERRY, ROYAL INDIAN ARMY SERVICE CORPS.

183374 LIEUTENANT COLONEL FREDERICK DONALD PEACOCK, INDIAN ENGINEERS.

The following officers and other ranks were Mentioned in Despatches in recognition of their Gallant or Distinguished Services during the Burma Campaign, which would also have included their involvement in the action at Lion Box Kanglatongbi.

IA/557 LIEUTENANT COLONEL HERBERT IAN CUNNINGHAM, INDIAN ARMY ORDNANCE CORPS.

121020 LIEUTENANT COLONEL EDWARD STYRING FIELD, ROYAL ARMY SERVICE CORPS.

IA/16 LIEUTENANT COLONEL HENRY NORMAND MACLAURIN MBE, 1st DUKE OF YORK'S OWN CAVALRY (SKINNER'S HORSE).

109320 MAJOR JOCELYN WILLIAM MAXIM ALEXANDER, ROYAL ENGINEERS.

70320 MAJOR THOMAS LINDSAY GRAY OBE, ROYAL ENGINEERS.

163100 MAJOR HERBERT JAMES WILLIAM SCANES, PIONEER CORPS ATTACHED 15th PUNJAB REGIMENT

176002 CAPTAIN DENNIS GRANVILLE BUCKINGHAM, ROYAL NORFOLK REGIMENT ATTACHED INDIAN ARMY ORDNANCE CORPS.

1467 CAPTAIN EDWARD CORNELIUS HUBBARD, INDIAN ARMY ORDNANCE CORPS.

4201 CAPTAIN BRIAN HOPE WINSTANLEY, 14th PUNJAB REGIMENT.

242336 LIEUTENANT JOHN ALLAN COLE, ROYAL ARMOURED CORPS ATTACHED 3rd PRINCE OF WALES DRAGOON GUARDS (CARABINIERS).

151782 LIEUTENANT KEITH FREDERICK DORMAN, ROYAL ENGINEERS.

LIEUTENANT RICHARD STEWART BIDDULPH MADELEY, INDIAN ENGINEERS.

184709 LIEUTENANT GEORGE BAZELY SCURFIELD, ROYAL ARTILLERY ATTACHED 'V' FORCE.

2007 LIEUTENANT JOSEPH ROSS SEVERN, INDIAN ARMOURED CORPS ATTACHED INDIAN ENGINEERS.

227671 LIEUTENANT JOHN COOPER SOMERVILLE, ROYAL ENGINEERS.

797522 WARRANT OFFICER CLASS 1, EUGENE CHARLES FRENCH, ROYAL ARMY ORDNANCE CORPS.

7622498 WARRANT OFFICER CLASS 1, CHARLES SLANEY, ROYAL ARMY ORDNANCE CORPS.

4541292 CORPORAL WALTER PEARSON, 2nd BATTALION WEST YORKSHIRE REGIMENT.

7945760 TROOPER MALCOLM LEONARD CONNOLLY, 3rd PRINCE OF WALES DRAGOON GUARDS (CARABINIERS).

Final observations

If it were still possible to talk to those who fought at Lion Box, they would almost certainly to a man say it was indeed a battle (and a bloody one at that), but sadly there is no official battle honour of Lion Box. There is, however, the Battle Honour of Kanglatongbi, which was awarded to those units who 'took part in this subsidiary action, which covers the fight to re-capture Kanglatongbi, and all the operations up the Imphal–Kohima road, until contact was made with 2nd Division'. This is for the period from 21 April to 22 June 1944 only, which does *not* include the dates covering the action at Lion Box. Three British regiments and four Indian regiments were awarded the Battle Honour Kanglatongbi, of which some elements of the three actually fought at Lion Box as well: 3rd Carabiniers (Prince of Wales Dragoon Guards), 2nd Battalion West Yorkshire Regiment, and 3rd/9th Battalion Jat Regiment. (The other four regiments who were not present at Lion Box were 2nd Battalion King's Own Scottish Borderers, 3rd/2nd Battalion Punjab Regiment, 1st/11th Battalion Sikh Regiment, and 4th/8th Gurkha Rifles.)

Because of post-war defence reorganisations, these three British regiments no longer exist in name, swallowed up into larger formations upon amalgamation. Of their descendant regiments, only one still has emblazoned on the regimental colours the Battle Honour of Kanglatongbi, which is the Royal Scots Dragoon Guards, formed in 1971 with the amalgamation of the Royal Scots Greys and the 3rd Carabiniers.

ARMY ORDNANCE CORPS RAISING DAY

The present-day Army Ordnance Corps of the Indian Army can trace their history right back to the eighteenth century, when the British East India Company first realised the need for the proper support of an ordnance department due to its military expansion. A Board of Ordnance was raised on 8 April 1775 under the control of the Bengal Presidency, but by the 1870s, the British Crown influence in India had increased so much that in 1884 the Ordnance Department of India came into being.

Although not a battle honour or award, Raising Day is still commemorated and celebrated each year on 8 April by the AOC when the battle at Lion Box Kanglatongbi is remembered as its finest hour, when men of the RAOC and IAOC stood shoulder to shoulder, not only during the fighting, but also with their diligent work ensuring their vital stores were protected and continued to be issued to those dependant on them.

Presentation of a cast bronze plaque to senior officers of the Ordnance Corps from the Lion Cubs of Kanglatongbi.

Appendix Three

Discovering the Second World War in Manipur

Research, Discovery, Excavation, and Commemoration
Report by Rajeshwor Yumnam, MPhil (NET), Research Historian

Abstract

The Imphal Campaign was a critical turning point in the Burma Campaign, marking a significant Allied victory over Japanese forces. This paper focuses on the joint activities and research collaboration between this author and Christopher Johnson on the various battlefields in Manipur pertaining to Second World War, which in a short span of time change the awareness landscape of the Burma Campaign in general, and the Imphal Campaign in particular. Maps, war diaries, personal memoirs and various official and personal documents were used by both the researchers while finding various battlefield locations and the recording thereof.

Introduction

The author met Christopher over a review of his book in an online portal called 'Kanglaonline'. The author asked if he could get a copy of the book and Christopher generously sent a copy of the book by post. Through email they got to know each other and their common interest in finding new things brought them closer. It was in August of 2009 when the initial contact was made and within a few months, they were synchronised and started discovering many battlefield sites which were previously unaware to the public mass in general. Books were sent by Christopher to the author which were not available then in Imphal. After reading those relevant books, the author started exploring the battle sites after doing proper research on map and Google Earth. Other than battlefield research, both were keen in remembering the soldiers who died during the conflict as well. Remembrance Sunday was first observed by the author in Imphal War Cemetery in 2009 after due instruction and briefing with proper programme planning from Christopher.

First exploration of Kanglatongbi Battlefield

It was 2009, the author laid his first floral tribute at the Kanglatongbi War Memorial on the Remembrance Sunday after due explanation of the significance by Christopher. After that Christopher sent battle details and locations with stories of the soldiers. With that information the author wanted to conduct expeditions to excavate and see relics of the war. Locations were identified on the ground and first excavation was conducted by the author and his friends. The excavation was covered as news programme by Mr Prem Sharma, a good friend of the author who was working with ISTV (a local TV channel) then. The author and his team of friends found lots of artefacts from a single dig, and important locations on the ground were identified. The news programme broadcast a new interest to the viewers, and a significant aspect of the history of the region was highlighted with the single excavation and the programme. The relics were taken home by the author and later washed and preserved, before their eventual deposit in the developing Imphal War Museum.

Sangshak battlefield and the documentary film

The author was working with a mobile telecom company when he found Christopher. He travelled to the interior inside the villages in Manipur for Mobile Tower survey. He also was looking after USO (Universal Service Obligation) project. It was the Indian Government Project where private telecom companies were made mandatory to provide telecom network to very remote places where road and communication was minimal during that period. For this project, the author was, for most of the time, in interior villages, travelling from one village after another in his modified Jeep (made as lookalike to 1942 Willys Jeep). It was during this period that the author was introduced to the Sangshak Battle by the book *The Battle of Sangshak* by Harry Seaman which was gifted by Christopher. During his official work the author visited Sangshak many times and studied the battle location of Sangshak with the help of the book. Online co-ordination was made with Christopher during the research through emails. The author thought it was very important to record what they were doing, and he hired a camera crew to record the activity on the battlefield. Later the documentary was released by the title *Battle of Sangshak*. It was first released in Imphal in 2010 on 26 March, the battle day of Sangshak. The author was introduced to many veterans of Sangshak Battle and mention may be made of veterans like Basil Seaton, Maurice Bell, Bill MacKay and others, who helped the author in completing his documentary film. All these veterans became very good friends of the author until they left for their heavenly abode.

Exploration and excavation of Isaac

A peak codenamed Isaac during the conflict, located east of present-day Motbung, was an important battlefield. Part of the Japanese 15th Division which disturbed the movement of soldiers at the national highway (Imphal–Dimapur road) were stationed at Isaac and nearby areas. They harassed the Allied troops moving along the highway. In June 1944, tanks were used to attack the Japanese force up on the peak. A tank was destroyed, and later during his research, pictures of the tank taken during the war were sent to Christopher by a veteran named Malcolm Connolly. Finding the location where the picture was taken was very important. So, the author and his team went up the mountain to find the peak Isaac. After two explorations, the location was found where the picture of the destroyed tank was taken. The location was confirmed with the mountain contour at the background of the picture. On that day when Isaac was discovered, Christopher was all the time guiding the author and his team through online video call. Later in April 2014, when Christopher came to Imphal, the author took him and his friends from the UK to Isaac, to witness the bunkers and foxholes present at that battle site. The team excavated the battlefield that day and found many remains of the war. The relics recovered that day were washed and preserved at the Imphal War Museum as well.

Establishment of Imphal War Museum

With excavations from various battlefields in Manipur, the author's house was piling up with relics. The author joined hands with his friend Mr Arambam Angamba and started designing and constructing the 'Imphal War Museum' during later part of 2013. An organisation called Second World War Imphal Campaign Foundation was established and registered. Under the banner of the organisation, the Imphal War Museum was established at the residence of Mr Angamba. The Museum displays collected items from various battlefields and relics bought by Mr Angamba and the author from various interior villages. The museum was later inaugurated by Christopher Johnson in April 2014, to mark the 70th anniversary commemoration of Battle of Imphal. The Museum now has visitors from around the globe. Many inspired students from various schools, college and university throng to make study of the Burma Campaign. The museum also contains various maps and personal artefacts donated by generous families of the soldiers from both sides of the conflict.

Discovery of Runaway Hill

Runaway Hill was an important position during the Imphal Campaign. A soldier of the 3/9 Jat Regiment named Abdul Hafiz received posthumously the most coveted Victoria Cross for his raw valour while fighting and simultaneously encouraging his fellow soldiers to attack a Japanese position. He was the first Indian Muslim to receive a Victoria Cross. The story was known to many scholars and veterans, but none of the books available ever mentioned the exact location where the hill was located. Most of the books mentioned it was at the northern end of Nungshigum hill range. It was a map which Christopher found showing the various jurisdiction and patrolling boundaries of adjoining regiments and battalions that Runaway Hill was marked. The author with his friends scaled the position on a hot sunny day of 20 July 2013. When they reach the highest point, they found dug in positions and various spent cartridges and personal artifacts. Excavations were done the whole day and relics were later brought for preservation at Imphal War Museum. Christopher and the author confirmed that it was the Runaway Hill.

Discovery of first battlefield of the Second World War in India

The Japanese 15 Army crossed the Chindwin and launched an all-out attack on the allied force in India on 15 March 1944. The operation was named U-Go. First, they entered the Ukhrul District in Manipur and reached Pushing, a border village on 17 March. When the Japanese three divisions crossed the Chindwin River and attacked Imphal and Kohima (Operation U-Go), the first engagement in Indian soil with the Japanese tidal wave was encountered by C Company 152 Indian Para Battalion under Major J. Fuller at Point 7378, Ukhrul, Manipur on 19 March 1944. 152 Indian Para Battalion was under the command of Brigadier Hope Thomson's 50th Para Brigade.

In mid-March 1944, the 50th Para Brigade under Brigadier M. Hope Thompson arrived at Ukhrul to relieve the 49th Indian Brigade. The newly arrived Paras took over a range of scattered hilltop positions once occupied by the 49th Brigade. Lt Col Paul Hopkinson's 152 (Indian) Para Battalion moved up to the position called Kidney Camp. From Kidney Camp, on 18 March he sent two companies out to occupy hilltop positions and relieve 4/5 Mahratta Light Infantry. 4/5 Mahratta Light Infantry went as reserve at Kidney Camp. Major Webb's B Company was dispatched to Point 7386 (Badger) and Point 7000 (Gamnom). While Major J. Fuller's C Company was sent to the unnamed Point 7378. All these positions dominated the two east–west jeep tracks over the hills in the area. The first two days were spent improving their trenches, dugouts and firing positions.

Major John Fuller's small company at point 7378 consisted of a section of three-inch mortars from the support company and a pair of medium machine guns from the brigade's machine gun company but no artillery was far enough forward to give them support; in total they numbered about 170, including seven British officers. Major Fuller's order had been to hold the hill until relieved to be on his guard against small Japanese patrols that might percolate from Burma and meanwhile to continue improvement of the defences. As a matter of prudence Fuller had positioned a three-man observation post about a mile ahead of Point 7378, on the track to Pushing.

C Company was eliminated, but the Japanese suffered 160 casualties including seven officers. By midday on 20 March the engagement was over, a tragic sacrifice of a fine fighting unit because of incompetence in providing supplies, barbed wire, ammunitions and above all, up-to-date intelligence.

In 2009, after making deep study over map, war diary and speaking with the surviving veterans, the author found the battlefield location of point 7378. The locals called the peak 'Harvakhangai'. The peak is located east of village Khangkhui in Ukhrul district. A team consisting of a camera crew, author and his friends climbed up the peak and found many foxholes and dug in positions. Many remains of the battle were found.

Discovery of Johnson Star

Christopher and the author were discussing battle locations most of the night after they became acquainted. One such night was discussed on Facebook messenger over an aerial reconnaissance picture of Kanglatongbi battlefield. Luckily Christopher found a star-shaped earthwork on the aerial picture taken in 1944. That was not natural and next morning the author went to the location and found that it was an ancient man-made structure more like for defense and made for a purpose. The author did research on the ground and presented the information to a seminar organized by the Government of Manipur. The author named the structure as Johnson Star, in the name of his friend, Christopher Johnson, who discovered the structure.

Commemoration of the 70th and 75th anniversary of Battle of Kanglatongbi

The commemoration of 70th anniversary of battle of Imphal was done with great pomp and show with dignitaries participating from various nations of the World. As part of the commemorations, the battle of Lion Box Kanglatongbi was also recognised on 7 April 2014. Christopher and the author liaised with the Ordnance Corps of India, veteran families and dignitaries who are relevant with the Battle of Kanglatongbi. A programme of events was also drafted by these two individuals and executed. Various retired generals and important dignitaries gathered that day to commemorate the battle. It was an idea formed and executed as a result of research and dedication by Christopher and the author.

It was found that the writings on the plaques and walls of the Kanglatongbi Memorial had some mistakes. Christopher sent the author relevant documents as proof of the mistake and the author submitted the documents to the Army Ordnance Corps officers in Manipur. Later before the 75th anniversary commemoration, the plaques and writings were rectified as per the corrected version.

Similarly, the 75th anniversary commemoration of Battle of Kanglatongbi was organised on 7 April 2019 at the Kanglatongbi War Memorial. Many dignitaries and families of the soldiers who fought at Kanglatongbi were also invited. The Indian Ordnance Corps were so happy with the function and dedication that Christopher was invited to lay wreath at the newly inaugurated Indian National War Memorial in Delhi, on the occasion of the Ordnance Raising Day on 8 April 2019.

Formation of Lion Cubs of Kanglatongbi

An organisation called Lion Cubs of Kanglatongbi was formed with the initiative of Christopher Johnson somewhere around the year 2017. Families from around the world who are related with Battle of Kanglatongbi were invited to join the group. The author was made an honorary member of the group. The group members from UK jointly travelled to India during 2019 to participate in the 75th anniversary commemoration of Battle of Kanglatongbi.

The author participated in the 80th Anniversary of Battle of Lion Box Kanglatongbi commemoration service at the National Memorial Arboretum at Birmingham, UK. He was given the onus to call the roll of Indian Soldiers who died during the battle.

Activities of Second World War Imphal Campaign Foundation

The Organisation organised a seminar on international peace and reconciliation in Imphal during the 75th anniversary commemoration of Battle of Imphal. It was participated by the Chairperson of the Burma Campaign Society, renowned historians and many families whose parents have participated in the Burma Campaign. All the participants unanimously pledge for World Peace and reconciliation. Every VJ Day, the organisation had been organising wreath-laying ceremonies and talks. Talks were organised with participation from students from various schools and colleges.

During the Covid days, the organisation of Remembrance Sunday took place on a grand scale with the participation of Member of Parliament, Inner Manipur Constituency Shri Raj Kumar Ranjan Singh as the Chief Guest of the Function. Every year the Remembrance Sunday is commemorated with wreath laying and floral tribute at Imphal War Cemetery by members of the Second World War Imphal Campaign Foundation. On this day all those Civilians, Soldiers of All Ranks and living beings in the world who died during the First and Second World Wars are remembered and offered prayer for their eternal peace.

Conclusion

Some 25 years ago, the people of Manipur were not much aware of the exact dates and regiments which participated in each battle which happened in the geographical area of Manipur. It was a general knowledge that the war happened in Manipur which was commonly called 'Japan Laan'. Everyone heard stories of the 'Japan Laan' from their grandfather and grandmothers. There were stories of flying Japanese, black soldiers who cut big meat, tall soldiers with pointed big caps, the Iron Elephants (tanks), communication with British soldiers with sign language etc. It was more like a folk tale where the youngsters gather around a fire with an elderly eyewitness to hear the war telling stories about what they heard and saw during the war. With the above activities, and many more besides, taken up by the Second World War Imphal Campaign Foundation, many people were given the primary source and information on the dates, and formations of armed forces involved in each battle. With the organisation of many functions and establishment of contacts with various veterans' families and researchers, the tourist flow in Manipur have increased manifold post 2014 when the anniversary commemoration of Battle of Imphal was first started. To meet the market demand, many tour operators with specialisation in battlefield guiding started their operation in Manipur. Overall, all the activities have contributed to peace, reconciliation and welfare of the people and the economy.

Appendix Four

The Kanglatongbi War Memorial

After hostilities had ceased, thoughts turned to those whose sacrifice helped earn this victory in the Far East, and during the autumn of 1945 an idea was conceived by Brigadier Cecil Herbert Speer, OBE, of the Indian Army Ordnance Corps Eastern Command, for the erection of a memorial for those of the RAOC/IAOC who had given their lives during the war, and planning began. Major Robert George Madeley, Royal Engineers, an architect by profession, and Captain Charles William Tranter, also Royal Engineers, were consulted and were tasked with the drawing up of plans for a memorial befitting those corps.

Major Robert George Madeley, Royal Engineers, designer of the Kanglatongbi War Memorial.

The location for this memorial was to be near to the entrance of 221 Advanced Ordnance Depot at milestone 118 on the main Dimapur–Imphal road. What better location than this, the site of the fierce action in April 1944 where the men of the Ordnance earned their place in military history, saving vast amounts of stores and ammunition from capture by the advancing Japanese forces, inflicting heavy casualties in the process.

Under the supervision of Major Madeley, an Artisan Company of Indian Engineers was used to build a masonry plinth from local materials, onto which was placed a large, rough-hewn monolith of Naga stone. The area surrounding this was landscaped with stone pavers and a low wall built to the rear. A bronze plaque, to be fixed to the stone, was cast by an Indian Electrical and Mechanical Engineer Company, based in Calcutta, upon which were superimposed the badges of the RAOC and IAOC. The Crusader Sword of the XIV Army and the emblem of the Eastern Command, a horse's head, were also placed upon the plaque. A bold inscription was the centrepiece, which read:

ERECTED BY THE DOS., INDIA, AND MEMBERS OF THE
R.AOC AND IAOC. TO THE MEMORY OF THE OFFICERS
AND MEN WHO GAVE THEIR LIVES IN THE IMPHAL
DIMAPUR AREAS DURING THE YEARS
1942/45 OF THE SECOND WORLD WAR.
TRIUMPHANT OVER FLESH AND PAIN THEY DIED OUR
DAY OF
PEACE TO GAIN.

Because of some unforeseen difficulties with the preparation and casting work of the plaque, the unveiling ceremony had to be put back from January 1946, when it was hoped that the Director of Ordnance Services, Brigadier Speer, would do the honours during his planned visit to the area. Now put back until March at least, the ceremony would be too late for Brigadier Speer to attend, as unfortunately his health had deteriorated, and he was repatriated without seeing his conception completed.

By the middle of April, everything was in place for the unveiling ceremony with Colonel Cunningham, the former CO of 221 AOD, and Brigadier Frank Leslie Harry, the new DOS, being chosen to officiate. A few days earlier the plaque had been ceremonially fixed to the stone by the detachment of the IEME, with a guard of sepoys from the IAOC being mounted at the same time. Unfortunately, at the last moment, the DOS was called away owing to the pressure of work, and it fell to Major William Edwin Hinge to represent him and deliver his address.

Dawn broke as a dismal grey day on Saturday, 15 April, but as the large contingent of officers and men from the Ordnance Corps began assembling at the memorial, the sun broke through the clouds and at 09.00 hours, Major Hinge stepped forward. Behind him was the memorial, draped with the Union Flag, with a sentry posted at each of the four corners, resting on arms reversed. A guard of honour stood to the rear. Major Hinge then spoke of how this memorial was dedicated to those members of the corps who had perished during the whole of the Burma operations, from the dark days of 1942 and the retreat from Burma through to the capture of Rangoon in 1945. He went on to explain how fitting it was that the memorial should be located here as a reminder of those whose bravery was awarded and those who gave their lives. He then invited Colonel Cunningham to do the unveiling.

> I therefore consider it fitting to ask Colonel Cunningham, who was himself in command of that devoted band of men, namely the staff of 221 AOD, who so ably defended their charge at Kanglatongbi to speak to you the final words before he performs the act of unveiling this symbol of our gratitude to those of the RAOC and the IAOC who so devotedly sacrificed their lives that we might live, and in loyalty to the best traditions of the corps. It is also a token of the mutual respect of one to the other of the RAOC and IAOC who worked so devotedly together throughout the war, always with the best interests of the corps at heart and of the Army, which it is our duty to serve.

Colonel Cunningham then responded to his invitation and stood to speak in front of the Memorial.

> This site marks the beginning and the end of a phase in the history of the RAOC and IAOC. It is here that a detachment of Ordnance personnel from Manipur Road first met the retiring Burma Army in 1942 and formed an Ordnance dump, which later became 56 OFD, and in October 1943 – 221 AOD. Subsequently during the Jap invasion of the Imphal Plain, this site was the scene of very heavy fighting during which the personnel of 221 AOD played a notable part. The site was evacuated on Good Friday, 1944 in the face of heavy Jap fire and the depot withdrawn into the Keep. During this action, Sergeant Campbell of the Seaforth Highlanders and Private Lawson of the Duke of Wellington's Regiment[1] were killed. Both displayed outstanding courage during the action. Mention also should be made of the forward OFDs, 51, 52 and 53. These units did sterling work during this period, as also did 63 OFD at Palel, who held their sector of the box against a number of Jap attacks and suffered casualties.

---

1. In his speech, Colonel Cunningham mistakenly referred to Private Lawson of the Duke of Wellington's Regiment as being one of the casualties from 221 AOD. It should of course be Private Lawton of the South Lancashire Regiment. It is unknown whether Colonel Cunningham made this mistake or whether it was the reporter of the event.

The Ordnance services, despite innumerable difficulties never failed to deliver the goods, but their hard work would have been as nothing had it not been for the magnificent work done by the Base Depot, 226 AOD, at Manipur Road, who never failed to get the stores forward. [Colonel Cunningham became the CO of 226 after 221 was flown out of Imphal in April 1944.] Ordnance personnel in this area endured many hardships, sickness took a

Lieutenant Colonel Cunningham laying a wreath at the Kanglatongbi War Memorial, April 1946.

Lieutenant Colonel Cunningham unveiling the Kanglatongbi War Memorial, April 1946.

heavy toll, but throughout the whole period, in spite of sickness, discomfort, and at times enemy action, they never failed and never let the troops down. We will never forget them and this memorial represents a permanent record of those who fell in a great service and those who worked and suffered despite all difficulties. In memory of our comrades, who made the great sacrifice, and in memory of all ranks of the RAOC and IAOC who served in this area, I now unveil this memorial.

With this, Colonel Cunningham removed the Union Flag to reveal the memorial as the Assam Rifles bugler sounded the 'Last Post' followed by the 'Reveille' while the whole ceremonial party were stood to attention, their officers saluting. A wreath was laid by Colonel Cunningham at the base of the memorial on behalf of the DOS and all officers and other ranks of the corps before the parade were dismissed and marched away. Then it began to rain.

Because the Kanglatongbi War Memorial was in such a remote area of north-eastern India, proper maintenance was limited, and it began to suffer the effects and ravages of time and climatic conditions. Added

Bugler playing the 'Last Post' and 'Reveille' at Kanglatongbi War Memorial, April 1946.

to this were the concerns of vandalism in an area where there was widespread unrest within the population at this time. In concurrence with the Commonwealth War Graves Commission, the DOS ordered that the memorial should be brought to India for its safekeeping and it was duly transported to the College of Materials Management at Jabalpur in 1976 and it now resides in the AOC museum there. A replica of the memorial was built there too, and another one was erected to replace the original at Kanglatongbi. However, this one has changed considerably over the years, having been refurbished many times to make it presentable for

Kanglatongbi War Memorial, 7 April 2019: (left to right) Mr Rajeshwor Yumnam, Lieutenant General Gautam Moorthy (Retd), former DGOS Indian Army, and the author.

commemorations and visits by VIPs. A 500m^2 compound has been formed, around which a gaily decorated high wall has been built with an entrance gateway of wrought iron. The memorial, a square three-tiered pink and black marble plinth surmounted by a stone replica of the original citation, is impressive in its simplicity. Situated at one end of the compound, it is easily seen through the gates as one passes by. A small pavilion has been erected behind the memorial, where the visitors' book is placed and where guests are invited to sign it in comfort. Also within the compound are low-growing hedges and pathways, which guide the visitor to an area where plaques, similar to those of the grave markers in the CWGC cemeteries in the region, record the visits of VIPs. A small open area surrounded by larger trees in the compound adds to the peaceful setting, while the ever-present traffic thunders past outside, along the Kohima–Imphal National Highway 1.

The Howard Memorial, Lion Box Kanglatongbi

Possibly the only personal memorial erected in the Imphal area, the Howard Memorial is dedicated to the memory of Private William John Howard, who was killed in action not far from where this memorial is located in the former Lion Box at Kanglatongbi. He has no known grave.

For many years, this author held ambitions to erect a memorial for Private Howard on the battlefield because of the fateful connections between the Johnson and Howard families. Once the difficult decision had been made to seek out the Howard family to inform them of the true circumstances of his death and, upon the successful search and with the family's blessing, the process of finding a suitable location for a memorial began. For several years, Mr Rajeshwor Yumnam had unsuccessfully sought out such a place for a small plot of land to use until local landowners, Mr Arjun Jogi and Mr Khem Pokhrel, most generously donated part of their land in the former Sector 3 area of Lion Box for this purpose in late 2021. Appropriately, the remains of a former defensive trench are still visible just a few yards away beside the escarpment that overlooks the paddy fields on the east side of Kanglatongbi and near to a track leading to the Imphal River and Picquet Hill beyond. Here, a small area was carved out by a mechanical digger, a concrete plinth constructed and a locally sourced stone monolith, weighing over 2 tons, placed upright on this plinth, upon which are carved the badge of the XIV Army and the following words:

IN MEMORY OF
PRIVATE WILLIAM JOHN HOWARD
THE BORDER REGIMENT (ATTACHED 20
REINFORCEMENT CAMP)
KILLED IN ACTION NEAR THIS PLACE WHILST PART OF
THE REARGUARD
DEFENCES DURING THE EVACUATION OF LION BOX
KANGLATONGBI 7th APRIL 1944
REMEMBERED WITH PRIDE BY HIS EVER-LOVING FAMILY
REMEMBERING ALSO ALL THOSE GALLANT BRITISH
AND INDIAN DEFENDERS OF LION BOX KANGLATONGBI
APRIL 1944

ERECTED IN CONJUNCTION WITH THE LANDOWNERS
(ARJUN YOGI AND KHEM POKHREL) AND 2WW IMPHAL
CAMPAIGN FOUNDATION. THEIR GENEROSITY IS MOST
GRATEFULLY ACKNOWLEDGED

Strong stone retaining walls hold back the loose stone and soil of the escarpment and a low metal railing around the site protects the memorial. A small gateway allows access for the laying of tributes and for maintenance, with a Gulmohar flowering tree planted to the rear, adding colour when it will blossom each spring.

Sadly, Private Howard's son Michael, a babe in arms when his father died, did not manage to see the finished memorial, passing away himself in January 2022 just before its completion. Because of the unprecedented tribal violence in Manipur since the memorial was erected, it has not been possible for any inauguration ceremony to be held by the families at the site. It is sincerely hoped that this situation will soon be resolved and visits to Manipur, and especially Kanglatongbi, will resume and be as safe and friendly as they have always been in the past. Meanwhile, floral tributes for anniversaries and remembrance will continue to be placed by friends living locally.

The Howard Memorial at Kanglatongbi.

The Eightieth Anniversary Commemoration of Lion Box

The seventieth and seventy-fifth anniversaries of the battle at Lion Box were commemorated in fine style by the Indian Army, especially the Army Ordnance Corps, at the Kanglatongbi War Memorial, with the eightieth anniversary eagerly anticipated to follow suit. It was a great disappointment to both the Indian Army and the Lion Cubs of Kanglatongbi (families of the veterans of Lion Box) that the unprecedented and tragic tribal violence in Manipur at the time of the anniversary meant that it was unsafe for any event to take place. Not to be beaten by this and determined that this significant anniversary should not go unmarked, the Lion Cubs set about planning an official commemoration service in the UK for the first time ever.

The Burma Star Memorial at the National Memorial Arboretum in Staffordshire was the venue chosen as being the most appropriate. Came the day of the service, Sunday, 7 April 2024, the weather was threatening, with the heavy rain clouds and blustery winds causing a certain amount of anxiety for the organisers and participants alike. This concern soon passed, as did the clouds, driven on by the strong wind, passing either side of the gathered throng. No one attending will forget the colourful spectacle of the many ex-servicemen's association standards fluttering in the wind as the bearers gathered around the memorial, opposite the uniformed ranks of serving soldiers. Regimental representatives from descendant units that participated at Kanglatongbi were on parade, under the supervision of Parade Marshall Squadron Sergeant Major Neil Ibbinson of the Royal Logistic Corps, itself descended from the RASC and RAOC.

Nearly 100 guests, mostly Lion Cubs, sat listening intently to the powerful address delivered by The Reverend Dr Andrew Sangster as he led this service of remembrance. Faith leaders from the Sikh and Muslim communities also participated in acknowledgement of those from these faiths who fell at the battle. Sadly, the Hindu priest was unable to attend. Another VIP who was unable to join at the last moment was Brigadier Clive Elderton, CBE, formerly British Military Adviser to India. However, the reading of his tribute on his behalf was by a fellow logistician and standard-bearer, Lieutenant Colonel Terry Byrne. The personal message from the present Director General Ordnance Services, Lieutenant General S.C. Tandi, VSM, written especially for this commemoration, was then read out by this author:

> Together with all ranks of the Army Ordnance Corps of the Indian Army, I convey my solemn homage to the officers and men of 221 Advanced Ordnance Depot who laid down their lives fighting a determined enemy bayonet charge on the night of 6/7 April at Kanglatongbi on the Imphal–Dimapur road and emerged victorious. The supreme sacrifice of those gallant men is a source of pride and inspiration for our future generations. On this day, we remember those brave men for their guts and fortitude. 'Triumphant over flesh and pain, they died our day of peace to gain.' Long live the Corps! *Jai Hind*!

Direct family descendants of the two Military Cross recipients of the battle were in attendance and took part in the ceremonies. Francis Boyd, a son of Major John Boyd, MC, called part of the roll of honour of the

The author reading the message from the DGOS India at the eightieth anniversary service at the National Memorial Arboretum under the leadership of The Reverend Dr Sangster.

British dead, including the names of some of those men under his father's command. The salutation was read by Caroline Jephcott, the daughter of Captain Keith Baker, MC. Other Lion Cubs also participated, adding greatly to the poignancy of the occasion. Richard Rawes called the name of his grandfather, Driver Matthew Rawes, when he read the remaining part of the roll of honour. The grandson of Warrant Officer Tom Ansell, Tim Vaughan, read a poem appropriately named 'The Forgotten Army', and Joan Bolton-Frost read excerpts from letters written home by her father, Sergeant Bernard Hargreaves, adding a personal aspect common to those men far away from their loved ones. Curtis Barrett, the great-grandson of Private William Howard, most ably read a poem entitled 'Unforgotten Men', the final verse being:

> They sleep eternal, calm and deep,
> Beneath the rocky hillside steep,
> A ghostly shroud their only keep,
> The cold grey mists of Manipur.

His great-grandfather still lies somewhere on that Manipur battlefield.

Another unforgettable part of the service was the calling of the roll of honour of the Indian dead by Rajeshwor Yumnam (flying in from Imphal specially for this commemoration) and Lance Corporal Sanjog Gurung of the Queen's Gurkha Signals. Together, they each took turns calling relentlessly the names of over eighty men. After the stirring sounds of the 'Last Post' and 'Reveille' had been played by bugler Bob Kerry (ex-Royal Anglian Regiment), an invitation to lay wreaths at the memorial was given, and queues were formed as wreath layers awaited their turn, accompanied by the playing of a lament by Scottish Piper John Innes (ex-Corps of Royal Signals). John Ling (ex-Royal Norfolk Regiment) read the 'Kohima Epitaph' before The Reverend Dr Sangster gave the final blessing, and the parade moved off, led by the King's Colour Standard of the Royal Norfolk Veterans Association, paraded by David Westgate, the grandson of CSM George Johnson.

The gathering then returned to the hospitality suite within the National Memorial Arboretum complex for refreshments and another chance to engage with each other. All those present were agreed that this service had been most memorable, and were grateful to have attended this unique occasion.

Abbreviations and Acronyms

2 i/c	Second in Command
AAQMG	Assistant Adjutant and Quartermaster General
ADOS	Assistant Director Ordnance Services
ADS	Advanced Dressing Station
ADT stores	Armoured Divisional Troops Stores
AMU	Anti-Malaria Unit
AOD	Advanced Ordnance Depot
AOR	African Other Rank
AW	Artisan Works
BAD	Base Ammunition Depot
BGH	British General Hospital
BOD	Base Ordnance Depot
BOR	British Other Rank
BPT	Bulk Petroleum Transport
Brig	Brigadier
Capt	Captain
Carbs	Carabiniers
CBE	Commander of the Order of the British Empire
Cdtr	Conductor
CO	Commanding Officer
Col	Colonel
Cpl	Corporal
CQMS	Company Quartermaster Sergeant
CRE	Commander Royal Engineers
CSM	Company Sergeant Major
CWGW	Commonwealth War Graves Commission
DADOS	Deputy Assistant Director Ordnance Services
DDOS	Deputy Director Ordnance Services

DGOS	Director General Ordnance Services
DOW	Died of Wounds
DSO	Distinguished Service Order
Dvr	Driver
FFR	Frontier Force Regiment/Rifles
F/Lt	Flight Lieutenant
F/O	Flying Officer
F/S	Flight Sergeant
FSD	Field Supply Depot
GE	Garrison Engineer
GHQ	General Headquarters
Gnr	Gunner
GOC	General Officer Commanding
GOR	Gurkha Other Rank
GPT	General Purpose Transport
GREF	General Reserve Engineer Force
Hav	Havildar
HQ	Headquarters
IAMC	Indian Army Medical Corps
IAOC	Indian Army Ordnance Corps
IE	Indian Engineers
IEME	Indian Electrical and Mechanical Engineers
IGH	Indian General Hospital
INA	Indian National Army
IOR	Indian Other Rank
JIF	Japanese Indian Force
Kangla Admin Commandant	Kanglatongbi Administration Commandant
KANGLA OPS	Kanglatongbi Operations (L of C)
KIA	Killed in Action
KOYLI	King's Own Yorkshire Light Infantry
L/Cpl	Lance Corporal
LMG	Light Machine Gun
L/Sgt	Lance Sergeant
L OF C	Lines of Communication

Lt	Lieutenant
Lt Col	Lieutenant Colonel
Maj	Major
Maj Gen	Major General
MBE	Member of the Order of the British Empire
MC	Military Cross
ME	Mechanical Equipment
MEx	Mechanical Excavation
MT	Mechanical Transport
NCO	Non-Commissioned Officer
OBE	Order of the British Empire
OC	Officer Commanding
OFD	Ordnance Field Depot
OWL	Operator Wireless and Line
POL	Petrol Oil Lubricant
Pte	Private
QMS	Quartermaster Sergeant
RAMC	Royal Army Medical Corps
RAOC	Royal Army Ordnance Corps
RASC	Royal Army Service Corps
RFT	Reinforcement
RIASC	Royal Indian Army Service Corps
RSM	Regimental Sergeant Major
Rtd	Retired
Sep	Sepoy
Sig	Signalman
Spr	Sapper
S&T	Supplies and Transport
Sub	Subedar
Tpr	Trooper
VCO	Viceroy's Commissioned Officer
VIP	Very Important Person
VRG	Vehicle Reserve Group
VSM	Vishisht Seva Medal
WAE	West African Engineers
WO	Warrant Officer

Index

The index is about the many people named in this book – British, Indian, Japanese, all mixed up as they were on the battlefield. They are marked by their surnames and ranks.